The New
Servants of Power

Keith Haring, UNTITLED

From *Village Voice*, **June 15, 1982.**

The New Servants of Power

A CRITIQUE OF THE 1980s SCHOOL REFORM MOVEMENT

EDITED BY

Christine M. Shea,
Ernest Kahane,
AND
Peter Sola

Foreword by Maxine Greene

New York
Westport, Connecticut
London

Library of Congress Cataloging-in-Publication Data

The New servants of power : a critique of the 1980s school reform
movement / edited by Christine M. Shea, Ernest Kahane, and Peter
Sola ; foreword by Maxine Greene.
    p. cm.
  Includes bibliographical references (p.).
  ISBN 0-275-93602-3 (alk. paper)
    1. Education—United States—Aims and objectives. 2. Public
schools—United States—Evaluation. 3. Educational equalization—
United States. I. Shea, Christine Mary, 1945- . II. Kahane,
Ernest. III. Sola, Peter Andre, 1940- . IV. Title: School reform
movement.
LA217.N47   1990
370'.973—dc20   90-30213

A hardcover edition of *The New Servants of Power:
A Critique of the 1980s School Reform Movement* is
available from Greenwood Press (Contributions to the
Study of Education, no. 28; ISBN 0-313-25475-3).

Library of Congress Catalog Card Number: 90-30213

ISBN: 0-275-93602-3

First published in 1989
Paperback edition 1990

Praeger Publishers, One Madison Avenue, New York, NY 10010
An imprint of Greenwood Publishing Group, Inc.

Printed in the United States of America

The paper used in this book complies with the
Permanent Paper Standard issued by the National
Information Standards Organization (Z39.48-1984).

10 9 8 7 6 5 4 3 2 1

Copyright Acknowledgment

The frontispiece, *Untitled* by Keith Haring, appears courtesy of Keith Haring (© 1982).
Although this print was published in the *Village Voice* (June 15, 1982), Haring holds the
copyright to the print.

TO

CLARENCE J. KARIER

"In conclusion let me say that . . . [his] . . . greatest
virtue was his committed empathy with all the oppressed and
his divine dissatisfaction with all forms of injustice."
From Dr. Martin Luther King,
"Centennial Address to Honor 100th
Birthday of Dr. W.E.B. Dubois,"
February 23, 1968.

Contents

Foreword

Maxine Greene

The New Servants of Power is in many ways unique in its critique of the educational reform movement of the late 1970s to late 1980s. The chapters that follow provide a scholarly, incisive, far-ranging account of the economic and sociopolitical factors that goes far to explain the anti-humanist and nondemocratic implications of the reports. These chapters break unapologetically through the mystifying claims that the reforms intend to reconcile equity and excellence. They assert flatly, sometimes in different idioms, that fundamental inequities—those suffered by Blacks and by women, for instance—are ignored in the reform proposals and may even be exacerbated over time. Fascinating material is presented on the differences among the various elites: those preoccupied with military dominance and those concerned about trilateral management of a global economy; those interested in using schools to repair character deficiencies and those interested in using them to upgrade competence and skills. Much of what follows, indeed, sheds a new and sometimes lurid light on what the reform reports actually imply when it comes to "learning to learn" minimal competency skills and the requirements for the dead-end jobs awaiting perhaps the majority of our young.

On one level, this book may be taken to be a profoundly thoughtful functionalist account of the "realities" being mediated and rationalized by the so-called reform reports and their impacts upon the schools. On another level, however, the various chapters (including those on work, discrimination, teacher education, and continuing education) may serve as provocations to the reader. Such a reader would reject the functionalist explanation along with explanations grounded in either economic determinism or necessity. Nowhere is it written that American schools are required to track, test, control, and sort out in response to the demands of the Pentagon or to those obsessed with exploiting markets overseas. It may indeed be the case that no educational system has yet fulfilled the demands of both equity and excellence. It may be the case that publics everywhere, deceived or undeceived, will insist that the primary object of the school is to prepare the young to meet "market demand." For all that, the educator who refuses mere submergence and mere acquiescence will refuse the claims of objectivity when it comes to official renderings of the realities confronting the schools. Interpretation is required, new ways of seeing from vantage points too seldom consulted. Questions regarding the quality of life and the quality of the workplace have to be opened, as do questions having to do with consumerism and the taken-for-grantedness with regard to America's dominance over (and superiority to) the Third World. The restless reader (even in the face of claims of hard-won "realism") may open questions as well that have to do with justice and with fairness—and with what happens to personal and collective self-esteem when gains are made at the cost of others' suffering.

The informed reader, finding a rich lode of information in the chapters to come, may also consider again the meanings of human consciousness and the human recognition that men and women are products of history, not nature alone. Consciousness signifies a reaching out beyond, a refusal of objectness, a realization as well as a refusal, a move to transcend. To read these chapters may well be to experience one's consciousness stirring in resistance and critique. What one can hope for is the launching of a dialogue. Who is to know whether the educational solution is to be found in Mortimer Adler's *Paideia*, in John Dewey's work, Paulo Freire's, Antonio Gramsci's, John Goodlad's, Ernest Boyer's? Who can be sure whether current proposals for civic education suggest the imposition of an unwarranted consensus? Who knows whether any such consensus can be thought to preexist or to emerge from what Jurgen Habermas calls competent communication, or from the ongoing "conversation" so many thinkers propose today in the place of objective truth? These and others are the kinds of wonderings generated by a reading of this book—generated at least in one reader. I can think of no better culmination for this scholarly work: It teaches, it enlarges, it disturbs. And then it launches readers into critical reflection, if they dare to take the risk.

Preface

The inspiration for collecting these essays into an anthology is to enlarge the scope of the contemporary debate about school and educational reform. Pursuant to this goal, these essays critically assess the national educational reports, books, and related policy that set parameters from which much of the contemporary educational debate proceeds.

In Part I, An Introductory Overview of the 1980s School Reform Debate, Christine Shea presents a provocative analysis examining the contemporary school reform debate as reflecting a conflict among dominant economic interest groups about the most efficient means of rebuilding labor productivity and American economic power. Her chapter "Pentagon vs. Multinational Capitalism: The Political Economy of the 1980s School Reform Movement," reveals areas of disagreement and consensus among economic elites and the implications for work, schooling, and social policy.

The relation among business, the state, and the 1980s school reform debate is examined from additional perspectives in Part II, A Critique of the Concept of Work in the School Reform Literature. Don Martin's "A Critique of the Concept of Work and Education in the School Reform Reports" shows how the concept of work within key reports will more likely support a narrowly based elite education rather than a marriage of "excellence and equity" for all students. Martin's examination of the arguments of the "latest reformers" within a historical context shows how educational rhetoric and policy mirrors social and economic constraints.

Edward Berman's "The State's Stake in Educational Reform" continues a critical analysis into the way external forces impact schooling. However, Berman reveals how the state's dual involvement in promoting international corporate competitiveness (accumulation) and mediating conflict within the system (legitimation) are crucial for understanding the direction, limits, and possibilities of meaningful reforms.

Ernest Kahane and Andrew Oram examine work within the high-tech environment in "Where Computers Are Taking Us in the Education Field." Kahane and Oram raise issues about the selling of high tech as a new and humanistic model for educators by examining traditional biases in hiring, promotion, and division of labor within a large computer manufacturer, and how a narrow, organizational short-term focus restricts the use and development of the new technology.

Concluding Part II is Peter Sola's "The Corporate Community on the Ideal Business-School Alliance: A Historical and Ethical Critique." Sola shows historically how business interest in school relationships have been aimed at preparing a qualified work force to generate greater economic productivity. Sola examines the cyclical nature of business and school relationships from the 1930s and goes on to elaborate an alternative set of priorities beyond private economic interests.

Part III, Educational Reform and "The New Equity," examines how groups and individuals who are traditionally less well-served fare within the national school reform reports. The essays examine the specific implications for constituents, raise critical questions about continued inequitable distribution of resources, and recommend alternative policies.

Beverly M. Gordon in "The Bootstrap Ideology of Educational Reform: What the Recent Reports Say about the Current and Future Status of Blacks in Higher Education" documents the limitations of current reform reports in addressing persistent racial problems. Gordon calls for the addition of a minority agenda for school reform, and presents an important argument for minority institution building by minority group members as a vehicle for empowerment and enriching the larger society.

Deficiencies in a commitment to meaningful school reform are examined by Timothy Reagan in his essay about American bilingual education policy. As he shows in "More of the Same Reforms of American Public Schooling and the Minority Language Student," neither the goals of "excellence" or "equity" seem well served by the prevailing assimilationist approach. Reagan provides strong arguments for an alternative multicultural approach that respects cultural diversity and supports current learning research in the classroom.

Kathryn Borman and Patricia O'Reilly, identify in "The Eighties Image of Girls and Women in the Educational Reform Literature: A Review of the Issues," the ways that the school reform reports fail to reflect sensitivity to the issues of sex equity and sexual discrimination as women and girls face them in educational institutions. Borman and O'Reilly propose specific recommendations for educators to effectively address the issues of sex discrimination.

Finally, to conclude Part III, William Pink shows in "The New Equity:

Competing Visions" how "equity" in the school reform reports becomes set in opposition and subordinate to concepts of "excellence." Pink points out how both "excellence" and "equity" are not well served in the reports and presents recommendations to meaningfully reconstruct these principles.

In Part IV, School Reform Proposals for the New Curriculum, the reform reports' treatment of aims, attitudes, skills, and disciplines embodied in specific curriculum proposals is analyzed. Stuart McAninich in, "Civic Education Reform and the Quest for a Unified Society: A Critique of R. Freeman Butts's Agenda for Civic Learning," examines an important articulation of "civic education" that reflects an agenda accepted by both liberals and conservatives. McAninch shows how the conception of common values by both groups can serve to subordinate individual reason to establish a wider loyalty.

Joseph DeVitis and John Martin Rich, in "An Evaluation of the Aims and Curriculum Proposals in Sizer's *Horace's Compromise*," appraise Sizer's curricula and place in it context of other contemporary studies. Though DeVitis and Rich acknowledge the strengths of Sizer's recommendations, they also provide a framework to analyze the limitations of Sizer's and other curriculum proposals.

"Is Continuing Education Anything More than a Yuppie Phenonemon?" by Paul Violas reveals how inequities for the poor are mirrored and reinforced by continuing education programs. By examining demographics, primary and secondary labor markets, and the types of barriers that impede access for these programs, Violas shows how the most affluent benefit disproportionately. He suggests an alternative community-based approach aimed at serving and addressing the needs and aspirations of disadvantaged groups.

Richard Altenbaugh concludes the volume with "Teachers, Their World, and Their Work: A Review of the Idea of 'Professional Excellence' in School Reform Reports." As Altenbaugh shows, teachers are a key element in initiating school reform, yet their voices are absent from the school reports and they remain at the bottom of the decision-making pyramid. By revealing how teachers can stifle and promote reform, Altenbaugh questions the "realism" of the reports and presents a way beyond them.

The editors wish to acknowledge the help of staff at West Virginia University, College of Human Resources and Education, in preparing this volume. Bonnie Blaney, Gail Martine, Kathy Robinett, and Kim Thomas willingly typed and retyped article drafts, and helped with the thankless task of preparing the book's bibliography. Christine, especially, is indebted to their support and good cheer.

Christine would also like to thank Dr. R. Bruce McPherson, Director, North Carolina Center for the Advancement of Teaching, who provided the ideal collegial environment necessary for the completion of this manuscript.

PART I

AN INTRODUCTORY OVERVIEW OF THE 1980s SCHOOL REFORM DEBATE

1

Pentagon vs. Multinational Capitalism: The Political Economy of the 1980s School Reform Movement

Christine M. Shea

INTRODUCTION

Once again the schools are embroiled in a national controversy concerning test scores, coursework, teacher preparation, school administration, and so on. Once again educational scholars and academics are engaged in a national debate over the intent and probable consequences of these reforms. The cry for both "excellence" and "equity" are common themes to those familiar with contemporary school reform rhetoric. Twentieth-century educational reform proposals have always been shrouded in the familiar cloth of these meritocratic principles. The school reform proposals of the 1980s have been no exception. One of the most consistent characteristics of the school reform literature has been its attempt to justify its reform proposals on the basis of both "excellence" and "equity." This rationale was set out in explicit meritocratic language by the initial reform report, *A Nation at Risk*, when it stated,

> We do not believe that a public commitment to excellence and educational reform must be made at the expense of a strong public commitment to the equitable treatment of our diverse population. The twin goals of equity and high-quality schooling have profound and practical meaning for our economy and society, and we cannot permit one to yield to the other in principle or practice. To do so would deny young people their chance to learn and live according to their aspirations and abilities. (National Commission on Excellence in Education 1983, 13)

A new equation, however, has been added to the school reform agenda, and that is the problem of how to ensure the continued viability of these traditional meritocratic principles in American society in the context of a dramatic shift in the world economy. Numerous research studies have attempted to describe the dimensions of this emerging world capitalist economy, the widespread adoption of new computer and telecommunications technologies, and the changing demographic structures of the American population. The resulting portrait has generated the fuel for the latest series of school reform activities and has catalogued renewed discussion in educational policy circles concerning the role and structure of educational institutions in the future American economy.

Within the past few years, much space and attention has been devoted to the arguments of the current school reformers and ideologues. Much of this writing has failed to reveal the growing debate between two competing ideological positions: the conservative sunbelt coalition vs. the northeastern liberal establishment. Although the achievement-oriented rhetoric pertaining to "excellence" and "equity" are common features in each theoretical paradigm, they present contrasting interpretations of these terms as they relate to the future American economy. In reviewing these competing world views, we must address a number of issues concerning the kind of American citizens that each system would likely produce and the advisability of supporting the type of world economy implied by each reform model. In addition, our ability to transcend each of these macroeconomic models may ultimately rest on our willingness to critique these models not on the superficial level of programmatic detail, but rather to submerge ourselves in the logic of the ideologies themselves—at the roots of their metaphysical, epistemological, and axiological assumptions, biases, and preconceptions. It is on this analytic level that the foundations disciplines are structured to provide their greatest service to the formation and evaluation of educational policy. In this chapter, therefore, we: (1) outline the new demographic statistics that form the underlying rationale for much of the school reform impetus, (2) sketch out the conservative sunbelt model and the northeastern liberal public policy positions that have been developed to respond to the problems identified in the demographic projections, (3) draw out the accompanying school reform proposals subscribed to by each position, and (4) suggest an alternative framework for school reform.

THE EMERGING GLOBAL ECONOMY

Since the early 1980s, public policy experts have become increasingly concerned that the performance of the American economy has not kept pace with other leading world powers. They have underscored the importance of the new international division of labor, in its formative stages, as a large share of the industrial base for the new world economy shifts to Third World developing nations. Analysts, referring to the "de-industrialization of America," generally agree that the United States has lost its competitive advantage in labor-intensive industries and manufacturing based on routine production methods. Conservatives and liberals alike support this process of international specialization on the premise that it is self-defeating to remain in markets that are being dominated by developing countries. Such a macroeconomic decision, however, inevitably involves related choices—resources must be transferred to high-skilled and/or mechanized production processes, whereas manufactured products involving low-skilled, standardized production must be imported. Similarly, it is in the competitive interests of U.S. industry to assemble finished products in countries that have a large, low-cost labor supply and are located close to overseas markets. Thus, for American public policy experts, the most crucial issue to be resolved in the development of a "competitiveness strategy" (conservative terminology) or "national industrial policy" (liberal terminology) is how America can (and indeed *must*) transfer labor-intensive, low-skill production to Third World developing countries, at the same time maintaining control over the entire world production process in ways that ensure the future competitive supremacy of the United States (Magaziner and Reich 1982; Thurow 1985; Committee for Economic Development 1984; McKenzie 1985; Phillips 1984).

According to both conservative and liberal social policy experts, unless the United States develops a comprehensive, coherent, broadly based national effort to control global markets, the American economy will not fully revitalize. For these planners, control over the shape and direction of this new world economy necessitates that the entire production process be piloted from the United States via an integrated network of electronics, robotics, computers, and telecommunications technology. It is further emphasized that this combined phenomena of capital flight to Third World developing nations and high tech mechanization of the workplace will have a dramatic impact in terms of the numbers, type, and skill level of the jobs available in the American work force.

THE NEW TECHNOLOGIES

For the past decade, there has been intense academic debate concerning the probable effects of automation, particularly as represented by "the new technologies" on the labor process. There is little doubt that the increased use of computers, electronics, robotics, and a vast new array of telecommunications equipment will have a major impact on corporate production and operation systems of the future. The new technologies have added a vast new language of production: computer-integrated manufacturing (CIM), laser technology, robotics, computer-assisted design (CAD), computer-assisted manufacturing (CAM), and flexible manufacturing systems (FMS). These automated production systems are envisioned as the new competitive technology that will enable American manufacturing firms to change their production processes through computer-based techniques in a matter of minutes and hours rather than months.

Most of the technical forecasts that have attempted to detail the impact of these new technologies picture a rosy future of technological growth and development—higher productivity, increased response to market demand, greater flexibility, and improved quality control (Lund and Hansen 1986; National Academy of Sciences 1983, 1984; National Science Board Commission of Precollegiate Education in Mathematics, Science, and Technology 1983; Servan-Schreiber and Crecine 1986). According to recent predictions, this Third Industrial Revolution will fuse design, manufacturing, and marketing into a single stream of information that will eventually permit us to automate just about anything now accomplished by human labor (Draper 1985, 48). These same optimistic forecasters tend to be equally positive about the social impact of the new technologies on the restructuring of work and the reorganization of the workplace. They posit an inexorable link between social progress and technological growth. They predict that work in the America of the year 2000 will more creative and satisfying and demand ever higher skill levels. According to one 1986 report funded by the U.S. Congress, Office of Technological Assessment, the list of factory worker skills required by the new computer/telecommunications technology includes visualization, statistical inference, attentiveness, conceptual thinking, understanding of process phenomena, and individual responsibility. This report also states that the direction of work skills is changing from physical, manipulative, tacticle, "hands on" type of work to work that is conceptual, cognitive, and based on an abstract understanding of the production processes (Lund and Hansen 1986, 95). Explicitly stated, optimistic predictions such as this one are typical of those found in the popularized literature of the 1980s school reform movement.

The opposing view of more skeptical forecasters is that the new technologies will only subordinate people to machines in a new and degrading manner. In a recent *New York Times Book Review* essay, Roger Draper culled from the critical research literature a more pessimistic scenario of the qualitative and quantitative impact of the CIM production technology on American workers. According to his calculations, the impact of this quest for the fully automated workplace will be felt by all levels of the corporate sector, including financial analysts, inventory controllers, marketing specialists, and service workers, as well as the traditional line production workers. In the words of one futurist, "unlike other technologies which increase the productivity of the worker, the robot actually replaces the worker. That indeed is one of the prime tasks for which robots are built" (Shaiken 1984, 47). Second-generation robots, capable of being used in a complete CIM process, are expected to have an even greater impact on the loss of manufacturing jobs. Volkswagen officials predict that these second-generation robots will soon perform 60 percent of all the work on auto production. They claim that half the jobs held by the country's 1.2 million production line workers might be at risk (Draper 1985, 49). GM's Roger Smith said that each one-dollar-an-hour pay increase makes it profitable for the company to install 1,000 additional robots (Shaiken 1984, 169). About nine-tenths of Apple's Macintosh computer is assembled automatically (Draper 1985, 48). It is interesting to note that America's huge multinational corporations are beginning to purchase their own robotics manufacturing firms. For example, Westinghouse, General Electric, General

Motors, Bendix, Renault, Volkswagen, and United Technologies have already done so (ibid., 48).

The CIM production technology will have not only a quantitative effect on the number of American jobs, but there will also be a qualitative effect regarding the kinds of jobs skills demanded of those workers lucky enough to be employed. To dispel any glib assumptions that these CIM jobs will require greater cognitive and technical skills for all American youths, more skeptical analysts have scrutinized recent technical forecasts for more hidden, often implicit assumptions. For example, one report (after the seemingly obligatory recitation of "the romance of technology" data) concluded with the following caveat: "It is deceptive to label such skills as highly technical. The situation is much like driving a car. One does not have to know the theory of internal combustion engines or how power gets to the wheels in order to get around in traffic. Similarly, workers connected with computer-managed processes will generally not be required to know very much about how computers work. They will have no need to learn conventional programming or anything about digital circuits" (Lund and Hansen 1986, 96). And as an illustrative example, they quote the remark of one survey participant:

I argue with some people in terms of the importance of the video game craze that we're in now. A lot of people are against it. My way of thinking is that it's part of this training. You get comfortable with sitting there playing the video game and it's much like sitting there having your production line going on out there and you're monitoring things on the tube. . . . You're dealing with the black box. . . . The kind of people that will be willing to do that kind of job are probably being trained in our video arcades today. (Lund and Hansen 1986, 96–97)

The 1980s school reform movement literature has continued to serve as a sounding board for both of these contrasting viewpoints of the new technologies impact on the American worker. Competing statistical data sets and ideological assumptions make any final resolution of the debate problematic.

THE NEW DEMOGRAPHICS

C. Emily Feistritzer, in the Preface to her book *Cheating Our Children: Why We Need School Reform*, emphasizes the importance of understanding why there must be radical changes in the American educational school system today as measured against the data of the early 1970s: "Today we deal with a new kind of child, from a different background, with a different set of values, hopes, and dreams. That child's parents are different. As surroundings have changed, so have the aspirations" (Feistritzer 1985, vi). The data analysis of Feistritzer, who is director of the National Center for Education Information, represents the kind of new statistical predictions that are being widely circulated within educational circles and that have been extensively used by the 1980s school reformers to justify proposed curriculum and structural changes. As Feistritzer explains, "What we have concluded after analyzing the data is that the biggest reason schools must change is to meet the demands of the children of the 1980s. These children come from vastly different family structures, economic conditions, and language and cultural backgrounds than did the children of only 15 years ago" (Feistritzer 1985, 59).

The statistical story presented can be found in some form in nearly all of the current reform literature. The story begins with a direct challenge to the statistical self-concept that Americans had of themselves during the 1970s—that they were an aging population with fewer children. This reactionary portrait was largely the product of data showing that the massive increase of women in the workplace had resulted in a significant number of young women postponing the start of their families. As a result, it was widely thought that there would be fewer children attending American public schools for the remainder of the twentieth century. However, a careful analysis of more recent data presents a somewhat different picture. It reveals that the population under five grew at a rate three times the overall population from 1980 to 1983 (9 percent), reversing a decline in population of this age group in the last fifteen years (Education Week Staff 1986, 14–39; Feistritzer 1985, 14, 59; Children's Defense Fund 1985, chapters 1 and 3).

The vision of American life in the year 2000 is presented in graphs clearly reminiscent of the race suicide charts of the 1920s—emphasis is placed on the dramatic growth in black and Hispanic populations. As Feistritzer dramatically relates, "The new baby boom is non-white" (Feistritzer 1985, 59). Using basic data from the U.S. Bureau of the Census, the school reform literature has highlighted data showing that minority populations are growing at a much faster rate than are whites. It is estimated that by the year 2000, about 38 percent of the under-eighteen population will be made up of Blacks, Hispanics, Native Americans, and Asians. It is also estimated that "their" portion of American children and youth is expected to grow for many years thereafter (Education Week Staff, 1986, 16–24). The school reform system never failed to point out that youngsters from these groups constituted less than 15 percent of the under-eighteen population in 1950 and less than 27 percent in 1980 (Miller 1986, 52). Thus the most significant demographic changes are considered to be the nation's changing racial and ethnic composition.

Having statistically established the recent population increases among black and Hispanic youths, the data analysts then seek to establish correlations between these changing racial and ethnic demographics and the startling growth in recent poverty. The most important data emphasized in these discussions is that children are bearing the brunt of the latest "poverty boom." According to these demographers, the richest nation in the history of the world, despite its much heralded attempt to end poverty and deprivation, has in recent years seen a tragic increase in the number of poor children: "In 1974, children became the poorest segment of American society, displacing the aged. Since then, child poverty has grown deeper and more widespread.'' (Education Week Staff, 1986, 25). One in five children in this nation now live below the poverty level; 23.3 percent of children under 6 are poor'' (Education Week Staff, 1986, 25–27; Feistritzer 1985, 59). In human terms, that means that our affluent nation had 34.4 million citizens living in poverty in 1982, of which 23.5 million were white, 9.7 million were black, and 4.3 million were Hispanics (Feistritzer 1985, 34). A 1985 report prepared by the Congressional Research Service and the Congressional Budget Office found that whereas half of all black children and a third of all Hispanic children are poor, five-sixths of all white children are not poor (Hentoff 1985, 5).

This new statistical portrait then makes it most celebrated and harsh indictments—if the victims of this ''new poverty boom'' are America's children, then the culprits are clearly American females. First to be cited for condemnations are female-single headed households:

> The rapid growth of households headed by single females has led to much of the overall increase (about 40 percent) in the number of poor families since 1980. One out of every 3 such families headed by single black and single Hispanic females live in poverty. (Education Week Staff, 1985, 25)

New York Senator Daniel Patrick Moynihan, whose 1965 report on the plight of black female-headed families stirred a national debate (and was criticized by many as blatantly racist), extended his analysis in a 1985 report to include the plight of all female-headed households. He argues that the nation must develop a bipartisan family-oriented policy to tackle growing poverty that ''is now inextricably linked with the family structure'' (Moynihan 1986, 18). In 1965 Senator Moynihan reported that disproportionate poverty among Blacks resulted largely from the breakdown of the black family. Today Moynihan warns that the problems facing families—particularly female-headed households—and children— now cross racial lines. He cites the 1983 data from the Congressional Budget Office in support of his position: children under eighteen years of age represent well over one-third (39 percent) of the total number of persons in poverty. The poverty rate for children in female-headed households was much higher (56 percent) than that for all children in other families. The number of female-headed and single-parent households has risen consistently since 1960. Between 1980 and 2000, the numbers of female-headed families are expected to increase at the rate more than five times the rate of husband-headed families (Hertling 1985, 8). The 1985 Congressional Research Service and the Congressional Budget Office likewise make a direct link between the increase in the number of female-headed households over the past quarter-century and the increase in child poverty. The report charged,

> If the proportion of children in female-headed families had not increased during the past 25 years, it is estimated that the number of poor children in 1983 might have been almost 3 million, or 22 percent lower than it actually was. (Hentoff 1985, 5)

The reform literature statistics cited in support of the present conditions in and social consequences of life in a single-female headed household are presented in a social vacuum. A number of reported female personality deficiencies in such households (i.e., sexual license, egocentricity, moral laxness, low IQ, lack of social responsibility, etc.) are made to appear as the major reasons explaining this "family breakdown." The statistics are unrelenting: one in five children now live with a mother with no father present. Over half (56 percent) of these children are poor. The number of female householders, no husband present, has doubled since 1970 and tripled since 1960. One-third of all female householders are poor (Feistritzer 1985, 59). The figures for the black female-headed household is subject to even greater concern—one in three female householders is black. Forty-seven percent of black women maintain families of their own children, but with no husband present. Almost always they live below the poverty level. Some 70.7 percent of the children who live with them are classified as poor (Feistritzer 1985, 60). As the Children's Defense League summarized the data:

Whether black or white, young mothers under age 25 heading families are very likely to be poor. The poverty rates in 1983 were 85.2 percent for young black female-headed families and 72.1 percent for young white female-headed families. (Children's Defense Fund 1985, 9)

This statistical portrait reveals a bleak landscape. America today is more illiterate, more hungry, more homeless, more unemployed, more alienated, more hopeless than ever before in our nation's history. Each of these phenomenon has also been highly correlated with urban cities and female-headed households (Children's Defense Fund 1985; Education Week Staff 1985, 1986; Feistritzer 1985; Hispanic Policy Development Fund 1984; Tugend March 1986 and April 1986; Uhlenberg and Eggbeen 1986). The connection between female-headed households and child poverty is especially high in urban areas. Again, according to the National Center for Education Information's analysis of the data—nearly 1 in 5 residents in inner cities is classified as poor. One-third of all children living in inner cities are poor. Two-thirds of all children with female householders in inner cities are poor. Over 72 percent of inner-city children under 6 years of age are poor (Feistritzer 1985, 35). It is estimated that since 1981, 2,000 urban children have fallen into poverty each day (Futrell 1986, 10).

Curiously, the feminization of poverty and the consequent victimization of children have occurred within an occupational environment that has likewise seen a dramatic increase in the numbers of women working and earning in the American labor force. The number of females, 14 years old and over, with an income rose from 51.6 million in 1970 to 83.8 million in 1983. The working "super-mom" has become a regular fixture in American culture—2 out of 3 of the 60 million children under 18 in 1982 had working mothers (Feistritzer 1985, 49). However, as participants in the secondary labor force, women experience little job security, occupational mobility, professional self-fulfillment or financial gain. The median income for the 24,668,000 female householders in 1982 was $10,970 compared with a median income of $24,376 for 59.25 million male householders that year (Feistritzer 1985, 46). Thus, although employment options grew substantially for women in the 1970s, the workplace—including educational access—remains predominantly sex-segregated and racially-segregated—and tends to depress women's wages and opportunities for advancement (Bridgman 1986, 10).

Not only have increasing poverty rates been correlated with the rise of female-headed households, but similarly, high school grades, SES quartiles, and achievement test scores have been correlated directly with the rise of single female-headed family structures. According to this research, "though we might wish it otherwise and might pledge to alter it, in our society success begets success and failure is usually the parent to failure" (Feistritzer 1985, 1). Such socioeconomic variables as family income, education level of parents, and whether a student lives with both parents, data reveal, have a direct correlation with how well that student performs academically in school. Students who live with both parents, come from high-income families, the top socioeconomic status quartile, have relatively highly educated parents—these students score highest on achievement test scores. Students who are poor, in the bottom SES quartile, live with one parent or have some other arrangement, and whose parents have little education—these students score lowest on achievement test scores (Feistritzer 1985, 1–2). Thus the reader is left to conclude that the recent decline in test scores and other measures of educational achievement is directly correlated to the dramatic increase in working moms and single female-headed households.

MEGATRENDS AND PUBLIC POLICY

These technical analyses of the emerging world economy, the nature of the new technologies, and the demographic characteristics of the future American population have been scrutinized especially by American economists, educators, social planners, industrialists, and personnel specialists for their likely impact on personnel demand and supply issues. According to John Ong, chairman and CEO of B. F. Goodrich Company and a spokesman for the nonprofit business-led National Alliance of Business, for the remainder of this century America will struggle with the problems of untrained workers in a technological workplace, stiff international competition, and demographic shifts in the composition of the work force (National Alliance of Business 1986).

For both liberals and conservatives alike, the lessons to be learned from these latest technical projections are clear: any future longevity for the United States in the new global marketplace depends on the ability of American public policy to resolve the dilemmas posed by a mismatch between the personnel demands of an emerging high tech, high skill economy and an increasingly ill-prepared personnel supply from largely poor, minority, single-family headed households. Within the framework of these new social forces, the theory of human capital plays a central role, emphasizing as it does the relationship between lower skills (i.e., either cognitive skills or personality traits) and lower productivity and profits. According to this analysis, American workers are making substandard contributions to economic productivity. Schools are indicted for undermining the nation's industrial, commercial, technological, and military supremacy in the world economy by turning out students who have antiquated personality habits and deficient academic skills. In order to restore military supremacy and economic predominance in the international economy, a more direct link is called for between a reformed educational system and a more productive economy.

Having achieved consensus about the nature of the problem facing the present American economy, conservative and liberal social policy experts proceed to part company over the most efficient manner to ensure a highly productive American labor force. The 1980s school reform debate can be seen, then, in its largest social context, as ultimately a dispute between these two groups as to the most efficient means to maintain "the American meritocracy" in view of these new social forces—the emerging global economy, the new technologies, and the changing demographic characteristics of the American populace.

THE POLITICAL ECONOMY OF SCHOOL REFORM: THE SUNBELT CONSERVATIVE AGENDA OF THE 1980s

> . . . we have been compelled to create a permanent armaments industry of vast proportions. . . . This conjunction of an immense Military Establishment and a large arms industry is new in the American experience. . . . In the councils of government we must guard against the acquisition of unwarranted influence whether sought or unsought, by the military-industrial complex.
> (President Eisenhower 1961, cited in Melman 1970, 237)

It was in 1946 that General Dwight D. Eisenhower, acting in his capacity as chief of staff of the United States Army, originally formulated the idea of a close continuing relationship between the army and civilian American scientists, corporate leaders, technologists, and university officials (Melman 1970, 231). However, by January 1961, in his "farewell address," President Eisenhower, observing some of the consequences of the collaboration he had set in motion in 1946, tried to caution his successor, John F. Kennedy, and the American people to be watchful of this military-industrial complex. Four years later, even the usually accomodationist liberal establishment figure of Robert L. Heilbroner had also become alarmed over the ascendance of the military establishment: "There is little doubt that a military-industrial-political interpenetration of interests exists to the benefit of all three. Yet in this alliance I have seen no suggestion that the industrial element is the dominant one. It is the military or the political branch that commands, and business that obeys . . . the role of business in the entire defense effort is essentially one of jockeying for favor rather than initiating policy" (Heilbroner 1965, 51). By 1970, Columbia University's Seymour Melman, in his book *Pentagon Capitalism*, had convincingly traced in detail the expanding grasp of this military-corporate-defense network, the operational ethic of America's new high tech military contracting firms, and the new weapons being designed and tested in the Research and Development (R&D) laboratories of the Department of Defense (DOD).

The conservative sunbelt group has a difficult brand of domestic and international policy to implement, depending as it does on the support of a close, continuing relationship between the Pentagon, major American weapons and aerospace military corporations, American universities, and an eager international community of weapons purchasers. By any measure of industrial activity, this new weapons production and distribution network in the DOD is considered to be the largest industrial management complex in the United States (Packard 1986, 11; Schiller and Phillips 1970; Yarmolinsky 1971). William Proxmire wrote of the Pentagon's military-industrial complex: "[it] has more tentacles than an octopus. Its dimensions are almost infinite. It is a military-industrial-bureaucratic-trade association-labor union-intellectual-technical-service club-political complex whose pervasiveness touches nearly every citizen" (cited in Navarro 1984, 245). By the early 1980s, it was estimated that one in every ten Americans was employed in a defense-related white or blue collar job (Navarro 1984, 246).

SDI AND PENTAGON CAPITALISM

Reagan's new Pentagon-run "Star Wars" weapons production industry has added vast new wealth to the conservative sunbelt weapons coalition. Since 1984 many of these loyal Reagan supporters have received lucrative weapons contracts to define Star Wars technology and battle management systems for their use. They include General Dynamics, United Technologies, General Research, Hughes Aircraft, Lockheed, Raytheon, Northrup, Martin Marietta, McDonnell Douglas, Rockwell International, Science Applications, Sparta Corporation, Teledyne, and TRW. Other major defense contractors benefiting from the Reagan brand of Pentagon capitalism include Boeing, LTV, Aerojet General, General Electric, Honeywell, Grumman, Litton (ITEK), RCA, and Westinghouse (Adams 1986, 264; Navarro 1984, 247). David Packard, cofounder and chairman of Hewlett-Packard Company, past deputy secretary of Defense (1969–1971), and chairman of President Reagan's Blue Ribbon Commission on Defense Management, explained in a recent Heritage Foundation publication the extent of the DOD defense acquisition and weapons procurement industry:

Defense acquisition is the largest and probably most complex business enterprise in the free world. Annual purchases by the Department of Defense (DOD) total almost $170 billion—more than all the purchases of General Motors, Exxon, and IBM combined. DOD's research and development expenditures are more than 15 times those of the French, German, or British militaries, and 80 times those of the Japanese. Defense acquisition involves almost 15 million separate contract actions per year—or an average of 56,000 contract actions every working day. (Packard 1986, 11)

The Strategic Defense Initiative (SDI), or Star Wars, consists of many new developing technologies that have been sold to the American public on the grounds of their ability to "render nuclear weapons impotent and obsolete." The supporting evidence is not convincing (Union of Concerned Scientists 1984; Velikhov 1986; Mohr 1985). Star Wars appears to be (as one commentator observed), instead, "an integral part of a nuclear strategy, increasingly oriented toward the offensive use of nuclear weapons as a strategy that includes imagining that a nuclear war can be fought, controlled, won, and survived" (Adams 1986, 262). As such, this vast new Star Wars system involves a mind-boggling assortment of high tech paraphernalia including power stations, tracking equipment, adaptive optics technology, telecommunications, electronics, sensor technology, and battle management software. The new weapons of war include a horrifying and frightening array of devices that promise to deliver certain global destruction and nuclear holocaust: ground-based, chemical, free-electron, and space-based lasers; space-based neutral and ground-based charged particle beams; kinetic kill weapons technology, the nuclear pumped X-ray laser, and the battle management and computer coordination required to operate and coordinate these different defenses. This, in turn, has spawned new counteroffensive, Pentagon-directed weapons R&D teams funded to develop anti-SDI defenses: depressed (lower) trajectory missiles, dummy warheads and decoys, chaff and other atmospheric junk, more sea-based missiles, accelerated launch land-based missiles, nuclear space mines, killer satellites, and so on (Robinson 1986, 16–23 passim; Union of Concerned Scientists 1984; Thee 1986).

"COMPETITIVE SUPREMACY" AS PUBLIC POLICY

During the Reagan administration, Pentagon capitalism has been raised to a new level of public policy acceptance and support. Economists, public policy specialists, and educational leaders committed to Reagan's strategies are convinced that the continued longevity of "the American dream" can be achieved only by a unified military-political-social policy based on a global strategy they refer to as "competitive supremacy." The hawkishness of the administration leaders on nuclear weapons policy, the "Rambo" doctrine of illegal, covert aid to the contras, and the Star Wars strategy against the Soviet Union reflects the kind of "competitive supremacy" ethos that they have found so agreeable to their conservative nationalist anticommunism. As such, they support a public policy position that relates to the world community in an adversary relationship.

There is much controversy about the strengths of Reagan's competitive militaristic model versus the liberal dream of a global economy managed in the world interest by the high tech Trilateral leaders. Two divergent views of the individual and society underlie the differences between these groups. For the conservative, the individual is viewed essentially as a creature of self-interest as evidenced in the work of Adam Smith, Edmund Burke, Thomas Hobbes, and Alexander Hamilton. In this model, war is viewed as a rational activity; it is only natural that nations should have clashing interests. To deal with aggressors (real or imagined), the United States should be militarily prepared and should encourage in its people a willingness to fight. The watchword here is deterrence through military strength and supremacy.

According to the administration's "competitive supremacy" model of development, the United States' continued role as the world's dominant economic and political force can be maintained only from a position of military strength and dominance. Reagan's model of "international development" depends on an autocratic development policy that is not bound to promote the living standards of any Third World developing nation with which they seek economic alliances. In a recent booklet entitled *The United States and the World: Setting Limits*, former UN Ambassador Jeanne Kirkpatrick argues that "national interest" alone should determine our choice of foreign policies, particularly in regard to U.S. military defenses and access to necessary raw materials abroad (Kirkpatrick 1986, passim). Autocratic Third World dictatorships, friendly to American interests, are considered best equipped to guarantee both a continued supply of raw materials needed by U.S. heavy industry and a ready market for the finished military hardware. To operationalize this worldwide Pentagon network has necessitated the development of a tenuous alliance among an assorted coterie of international finance capitalists, arms dealers, military security specialists, Third World dictatorships, and Pentagon-supported sunbelt military contractors. Together, they have developed a particular strategy to achieve military control and dominance over the emerging world economy, the new technologies, and the expanding Third World populations at home and abroad (Chomsky and Herman 1979).

It is not difficult to understand the public policy implications of these "heavy industry" conservative sunbelt corporate/defense industries. Nor is it difficult to understand that these capital-intensive munitions and aerospace industries do not have the same economic interests or the same geopolitical concerns as the more flexible, high tech computer chip assembly or light industry plants of the northeastern liberal capitalists. Due to the massive initial capital investment needed to equip these defense production plants, along with the huge R&D costs, economic profitability for the heavy industry capitalists demands long-term social stability and monopoly control over the raw materials necessary for their production systems. Given the nature of these production variables, it is not surprising to discover that the Pentagon-dependent firms tend to specialize in a few weapons or weapons systems—e.g., United Technologies in military aircraft engine and helicopter manufacturing, Raytheon in missiles and electronics, General Dynamics in F–16 and F–111 jet fighters, and so on. This situation led one observer to conclude that "while there would appear to be enormous competition for shares of the overall defense budget, many firms have carved out a comfortable niche in the market where they bid, often with very little or no competition (Navarro 1984, 246). The combination of heavy capital investment in production systems and the need to protect high tech military security systems means that these Pentagon-controlled industries have little geographic mobility, and certainly have little to gain from an integrated system of world capitalism. Thus it is in the self-interest of the Pentagon-dependent coalition to visualize the international world market from a position of competitive superiority. In addition, because a large part of the growth of Pentagon capitalism is based on foreign weapons and aerospace orders, a foreign policy that glorifies a Rambo-style policy of imperialistic adventure and sabre-rattling Cold War defense tactics, plays directly into their economic interests.

COMPETITIVE SUPREMACY AND THE NEW FEDERALISM

During the Reagan administration, a new conservative approach to domestic social policies was articulated for the purpose of revitalizing the competitiveness of the American economy and restoring America's eroding position as the leading world power. Unlike traditional classical/libertarian Republican party solutions, this New Right coalition called for a much more centrally controlled, activist federal government to provide the framework for renewed national supremacy (Bohannon, Buckley, and Osborne 1983). Under a concept referred to as the "New Federalism," the roles and responsibility of federal and state governments, public educational institutions, and private sector corporations were redefined in order to achieve a new consensus for social action. President Reagan stressed the importance of strengthening this business-academic-government partnership nexus as a necessary structure to restore American supremacy and economic competitiveness (Business-Higher Education Forum 1983, 1985; Bohannon, Buckley, and Osbourne 1983; Doyle and Hartle 1985; Packard 1987; Committee for Economic Development).

The New Federalism was conceived as a political arrangement whereby federal level policy experts were empowered to prescribe the "consensus goals," whereas individual states, school systems, and local business groups were delegated to compete between and among themselves over the most efficient means to implement these natural goals (Finn 1986; Doyle and Finn 1984; Reagan and Sanzone 1981). Furthermore, there was a commitment to achieve these goals not through liberal-style monolithic federal level "give-away" programs, but rather through a series of federal level *incentive* programs in the areas of tax, trade, R&D, patent, antitrust policies, and the like (Business-Higher Education Forum 1983, 33; Committee for Economic Development 1984). On the state level, therefore, the principles of the New Federalism worked to play off one state economy against another, thereby extracting tax breaks and labor concessions in order to attract large multinational, corporate industry and huge Pentagon-controlled defense production plants. In this way, the national level big business-labor-academia-government coalition establishes national goals and macroeconomic policies, and then works to ensure that a decentralized market economy of numerous small manufacturing firms is allowed the "freedom" to openly compete for subcontracting work with the large multinational conglomerates.

Foundations closely linked to the defense and aerospace industries have contributed huge amounts of money during the 1980s to conservative think-tanks and activist secular and religious groups advocating these policies. Represented by the National Association of Manufacturers, the Chamber of Commerce, the American Enterprise Institute, the Moral Majority, the Hoover Institute, the Manhattan Institute, and the Heritage Foundation among others, the conservative sunbelt coalition has redirected huge sums of money from liberal welfare programs to conservative Pentagon-related defense projects. These conservative think-tanks have been sharply critical of liberal welfare programs and their harmful effects on the work ethic (Murray 1984; Gilder 1981). According to these analyses, the growth of the public sector has been associated with reduced economic vitality. The result, they charge, has been a deterioration of business profits: trade unions protected by government action drove up wages; government regulations reduced the ability of business firms to respond to changing market conditions; the vast social safety net increased taxation; and the widespread adoption of the "welfare mentality" has had an injurious effect on work discipline. Thus, according to conservative economists, liberal advocates of national industrial planning want to give America more of what weakened its economy in the first place: more federal restrictions on domestic and international trade, more taxes and government expenditures, and more centralized decision making. For these conservatives, the liberals offer the problems as the solution (Murray 1984; Gilder 1981).

However, the new conservative policy approach seemingly contains some contradictions of its own. In the process of formulating the competitiveness strategies of the New Federalism, the conservatives fully embraced the need for national industrial policies, without being willing to use the liberal terminology, or as Thurow (1985, 101) rightly noted, "what is thrown out by the front door is dragged in by the back door." Our analysis of the Pentagon model of capitalism revealed the extent to which the DOD clearly controls defense-related corporate industries. It is understandable why liberals argue that such marketplace intervention clearly constitutes centralized government targeting and control. Reagan administration apologists counter that such government control over the defense production establishments is justified primarily on national security criteria: "Defense expenditures are primarily a public good to increase national security. Because the primary beneficiaries of U.S. defense expenditures are U.S. citizens and their allies, these expenditures do not constitute a targeted industrial policy" (Committee for Economic Development 1984, 28).

The debate cannot be reduced to a matter of semantics. The concept of totalitarian governmental control over the economic sector has become acceptable to both conservatives and liberals as the inevitable price that must be paid to maintain global supremacy in the emerging world economy. Thus the notion that the New Right supports a shrinking role for government is a misleading characterization of Reagan's policies—as is his "happy trails" rhetoric about "getting the government off the people's backs." The intent of this new conservative sunbelt coalition is to clear the stage for two of Reagan's favorite actors—the more coercive branches of the military state and the monolithic grasp of the huge Pentagon-linked corporate industries and production plants. "Irangate" was only a more visible exposure of the ways in which coercive agencies of state power were encouraged to grow at the expense of basic civil rights and democratic liberties. The Reagan administration has vastly expanded the powers of the FBI to spy on ordinary Americans and of the CIA to involve itself in illegal covert activities. Federal level watchdog agencies, consumer protection groups, civil rights and affirmative action programs have had their budgets slashed and have been staffed with Reaganite appointees hostile to their basic principles. In conclusion, the Reagan policies have dramatically reshaped traditional classical/libertarian/conservative notions of limited government and the protection of private spheres of personal autonomy (Piven and Cloward 1982; Rule 1986).

MANAGING THE CONSERVATIVE MANDATE

The management model developed to ensure the effectiveness of the New Federalism was articulated in detail in the Heritage Foundation's influential volume *Mandate for Leadership II: Continuing the Conservative Revolution.* The Heritage Foundation's *Mandate for Leadership (I)* was designed to be a detailed road map to help the fledgling Reagan administration steer the nation into a sound future, guided by conservative principles (Butler, Sanera, and Weinrod 1984; Heatherly 1981). The positivist model of scientific management adopted by these sunbelt conservatives tends to view all problems as amenable to technical solutions. This system of Taylorism, often called in the business literature "managerialism," finds its greatest success in exactly the type of industrial production systems needed by large-scale weapons production firms, that is, standardized, high-volume production in capital-intensive manufacturing.

The Heritage Foundation manual identified the well-entrenched liberal federal bureaucracy as the most formidable challenge to be surmounted by the first-term Reagan administration. The problem of "controlling subordinate discretion" was identified as the missing link in the formation of an effective government operation. The Heritage Foundation's favored model of public administration and management called for an autocratic system of top-down control piloted by conservative policy experts that explicitly eliminated democratic participation. "Effective control begins with issuing orders. The less ambiguous and general they are, the less discretion is delegated to subordinates" (Butler, Sansera, amd Weinrod 1984, 532). Especially cited for administrative effectiveness was the Management-by-Objective (MBO) system of Secretary of Interior James Watt. The particular strength of this system, according to the Heritage Foundation report, was its ability to confine policy-making to top-level staff executives and its ability "to take initiative away from the bureaucracy, which is quickly set to work developing the administration's agenda rather than its own" (Butler, Sansera, and Weinrod 1984, 548). In light of the recent revelations concerning Reagan's "secret government" operations, apparently even these Heritage Foundation proposals were not sufficiently covert.

Reagan's conservative management proposals have been (without fail) articulated to the general public in the familiar meritocratic veneer. Thus proposals calling for more centralized policy development are explained in the New Federalism literature as a way to make decentralization work better. According to David Packard, "Rather than create more centralization, our proposals will create a climate in which real decentralized execution can take place" (Packard 1986, 15). In these ways, conservative public administration management policy relies heavily on a variety of public relations strategies implemented to ensure top-down management control while maintaining the symbolic vestiges of traditional democratic participation and decision making.

CONSERVATIVE SUNBELT SCHOOL REFORM POLICIES

Contemporary Reaganite conservatives have become convinced, however, that a new unified cultural system must be developed and coherent, rationalized worldview promoted if a compliant, adaptable, submissive, mobile citizenry and work force is to be maintained. Although the question of skill development, especially the development of both basic literacy skills and advanced technological expertise, is a central part of the conservative school reform agenda, conservative reformers have concentrated most attention on the question of the role of the American schools in character and citizenship training.

Regardless of the rhetoric highlighting the primacy of the family, conservative sunbelt school reform policies have recognized that, in terms of long-range social strategies, the family unit must be abandoned as the primary locus for the development and transmission of socially desirable cultural norms and personality traits. According to the blatantly sexist assumptions underlying their rationale, the growing number and weakening influence of single female-headed families have put the burden of socialization directly on educational institutions. The conservative sunbelt coalition has concluded that America's educational institutions must become important vehicles for socializing and instilling the necessary personality traits.

Therefore, conservative educational theorists have begun to focus more and more on the portion of the educational process we call "character development" as the missing equation in human capital theory. To conservative intellectual James Q. Wilson, the influential professor of government at Harvard and UCLA professor of management, the most significant development in public policy in the past twenty years has been a growing awareness that many public problems can be addressed only "if they are seen as arising out of a defect in character formation.'' In his *Public Interest* article ''The Rediscovery of Character: Private Virtue and Public Policy,'' Wilson observes that ''a good school is one that takes up and continues in a constructive manner, the development of character begun in the family'' (Wilson 1985, 33). Likewise, in his report for the National Chamber Foundation entitled *Self-Discipline, Schools, and the Business Community*, Amitai Etizioni also emphasizes character traits as the primary goal of school reform:

In their preoccupation with the cognitive, most parents and educators have ignored the importance to schooling of psychic development. It ought to be the first criterion we use in assessing schools: their contribution to the development of character of personality, to the formation of habits of thought and behavior which enable the student not only to acquire cognitive skills but also to act constructively in any situation. (Etzioni 1984, 6)

COMPETITIVE SUPREMACY AND CHARACTER DEVELOPMENT

William Bennett, Diane Ravitch, and Chester Finn have set forth many of their ideas on these issues in three books, *Against Mediocrity*, *Challenges to the Humanities*, and *The Schools We Deserve*. They see their theoretical task as that of developing a new utilitarian justification for a common core curriculum based on an assumed public consensus as to the proper aims and purposes of education. U.S. Secretary of Education William J. Bennett has urged the schools to stress the three C's: character, content, and choice. According to Secretary Bennett, ''Common culture—common values, common knowledge, and a common language—are essential to sharing dreams and to discussing differences. There are some things that we must all learn and learn together'' (Bennett 1986, 23). According to that perspective, the common core public school curriculum must be re-evaluated in terms of its utility in serving new societal goals: (1) every American youngster should be enrolled in essentially the same history course, learning the same historical facts; (2) a broad consensus exists in American society on the particular body of historical knowledge that is most worth knowing; (3) this shared cultural heritage must be absorbed by each student for the individual to be called ''literate'' and for education to be regarded as truly useful; and (4) the purpose of this new core curriculum should be presented in such a fashion as ''to realize a common political vision'' (Finn, Ravitch, et al. 1985). Their arguments dovetail neatly with the recent research of E. D. Hirsch and his University of Virginia colleagues. In a recent publication, *Cultural Literacy*, Hirsch argues that America's literacy problems stem from children's lack of knowledge about the common culture—not from a lack of mechanical reading skills. According to Dr. Hirsch, schools must return to a much more traditional, facts-oriented cultural curriculum that systematically teaches children the core information they need to know in order to read with comprehension and in order to become more productive members of American society.

Within these appeals for a common core curriculum is a subtle cry for a new kind of civic religion—a civic religion that supposedly blends the Judeo-Christian moral code, the patriotic fervor of traditional democratic beliefs, with a facts-based, skills-oriented curriculum. Gary Bauer, under secretary of Education and chairman of the Presidential Task Force on the Family, made this clear in a *Policy Review* article entitled "The Moral of the Story":

The most important values that our public schools must teach, I believe, are the fundamental principles that are the basis of our free society and democratic government. In our effort to identify values that can be taught in public schools, we should attempt to discover a common body of ethical knowledge that, even if it has religious origin, serves the purpose of maintaining and strengthening devotion to our country. (Bauer 1986, 26)

And what is the nature of this new civic religion that the sunbelt conservatives propose should be taught in educational institutions? Throughout his administration, Secretary of Education William Bennett has reiterated time and again that federal level liberal-style programs and spending are not the keys to boosting America's economic competitiveness. According to Bennett, "Gimmicky programs or new labels aren't going to make us more competitive—any more than new uniforms will make a football team play better. . . . The roots of competitiveness lie in the character of our people" (Wilson 1987, 29). He continues, "qualities such as honesty, a sense of responsibility, fidelity to task, regard for the rights of others form the core of good citizenship," and "are the real elements that will help Americans compete in world markets" (Wilson, 1987). If there remain any nagging doubts about the focal point of concern in Bennett's "common political vision," he elaborated clearly his position in a March 1985 speech to the AASA: "In my view, there are still too many schools in which our students are taught that this country's past is primarily a history of racism, pollution, oppression, and inequality" (Education Week 1985, 16).

If the roots of the "competitive supremacy" policy are interpreted to lie in the social construction of "a common political vision," it is little surprise that the conservative educators would emphasize the importance of these same values in their school programs and curricula.

The recent projects Bennett has financed via his discretionary funds appear intended to support a research and policy agenda in which this new civic religion will be taught via revised school curriculum texts and materials. The Ethics and Public Policy Center has received large grants to convene educators and prominent experts in foreign and military policy in an effort to develop instructional materials relating to U.S. foreign policy. The Center's project director said his group would " . . . try to avoid the mistake of starting by scaring the kids about nuclear war. That's the last thing we want to do." He said the aim of the project would be " . . . to help students understand the essence of foreign affairs, such as nuclear deterrence" (*Education Week*, March 19, 1986, 13). This same desire to use the school curriculum to form the kind of "competitive personality" thought best fitted to the needs of the sunbelt conservative culture is also found in a 1985 speech by Secretary Bennett where he suggested that if students received better history instruction, they would be more likely to support President Reagan's policy of aiding counterrevolutionaries in Nicaragua (*Education Week*, May 1, 1985). Whereas conservative educators may argue over the proper way to teach this new civic religion, there is broad consensus that it will be centered on the creation of a new competitive personality structure to be socially constructed via the study of American heroes in all school subject areas—American heros that produce well, work hard, go to church, form strong patriarchial family units, and, most of all, have the kind of "American character" that fights with patriotic fervor for "American values" around the world (Bauer 1986; Bennett 1986). The culture of Pentagon capitalism is thought to be best preserved through the educational socialization of the "new American character."

A unified educational strategy has been developed during the Reagan administration to ensure that the kind of "American character" compatible with the culture of Pentagon capitalism will be a central part of their school reform agenda. Two integrated school reform policies have been promulgated by the conservative sunbelt coalition: the first, competency-based education (CBE), and the second, maximizing parental choice. Competency-based education maintains that "consensus" standards can be implemented only through more central direction and control, whereas the second strategy claims that these "consensus" standards can be achieved only if individual schools, parents, and such are enabled the "freedom" to compete with one another for the most efficient realization of these standards. Thus the New Federalism finds its happy complement in the conservative school reform agenda. As Chester Finn explains:

Today the state which has always borne the formal constitutional responsibility for education—is the settor of norms, prescriber of ends. . . . But those within the individual school should become the forgers of means—curricular, pedagogical, organizational— and the appropriate unit of accountability for performance. (Finn 1986, 59)

In these ways, the conservative New Federalism educational program is specifically designed to implement related economic and political goals.

THE POLITICAL ECONOMY OF SCHOOL REFORM: THE NORTHEASTERN LIBERAL ESTABLISHMENT AGENDA OF THE 1980s

To some extremists, the Trilateral Commission is pictured as a nefarious plot by an Eastern Establishment of businessmen in the service of multinational corporations . . . [or] a scheme to subject the working people of the world to the machinations of rapacious capitalism. . . . My point is that far from being a coterie of international conspirators with designs on covertly ruling the world, the Trilateral Commission is, in reality, a group of concerned citizens interested in fostering greater understanding and cooperation among international allies. (David Rockefeller 1980, cited in Sklar 1980, xi)

The Reagan years have seen a major public policy split between the northeastern liberal establishment and the sunbelt conservative interests. Whereas there are many overlaps between these two competing philosophies, there are also a number of important distinctions that must be established. The northeastern liberal establishment has heavy interests in international banking and multinational corporations operating in the third world. In 1973 the Trilateral Commission was founded by David Rockefeller (Chase Manhattan Bank chairman), Zbigniew Brzezinski (President Carter's national security advisor), and a selected group of 300 like-minded prominent corporate executives, labor union leaders, university professors, and research institute directors from North America, Western Europe, and Japan. According to Bill Moyers, "David Rockefeller is the most conspicuous representative today of the [liberal] ruling class, a multinational fraternity of men who shape the global economy and manage the flow of its capital" (Sklar 1980, xii). As such, this international alliance is committed to the establishment of an integrated system of multinational world capitalism.

THE TRILATERAL LIBERALS AND WORLD CAPITALISM

The global strategy of the Trilateral Commission, set forth in their 1977 report, *Toward a Renovated International System*, argues that the "public and leaders of most countries continue to live in a mental universe which no longer exists— a world of separate nations—and have great difficulties thinking in terms of global perspectives and interdependence" (Cooper, Kaisar, and Kosaka 1977). Liberal corporate policy since the 1970s has focused on the international economy. It emphasizes the need to reorganize corporate management in the United States with a view to enabling U.S.-based corporations to accommodate rationally to the changing structure of international trade. Beginning in the 1960s, the traditionally large U.S. trade surplus began to erode. Trade rivalry was mounting among the United States, Japan, and Western Europe (Sklar 1980, 7). In addition, during the same time increasing numbers of Blacks, Chicanos, Native Americans, Puerto Ricans, and women were beginning to mobilize wide public support and effective political self-help campaigns. The rout of the U.S. military from Vietnam seriously undermined the confidence of the American public in elite control of their social and political institutions. As a result of the Church Committee investigations, congressional constraints were finally placed on direct and covert U.S. military action both at home and in Third World developing nations. The effect of this combined broadly based public reappraisal of governmental action and "morality" in the post–Vietnam/post–Watergate era was to mobilize a public questioning of the legitimacy of American operational policy and objectives— its hierarchy, its coercion, its secrecy, its covert activities, its leaders, and so on. Referred to by the liberal Trilateral alliance as a "crisis in capitalist democracies," their international policy solutions were designed to reassert the United States' role as the supreme architect and engineer of the emerging multinational world economy (Crozier, Huntington, and Watanuk: 1975).

The Trilateralists argue that the disturbing employment, profit, and growth statistics from the 1970s through the mid–1980s are the consequence of corporate management's emphasis on short-run profits rather than long-run growth. They condemn the militaristic model of competitive world capitalism that is supported by conservative Reaganites and have become alarmed by the threats that nuclear war, SDI world militarization, and cries for American competitive supremacy and global domination pose to the continued world accumulation of capital. Thus the liberal agenda for the 1980s has realized that the Reagan administration's cry for global militarization may not be in the long-term interests of continued multinational capitalist business and leisure-time pursuits.

"MUTUAL BENEFIT" AS PUBLIC POLICY

During the late 1970s, influenced by the Trilateral agenda, a team of neo-liberal politicians, economists, social policy experts, and think-tank researchers strove to reinvigorate declining liberal Democratic party policies that had begun to be identified with corrupt union activity, pork barrel welfare support programs, and an overly ambitious Federal enforcement of Supreme Court decisions in state and local arenas. By the early 1980s, the ideas of Gary Hart (D-Colorado), Robert Reich (Harvard), Walter Mondale (D-Minnesota), Felix Rohatyn (New York banker), John Naisbett (Washington, D.C.), and Lester Thurow (MIT) had become widely discussed in academic and political circles in conjunction with their advocacy of a "national industrial policy" to restore America's international competitiveness in the emerging international global economy.

The basic tenet of twentieth-century corporate liberalism has always rested on the principle that the excesses of capitalism can be reformed only by wise state and federal intervention. Thus in true neo-liberal style, Senator Gary Hart's NIP proposals are presented as an attempt to blend the Jeffersonian principle of a free competitive economy with the Rooseveltian principle that economic success cannot be divorced from social conscience (Hart 1983, 8, 10). Harvard professor Robert Reich, a founding father of the industrial policy approach, agrees with this position: "in the emerging era of productivity, social justice is not incompatible with economic growth, but essential to it" (Reich 1983, 20). In his book, *The Zero-Sum Society*, Lester C. Thurow develops a similar thesis that equity and efficiency are not mutually conflicting goals. He writes: "The world is full of empirical evidence that efficiency does not require less equity. Quite the contrary, to obtain the efficiency the United States needs, it is going to have to promote equity" (Thurow 1981, 120).

Liberal development economists are convinced that the main task facing poor nations is economic growth. If per capita income could be initiated and sustained, other problems of underdevelopment could be solved. However, the experience of developing nations over the past few decades revealed the futility of liberal economic theories that hypothesize an inevitable correlation between growth and the amelioration of mass poverty or social inequality. To solve this dilemma, liberal development economists searched for a new development strategy specifically constructed to deal with Third World poverty. Their response, widely referred to as the "basic needs approach," was popularized and disseminated by the Trilateral-controlled World Bank. As one well-known authority explained:

The evolution, from growth as the principal performance criterion, via employment and redistribution, to basic needs is an evolution from abstract to concrete objectives, from preoccupation with means to a renewed awareness of ends, and from a double negative (e.g., reducing employment) to a positive (i.e., meeting basic needs). (Streeten 1978, cited in Sameter 1984, 4)

Proponents of the "basic needs approach" agree that at its most fundamental level, any development strategy for Third World nations should include satisfying minimum levels of material needs such as consumption of food, shelter, and clothing, and access to such essential public services as pure water, sanitation, public transport, health, and education. Having articulated a long-range development plan to meet these basic needs, the northeast liberal establishment is then free to extend its control over Third World manufacturing and trade facilities. The result is a symbiotic union of the indigenous ruling classes and the multinational firms. Third World capitalist development as sponsored by the northeast liberal establishment is not geared to embark on a real systemic assault on poverty (Sandbrook 1982).

John Naisbett's *Megatrends* is a book often cited in the liberal reform literature and used as an authoritative framework and source for identifying the major defining characteristics and trends in the emerging future world economy. Naisbett himself summarizes the results of his content analysis of more than 2 million local newspaper articles from American cities and towns over a twelve-year period as follows: "It's becoming clear that yesterday is over, and as the Third World prepares to take over the major industrial tasks, the developed countries must move on to new enterprises" (Naisbett 1982, 72). The control over this new information technology by the Trilateral nations was thought to be the key to maintaining control over the new multinational capitalist world economy. Thus, according to the liberal model, it is critically important for American foreign policy to be based on an ethnic of "mutual benefit." Only by developing the Third World will Americans be assured of both goods and markets, or as Naisbett put it, "in an interdependent world, aid is not charity; it is investment" (Naisbett 1982, 77).

Thus, whereas both liberals and conservatives now support the abolition of labor unions and the shift of low skill production to the Third World, the liberal position holds that a system of multinational capitalism can work only if corporations from the advanced capitalist nations treat Third World workers well and if continual innovation and mechanization is encouraged. Thus the liberals continued to explicitly claim (as they have throughout the twentieth century) that social welfare programs are not only humane but that they make good economic sense. The liberal concept of the "good" multinational is committed to providing "social uplift" in the living standards for the Third World countries within which they construct their huge corporate conglomerates.

AMERICA'S HIGH TECH FUTURE AND TRILATERAL NATIONAL INDUSTRIAL POLICY (NIP)

Liberal theorists argue that the failure of macroeconomic policy in the 1970s was due to the increasing integration of the United States into the world economy. This growing integration exposed the inefficiency of many domestic American markets in contrast to foreign rivals. As these rivals captured a greater share of the world markets in steel, autos, and other industries, permanent layoffs and shutdowns occurred, especially in the high-wage, union-controlled manufacturing industries in America. The NIP proponents fear that as the heart of the nation's old manufacturing base (high-wage, labor-intensive, unionized, routine production manufacturing industries) is dramatically reshaped through capital flight and mechanization, the United States will more and more become a nation divided between the rich and the poor. They see a society in which the high-paying jobs of automobile and steel workers are rapidly being supplanted by low-paying jobs as janitors and fast-food waiters. Thus the NIP analysts believe that the introduction of the "new technologies" into the workplace (via robotics, computer-integrated manufacturing processes, and telecommunications technology), the growing mobility of capital on a global scale (via multinational corporations), and the lack of governmental controls on short-term profiteering are the key reasons for the present U.S. economic decline. However, the solution, for the NIP planners, is not to oppose these global economic trends but to exploit them to the competitive advantage of the United States and its allies (i.e., Japan and Western Europe). The challenge of the new international order will be to tie government programs and policies more closely to the new world economy. The emerging multinational corporate community is envisioned to replace the present geographically based system of national capitalism (Cope 1985; Thurow 1985; Magaziner and Reich 1982; Naisbett 1982; Cooper, Kaiser, and Kosaka 1977).

The work of MIT's Lester Thurow in *The Zero Sum Society*, Harvard's Robert Reich in *The Next American Frontier*, futurist John Naisbett in *Megatrends*, and Colorado's Gary Hart in *A New Democracy* are frequently referred to in the liberal reform literature for their utopian visions of the future U.S. high tech society. Although each of these theorists attributes the reckless "deindustrialization" of the country to a free market economy wherein private firms are encouraged to seek exclusively their own economic self-interest, their remedies do not involve a radical restructuring of either small entrepreneurial, large-scale nationally based, or multinational corporations. Rather, their solutions involve a combination of government intervention on the individual, local, and/or federal level to deal with the "aftershock" of capital flight and mechanization. As such, their proposals do little to challenge "deindustrialization," but rather, use the governmental structure to pacify the resulting social turmoil that inevitably follows such corporate irresponsibility. In other words, the federal government is given the task to be the "social conscience" for America's corporate capitalist institutions—a "social conscience" that itself is valued for its economic payoff.

The national industrial policy (NIP) proposals of the multinational liberals are not difficult to summarize: (1) that the principal obstacle facing the United States in restructuring its economy is the development of a national consensus on the value of a coordinated multinational industrial policy; (2) that the main task in restructuring the liberal interventionist state is to adopt government policies in Japan, Western Europe, and the United States that will promote a new kind of collaborative multinational world economy; (3) that international specialization of labor is the most efficient method to promote international global growth; (4) that the American business-government-academia coalition must concentrate its energies on the development and protection of capital-intensive, high tech, flexible manufacturing systems—complex technological systems in which the United States has a global competitive edge; and (5) to reduce the impact of capital flight and mechanization through increased funding for job training programs, research and development, regional development banks, and local business-government councils (Thurow 1982; Reich 1983; Naisbett 1982; Hart 1983; Committee for Economic Development 1984).

Central to the neo-liberal NIP proposals is their commitment to the idea of "targeting"—a government strategy to assist certain American industries to ensure their "competitive advantage" in the world marketplace. They emphasize that German and Japanese companies, in particular, have used government as an active business partner to better compete in the international marketplace. Thus the conservative refrain "liberate the entrepreneurs" is the problem not the solution. There may be ways in which entrepreneurs need to be liberated, according to these neo-liberals, but America is not being beaten in international competition by countries who have liberated their entrepreneurs and emphasized rugged individualism (Thurow 1985, 123). The liberal rejects the idea that the market is self-correcting: the real problems of our present economy—inflation, unemployment, lagging productivity, deficit spending—will not simply evaporate under the pressure of marketplace competition. So, too, the liberals point out that in the absence of strict regulations during the Reagan administration, the free market has produced short-term profits, but at the expense of pollution, hazardous wastes, dangerous workplaces, and human exploitation. Thus the liberal approach prefers a more regulated and planned economy that is better able to promote efficiency than any blind faith in "the invisible hand" in a marketplace crippled by oligopolies and monopolies.

MANAGING THE LIBERAL HIGH TECH UTOPIA

The liberals pin their hopes on a bright new high tech multinational corporate work environment that stresses adaptability, innovation, and productivity—the necessary components of success in the new international economy. Corporations will invest in new skill-intensive technologies, while farming out low skill, standardized production to the underdeveloped Third World nations. Liberal futurist planners envision nonhierarchical relations with their employees, lifetime employment in some sector of these multinational firms, and continual training and retraining benefits. This new womb-to-tomb liberal management utopia is superficially very convincing. It seemingly has the capacity to do what all twentieth-century liberal models attempt to do—ensure continued corporate economic growth, and at the same time create a more stable, meritocratic social order.

In the end, the case for the Trilateral's reliance on a national industrial policy (NIP) is simple. In the new world economy, America must do what is necessary to be competitive. When it comes down to conceptualizing the problem, there is a lot of agreement between the sunbelt conservatives and the northeastern liberals. Both propose an industrial policy, whatever words they choose to use and no matter how forceful their rhetoric to the contrary. Where they differ is in their procedures to resolve America's loss of international competitiveness— procedures that differ due to competing visions of human nature combined with competing economic and geopolitical strategies for world supremacy.

THE NORTHEASTERN LIBERAL ESTABLISHMENT APPROACH TO SCHOOL REFORM

Liberal corporate and philanthropic involvement in the school reform movement reflects a similar concern to create an harmonious world order via Trilateral control over developing Third World countries. The school reform reports have reached remarkably consistent conclusions regarding the impact of a high tech society on the need for increased skilled labor. There is a general agreement in the school reform literature that America's present demand for more technical skills has been necessitated by a number of recent events—rapid domestic industrial change caused by automation, robotics, and widespread use of computers; greater international technological competition from Japan, South Korea, and West Germany; and increased teen and adult illiteracy. Given the high tech nature of America's future, the school reform reports are especially concerned that American schools train the majority of youngsters to higher levels of academic excellence. They contend that the sophisticated nature of these new technologies requires increased education and training. For example, the *A Nation at Risk* report stated that "One estimate indicates that by the turn of the century, millions of jobs will involve laser technology and robotics" (NCEE 1983, 10). The *Action for Excellence* report expresses a similar position: "The advance of technology will greatly increase job requirements. Jobs which offer upward mobility will increasingly be those which require the creative use of technology" (ECS 1983, 16). The U.S. Chamber of Commerce report in *Business and Education* is even more explicit:

The current information-technology boom, coupled with immense domestic and international competition, pose increasing demands for skilled workers. The use of new production methods that allow more goods to be produced by fewer workers will limit employment for unskilled and/or semi-skilled workers. (Martin 1984, 5)

The National Academy of Sciences' *High Schools and the Changing Workplace* and the College Entrance Examination Board's *Academic Preparation for the World of Work* are also written on the assumption that our economy is headed in the direction of higher skill levels and that job opportunities in the future will favor the well educated. Although they admit that the "new technologies" may eliminate some jobs, nevertheless, they predict that future economic growth will more than offset these initial losses (National Academy of Sciences 1983; College Entrance Examination Board 1983).

These surveys never fail to point out that high tech will provide substantial new job opportunities in occupations and industries associated with these new technologies. The Bureau of Labor Statistics estimates that America is moving from a society that in 1982 required 38 percent of its labor force to achieve a high level of academic preparation, to a society in 1995 that will require over 50 percent of the labor force to have achieved high level computational, writing, speaking, and thinking skills. As Bill Honig, California state superintendent of public instruction, explained it:

Between 1982 and 1995, according to the BLS, 58.6 million job openings are projected to become available. Of these 27.1 million—or 46 percent of the total—are expected to require higher levels of academic preparation. In other words, broadly interpreted, the data show that we are moving from a work force in which 38 percent have the computational, speaking, writing, and thinking skills associated heretofore with the college-bound to a labor market in which nearly half the new hires will be expected to be so qualified. . . . I conclude from the BLS projections that we should be attempting to educate at least two-thirds to three-quarters of our students to these higher levels of academic achievement. (Honig 1985, 23)

Contemporary liberal theorists have found it necessary, therefore, to combine "the upgrading thesis" with traditional human capital theory in order to adequately explain the structure and functioning of their emerging high tech, multinational liberal utopia. This premise contends that the skill requirements needed to perform specified jobs throughout most of the occupational structure are constantly being upgraded in terms of their technical skills and cognitive abilities. In addition, the "upgrading thesis" contains a number of supplementary claims: first, that the technical skill requirements within occupations have been upgraded; second, that many new jobs requiring little in the way of technical skill have been eliminated; and third, that increased automation and mechanization result in an upgrading of the labor force. Thus, whereas conservative social theorists tend to emphasize "character development" as the missing productivity equation in the schools, the liberal theorists focus on the idea of "upgrading" cognitive skills in human capital.

At first glance, one would certainly be inclined to argue that the cry for "upgraded" cognitive skill development is perfectly tailored to meet the high tech demands for control over the emerging global economy by the Trilateral leaders. As expected, liberal theorists will tend to downplay the economic motivation underlying these proposals while emphasizing their academic payoffs. The school reform reports written from such liberal assumptions, therefore, demand that every school program be justified in terms of its "cognitive productivity"—that is, the ability to produce the degree and amount of cognitive skills with both an individual and social rate of return. Of course, it is implied but never stated that it would be unproductive, dysfunctional, and inefficient to develop individual skills that had no social rate of return. Thus programmatic investments especially cited for their potential "to produce a very high return for the nation" include preschool, basic skills, student counseling, work-study, school dropout, and minimal competency programs. In fact, many of these reports (e.g., Committee for Economic Development 1985; Goodlad 1984; Boyer 1983) urge that the business community be used to help school districts identify, select, and train principals as "productivity engineers." Together, these reports propose a comprehensive model for business involvement with the public schools: (1) financial involvement (via minigrant programs, teacher recognition programs, public relations campaigns, experimental curriculum development programs, etc.); (2) programmatic involvement (via adopt-a-school programs, school-to-work programs, magnet school development, career development programs, and staff management training programs, etc.); and (3) policy involvement (via local school board participation, state education taskforces, and major state policy initiatives, etc.). In redefining the educational enterprise as largely a preoccupational training center whose function is to produce the kind of applied skills immediately needed by the emerging model of world capitalism, these school reform proposals further denegrate American education.

The issue becomes even more complex and problematic when one examines in detail the school reform agenda that accompanied these new institutional partnerships and shared educational responsibilities. A number of subtle connections must be uncovered and subjected to further critical review in this liberal "workfare" (as opposed to "welfare") state and the new school work culture. First, a distinction must be made between the "new basics" curriculum, intended largely for the primary labor force, and the "minimal competency" curriculum, intended largely for the secondary labor force. First the "new basics" curriculum appears through its school intensification lists merely to be attempting to provide the social criteria for the acquisition of more advanced critical thinking skills and disciplinary-based achievement. Surely, the "new basics" recommended for high school students—that is, four years of English, three years of mathematics, three years of science, three years of social studies, and half a year of computer science—seem only faintly determined by a utilitarian calculus. From this perspective, the multitude of "school intensification" reforms are explained by the need for a future labor force with a greater degree of cognitive skills. The following school intensification recommendations can be found in some form in most all of the school reform reports:

—Lengthen the school day and the school year.

—Extend years in school.

—Give students more homework.

—Raise graduation academic standards.

—Set higher requirements for admission to college.

—Eliminate "soft" subjects.

—Eliminate vocational education track.

—Mandate a common core curriculum for all students.

—Increase math/science/foreign language requirements.

—Urge the gifted to enter science/technology fields.

Unfortunately, this "new basics curriculum" is designed only for those increasingly few individuals headed for the primary labor force. For the majority of youngsters headed for the low-paying, dead-end jobs of the secondary labor force, the liberal school reformers promise only to provide the noncollege-bound/ minimal competency student with the "learning to learn" skills needed to occupy the new "learning to learn" jobs in the emerging high tech society.

The new "learning to learn" job category provides the key to understanding the subtle arguments at work in the school reform literature over the validity of the "upgrading thesis." The recent influential Education Commission of the States report entitled *Action for Excellence* provides an especially revealing discussion of this new job category and the educational implications surrounding its "upgrading" requirements:

The stiffening demands of advancing technology will almost certainly mean that real opportunity, real chances for upward mobility, will increasingly be reserved for those with "learning to learn " skills. . . . And it is here—in imparting the skills of analysis and problem-solving that constitute "learning to learn" skills—that our schools face their greatest need for improvement. (ECS 1984, 16)

The report then launches into a detailed description of the newly developed four-tiered occupational classification system that should henceforth be used to classify American workers. According to their calculations, future U.S. workers will find employment in one of the following four categories:

Unskilled jobs—can be performed adequately by people with less than today's basic skills: simple hauling and janitorial work.

Basic jobs—require "today's basics": employment, for example, as a clerk in a small, noncomputerized store.

"Learning to Learn" jobs—demand that the worker possess not only basic skills, but be capable of acquiring new ones. Most factory and service industry jobs in America today fall into this category. And it is here—in imparting the skills of analysis and problem solving that constitute "learning to learn" skills—that our schools face their greatest need for improvement.

Professional jobs—require adaptability—"learning-to-learn" skills—and more sophisticated intellectual skills as well. Professionals, scientific programmers and analysts, and middle-to-upper-level corporate managers are examples. (ECS 1984, 16)

For the vast majority of American children, schooling would terminate with the "learning to learn" skills. The *Action for Excellence* report describes in detail the entry-level minimal competency requirements demanded by this new job category. It is important to quote this paragraph at length and to critically reflect on whether these "learning to learn" skills would: (1) result in any significant increase in academic achievement for the vast majority of American children; and (2) result in any significant "upgrading" in the kind of technical skills supposedly needed to function in "tomorrow's technologically sophisticated workplace." The report continues:

Competency in reading, for example, may well include not only the ability to literally decipher a simple written passage, but other skills as well: the ability to analyze and summarize, for example, and the ability to interpret passages inferentially as well as literally.

Basic, minimal mathematical competency may well include, in the future, not just the ability to compute with whole numbers, but also more complicated computing and problem-solving skills: the ability to use arithmetic computations in solving practical problems.

Competency in writing may well comprise not just the ability to write a sentence or paragraph, but the ability to gather and organize information coherently. (ECS 1984, 17)

Thus, whereas the liberal reform agenda appears on the surface to have the potential to provide the cognitive basis for the acquisition of advanced educational achievement, in reality it has been designed for an increasingly small sector of American youth. For the vast majority of noncollege-bound/minimal competency students, the end of formal schooling is expected to occur as soon as they demonstrate acquisition of "learning to learn" minimal competency skills. As such, the school reform proposals are intended to do little more than to prepare minority children for a series of dead-end, low-paying jobs in the secondary labor market. In this way, the "learning to learn" jobs category functions to weld the reality of the "skill delution thesis" to the rhetoric of the "upgrading thesis." As such, it admits that highly skilled labor will not likely be in great demand in America's high tech future, but it "sugar coats" this bitter reality in the soothing rhetoric of "advancing technology, upward mobility, and increasing opportunity." As long as the basic economic and political structure of the United States remains unchallenged, superficially humane gestures, uplifting liberal rhetoric, and moralistic sounding imperatives will be twisted and villified to meet the "mutual benefit" goals and interests of its beneficiaries.

ALTERNATIVES TO PENTAGON AND MULTINATIONAL CAPITALISM: EDUCATION AND DEMOCRATIC HUMANISM

Critical revisionist scholars have subjected the goal of "competitive supremacy" and "mutual benefit" to intense scrutiny and review, skeptical of their obvious appeals for military control over Third World and/or Trilateral domination of the emerging world economy. Recent reviews of these two competing models of American global supremacy have emphasized that such strategies are not only economically exploitative but politically repressive both at home and abroad. In an April 1986 *Atlantic Monthly* article entitled "Do We Need to Be No. 1?" David Gordon argues that rather than aiming to beggar our neighbors, we should be seeking to explore alternative "Front Yard Strategies" that aim to nurture America's social welfare and democratic rights at home and would eschew the temptation to take advantage of the vulnerability or weakness of "others."

This emerging world struggle between the Pentagon and the multinational models of global supremacy has begun to appear more and more as a power struggle between two economically based American special interest coalitions. Each special interest coalition has framed its appeals for mass public support in terms of the rhetoric of the new high tech U.S. meritocracy—that is, that future social progress can occur only through more investment in and better use of high technology; through an integrated world economy; and through the education of a more productive U.S. labor force. The rhetoric of this emerging new American meritocracy has functioned to camouflage the more repressive aspects of these social ideologies, especially their impact on American working-class poor and Third World minority populations.

This chapter argues that there are good grounds for believing that the high tech rhetoric of both the conservative and liberal models is being used as little more than a Trojan horse in order to ensure worker compliance and to achieve further social division of labor. For example, the "upgrading thesis" has been severely challenged by a number of research scholars, including Harry Braverman, Henry Levin, Russell Rumberger, Mike Cooley, Joan Greenbaum, and Gregory Squires among others. In their recent book, *Forecasting the Impact of the New Technologies on the Future Job Market*, Rumberger and Levin charge that the impact of high tech industries and occupations has been oversold. Not only will high tech industries employ only a fraction of the nation's workers, but many of the jobs they do provide require little or no knowledge of high technology. Their statistical projections of future employment in the United States reveal that future job growth will favor service and clerical jobs that require little or no postsecondary schooling and that pay below-average wages.

In the same way, whereas the new school reform debate is framed in the familiar rhetoric of "excellence" and "equity," its social ideology is better understood within the context of the international quest for military supremacy and economic domination. In sum, it seems clear that the Pentagon and multi-national models of world supremacy appear to rely for their success on the ability of the American public school system to produce a highly productive labor force with the required work skills and character traits. Implicit in both models is the tendency to reduce social problems and crises to the level of the personal and the psychological. In the case of the Pentagon capitalism model, social problems tend to be reduced to personality defects, whereas in the Trilateral capitalism model, social problems tend to be attributed to individual skill deficiencies. Both models then attempt to correlate these deficiencies with the increasing number of female single-headed households. It is not surprising, then, that schools would be viewed as the high tech Paideia for the reform and remediation of these "deficiencies."

Thus it appears that the American working-class poor, in particular, are headed toward a school experience that seems designed to ensure a passive enslavement to the immediate, the concrete, and the instrumental. As such, it appears likely to produce a generation of American youth dominated by a technology they don't understand and guided by an elite group of their privileged peers capable of social engineering the vast wealth of the U.S. economy to the exploitative life-styles of the rich and famous. Given the primacy of these concerns, any paradigm seeking an alternative model for educational reform or a more democratic form of social development has been dismissed as the work of ivory tower idealists, out of touch with the "realities" of life in twenty-first-century America. In his book *The Eclipse of Reason*, Max Horkheimer, founder of the Frankfort Institute for Social Research, provided an uncanny futuristic vision of life in the emerging high-tech society, dominated by corporate greed and mass domination. He was troubled by a world that was losing its capacity for democratic modes of personal identity and social organization as meaningful forms of self-government. America in the 1980s seems headed toward the macabre nightmare he struggled so unsuccessfully to deter.

Our struggle to articulate a more equitable, just, economically viable reform paradigm remains. Our task demands changes in our ways of working, living, and thinking, especially as they relate to the world economy and the Third World developing nations. The history of the twentieth century has already taught us the bitter lessons of bomb diplomacy and the "Cola-colonization" of the world. All meaningful social change, however, must begin with a new dream—as Dr. Martin Luther King well understood in his "I have a dream" speech. Only by recapturing the moral, philosophic, and political principles upon which King grounded his dream for American society, can we reconstruct our social institutions in ways that empower ourselves and dignify our world neighbors.

Alternative paradigms must begin at the most basic level of analysis. Critical scholars have the responsibility not only to identify failures in basic principles, mistakes in empirical data collection, and misplaced value priorities in contemporary mainstream social ideologies, but also to identify the boundaries of the alternative dream—its universal principles, realistic social policy objectives, and improved value perspectives. Indeed, as Mortimer J. Adler has stated, "The exposition of these universal principles will, in effect, delineate the shape of the good society as a practicable, not a utopian ideal—one not yet achieved, but genuinely achievable" (Adler 1971, 29). This affirmation of the sameness of the specific nature in which all human beings participate as individual members of the species has many social consequences. For instance, Adler argues that such an alternative perspective means that in ethics, all humans "have the same natural needs; that real goods, corresponding to natural needs, are the same for all; and that all men have the same natural rights, based on the real goods that satisfy their natural needs" (Adler 1971, 36). In politics, Adler shows how these beliefs about human nature support the proposition that "all men are equal as men, equal in their humanity, in their dignity as persons, and in their natural right" (Adler 1971, 36).

The social policy implications of such an alternative ideology are as obvious as they are dramatically different from those of the contemporary Pentagon and multicapitalist paradigms. To begin, within the context of these basic universal principles, a multitude of alternative dreams are both possible and desirable. However, this more humane, just, and democratic world economy of the future will necessarily involve difficult policy choices. For example, as Francis Moore Lappe has pointed out in her gripping best-seller *Diet for a Small Planet*, the world cannot continue indefinitely to support an agricultural system that is "geared to the production of steaks for profit rather than of cheap food for us all" (Lappe 1971, 16). Neither can the world's people continue to sit idly by as the global military establishment positions its weapons of mass destruction for the final nuclear annihilation. We must fight for our own dreams, not the escapist dreams of Hollywood media moguls or Madison Avenue social policy planners. As Martin Luther King understood, the dream must be rekindled in a hundred thousand hearts and minds:

Today we are still challenged to be dissatisfied. Let us be dissatisfied until every man can have food and material necessities for his body, culture and education for his mind, freedom and human dignity for his spirit. Let us be dissatisfied until rat-infested, vermin-filled slums will be a thing of the past and every family will have a decent, sanitary house in which to live. Let us be dissatisfied until the empty stomachs of Mississippi are filled and the idle industries of Appalachia are revitalized. Let us be dissatisfied until brotherhood is no longer a meaningless word at the end of a prayer but the first order of business on every legislative agenda. Let us be dissatisfied until our brother of the Third

World—Asia, Africa, and Latin America—will no longer be the victim of imperialist exploitation, but will be lifted from the long night of poverty, illiteracy, and disease. (King, 1968)

PART II

A CRITIQUE OF THE CONCEPT OF WORK IN THE SCHOOL REFORM LITERATURE

2

A Critique of the Concept of Work and Education in the School Reform Reports

Don T. Martin

One of the most notable developments in American education in the last two decades has been the emergence of a large number of reports, documents, and books on educational reform. This chapter provides a detailed examination of selected key reform reports of the 1980s, making a limited comparison of them to the educational reforms of the previous decade. It also examines the underlying structural elements that have led to these urgent calls for reform of the schools and analyzes why the political fervor they generated have produced so many reports in such a relatively short period of time. Finally, this chapter attempts to show the social effects that these proposed reforms could have on the different social classes and minorities in our society.

Although the number of school reform reports reached record proportions in the 1970s, the amount and intensity of such reports in the 1980s already appear to be exceeding those earlier numbers. Why have we been inundated recently with so many publications urging public school reform? Surely proponents of the American public school system have known that both the schools and the larger socioeconomic structure have been embroiled in "crisis politics" for most of the twentieth century. What, then, are the particular social conditions affecting our present-day schools and society that have motivated so many prominent economic and political figures to call for public school reform? Why, suddenly, have congressional and state legislators, corporate barons, university presidents, governors, and even presidential candidates mounted a crusade to reform U.S. schools?

Several reasons are often cited. Widespread concern over a decade or more of declining test scores and achievement levels appears at first glance to be the leading cause. Another factor often mentioned relates to the mounting arms build-up and the resultant worldwide threat to peace, especially the threat of nuclear war. The National Commission on Excellence in Education (NCEE), in its report *A Nation at Risk* (1983), laments that "we have squandered the gains in student achievement made in the wake of the Sputnik challenge (NCEE 1983, 5). The report continues:

> Knowledge, learning, information, and skilled intelligence are the new raw materials of international commerce. . . . If only to keep and improve on the slim competitive edge we still retain in world markets, we must dedicate ourselves to this reform of our educational system for the benefit of all. . . . Learning is the indispensable investment required for success in the "information age" we are entering. (NCEE 1983, 7)

Although the problems of declining student achievement and school attendance would logically be the focal point for social reform, regrettably more emphasis has been given to the diminished capacity of the U.S. economy to dominate worldwide markets. This had rekindled new interest in the old idea that schools function mainly to increase the productivity of the American labor force. Quality schools producing better educated workers with more rigorous academic standards and disciplinary controls was thought to be the only way to dominate successfully in the international marketplace.[1]

For example, in 1982 President Reagan issued an invitation to a six-member task force of leading corporate and university chief executives to explore how the nation's international competitive position could be further strengthened through increased technology innovation and corporate productivity. In response to his appeal, the Business-Higher Education Forum prepared a report entitled *America's Competitive Challenge* (1983). Complete with specific recommendations, this report was designed to strengthen America's competitiveness in world markets.

Amid the early 1980s reform literature, the report was one of the first documents to explicitly link educational reform with the improvement of U.S. industry and labor to compete on an international scale. For example, the key report recommendation asserted that "our society must develop a consensus that industrial competitiveness on a global scale is crucial to our social and economic well-being" (Business-Higher Education Forum 1983, 2). To achieve this goal, the report contends that most workers will need continual skill training and retraining if they are to keep pace with the changing demands of the new multinational corporate environment. In the report section entitled "Human Resources," American workers are described as "the essential ingredient in the process of technological innovation and economic competitiveness," and as having "antiquated functional skills and deficient academic skills" (Business–Higher Education Forum 1983, 21). Thus, in the typically demeaning corporate management, human relations lingo that has now become commonplace (and widely accepted) in academic literature, workers are viewed as poorly prepared and ill-trained; they make substandard contributions to productivity and economic growth. As a result (as these reports never fail to conclude), American workers need to be better educated and better trained in order for them to be more productive (Business-Higher Education Forum 1983, 22). The report also warns that "The nation's education and training institutions are responding too slowly to the central role they must play in revitalizing the weak American economy.... Linkages between educators, training systems and employers are weak.... If the nation's education and training institutions are to play the role they must, major changes will be required" (Business-Higher Education Forum 1983, 27).

A more recent school reform report, *Investment in Our Children* (1985) by the Committee for Economic Development, also marshaled the services of a distinguished blue-ribbon committee consisting largely of corporate executives, leading American academics, and top-level university administrators to discuss a document written by educational specialists from the ultraconservative American Enterprise Institute. The report called for widescale, sweeping reform of the nation's schools. Schools were indicted for failing the nation's children and undermining the nation's international competitiveness by turning out high school graduates who have difficulty in learning new job skills and even in performing the most routine entry-level jobs successfully. American industry, the report charges, has been forced to spend huge sums of money on employee education and training programs because it can no longer assume that young people who graduate from high school can read, write, reason, calculate, communicate, or accept job responsibilities. The report, therefore, recommends that schools should more clearly define and prioritize their major goals—which are to teach students a basic set of academic competency skills and behavioral attitudes toward work so they later can be successful either in the work force, in postsecondary education, or in the military (Committee for Economic Development 1983, 3–6). Moreover, the report leveled its sharpest criticism at vocational education programs, which it charged have failed to prepare its students for useful employment. Not surprisingly, *The Investment in Our Children* report relieved the business community of any responsibility for assuming the burden of financing the schools, but, rather, chided the public sector for its apathy. However, the report did suggest that the business community could encourage their own employees to become active in the schools, share their corporate management expertise with school administrators, and provide schools with follow-up employment information and mobility patterns of their recent graduates (Committee for Economic Development 1983, 30–35).

In line with the reform agenda of other major documents, the report did not support the development of a narrow vocationalism but, rather, placed stress on the acquisition of broad-based literacy, mathematic, and problem-solving skills. Moreover, the "new reform curriculum" emphasizes the importance of socializing students for the acquisition of a basic set of social skills, especially "adapting to change," "self-discipline," "reliability," "team work," "responsibility," and "respecting the rights of others." These recommendations were obviously extremely important to the report's authors—why else would they have repeated these demands nearly verbatim at least three times in their report (Committee for Economic Development 1983, 6, 15, 30)? What also seems obvious is that the report authors are obsessed with the idea of improving American education so as to enable U.S. industry to better compete internationally. Japan is continually singled out and ceremoniously praised for its high level of educational and industrial achievements. Japanese students are praised for their hard work, their competitive predispositions, and their sacrificial spirit of self-discipline. In the same breath, their peer group cooperativeness is cited as the explanation for why Japanese students outperform all other nations in science and math achievement tests.

The Task Force on Education for Economic Growth established by the Education Commission of the States (ECS) also issued its report, *Action for Excellence* (1983), which called for better schools "to improve economic development." The report highlights some of the "reform statistics" that have now become so commonplace in the reform literature. For example, the report warns that "In the 1980s productivity in manufacturing industries grew nearly four times as fast in Japan, and twice as fast in Germany and France as in the United States" (ECS 1983, 14). Although signaling the alarm on lower U.S. productivity, the report was careful to point out that improved schooling could make the American labor force more efficient. The casual claims and educational "cure-alls" flowing from the reports are familiar rhetoric by now, responding as they do to the well-published complaints by industrialists about the quality of potential employees coming out of American high schools, and especially about their lack of adequate academic skills and proper work socialization.

In a newly revised book entitled *American Education*, Joel Spring (1985) shows how the recent concern by the American business community with the lack of worker productivity and student achievement is directly related to their concerns about larger adverse changes taking place in the global world economy. According to demographic statistics cited by Spring, the unusually high 1970s unemployment rates were caused by the post–World War II baby boomers entering the labor market. The resulting labor surplus in business and industry resulted in labor-intensive management practices, but the cycle was short-lived (Spring 1985, 21–22). By the 1980s, a near reversal in personnel needs occurred: "the labor surplus" of the 1970s became "the labor bust" of the 1980s. Business responded with a series of school-business alliances designed to "cool out" excess labor resources via an increased involvement in "adopt-a-school" programs, "jobs-for-America's graduates," numerous alliances between business and schools, and an increased emphasis on career education.

This involvement of the American business community in public school education is not without historic precedent; for most of this century its influence has permeated the schools. Public schools have long been modeled after business and industry, and school managers and their policies have often been guided by business and professional leaders. However, the influence of business declined sharply between the mid–1960s and the late 1970s as corporate priorities temporarily shifted toward higher education. During these years, business and industrial leaders became increasingly distant from the public schools and had little contact with them. Nevertheless, as Michael Timpane has recently pointed out, they continued to assert that schools were failing because of unruly students, uncooperative teachers, and ineffectual administrators. Timpane concluded that "during these years, business leaders felt they could afford to be passively critical of education because of the plentiful supply of qualified entry-level workers among the very large numbers of young people born during the post-war baby-boom and among women reentering the labor market" (Timpane 1984, 391–392). In addition, Timpane concluded that changes in the labor supply was the most significant reason for the renewed interest by business leaders in the public schools. In particular, they came to realize that there would be: (1) 20 percent fewer high school graduates in 1990 than in 1980; (2) a slower rise of women in the labor market than in recent years; (3) increasingly complex skills needed because of the impact of technological advances; (4) the need for increased worker productivity in order for them to compete internationally; and (5) an emerging labor supply problem that only the public schools—not employment training programs—could deal with effectively (Timpane 1984, 392).

Whereas the 1980s can be characterized as the decade of the conservative "back-to-the-basics" school policies, one related development, which has been even more important, is the increased involvement of business in the public schools. Timpane describes its significance:

Of all the recent changes in the landscape of American education, none has been more dramatic and swift than the reappearance of the business sector. Nowadays, no analysis of educational performance fails to mention either the need for improved skills in the labor market or the need for improved productivity that will enable the U.S. to compete successfully in the global economy. No panel or state commission on education fails to include among its members—or to consult most carefully with—prominent business executives. No convention of educators fails to feature speeches and workshops on expanding and strengthening the "partnership" between business and education. And few communities fail to launch projects to build cooperation and understanding between business leaders and educators. (Timpane 1984, 389)

In a related study for the Carnegie Corporation, Timpane details the rapid growth of the new school/business cooperative programs, attributing its recent success to the growing shortage of entry-level workers. According to Timpane: "For the first time in a generation there will probably be, in several urban locations, an absolute shortage of labor supply for entry-level positions. Urban employers already report great difficulty in locating qualified employees for entry-level positions" (Timpane 1981, 28).

A further indication of the consolidation of the school/business nexus is provided in the new brochure of the U.S. Chamber of Commerce. *Business and*

Education (n.d.) exemplifies the goals of the recent involvement of business in educational reform. It supports the idea that business needs to become more involved in education reform so as to ensure that scarce societal resources are most effectively used in the schools to produce a highly productive and mobile labor supply. Business is viewed as being adversely affected by low student achievement and motivation. According to their rationale, the boom in the information and high tech industries and rising domestic and international competition creates new demands for more highly skilled workers. The new high tech production methods are viewed as having little use for unskilled and/or semiskilled workers, whereas skilled workers are judged to be less likely to be displaced by the new technologies (Chamber of Commerce 1984, 5). Specifically, this pamphlet provides an excellent example of the growing public consensus about the reasons for the rationale behind the new school/business partnership programs. As the report explains:

The business community has come to realize that increased involvement in education, at all levels, is essential to long-term economic growth. Business-education cooperation must be strengthened if the nation is to address properly the training and the retraining of future and existing workers, and help students develop effective "school-to-work" and "school-to-college" skills. (Chamber of Commerce 1984, 5)

In what has now become monotonous business rhetoric to those familiar with the school reform literature, the report provides the reader with the well-known "scare" tactics of school reform:

[We are] encountering increasing international competition, shortages of skilled workers, and increasing . . . illiteracy rates. Rapid rates of industrial change caused by automation, robotics, and widespread use of computers are dramatically altering the composition of the American workforce and the needs of American businesses. This reindustrialization is shifting employment opportunities, increasing the need for better prepared workers, and demanding that educational institutions be more responsive to national and international economic trends . . . no longer can a new employee expect to perform a single rudimentary function for an entire career. Rather, current and future employees will be called upon to continually update and retool job skills through training, retraining and education. The key to future job and career growth will be personal flexibility. (Chamber of Commerce 1984, 6–7)

This Chamber of Commerce pamphlet is representative of the new school/business partnership concept of school reform that is sweeping the country. In fact, a major portion of this small publication (43 pages) is devoted to a favorable review of this concept in eight other major reform reports.

Spring's (1985, 24) recent analysis of the 1980s school reform proposals led him to conclude that they were largely the result of concern over a pending economic crisis. Of course, these reports contain more than proposals aimed at dealing with the current economic crisis; nevertheless, I contend that this is the major causal factor for the recent flurry of reform activity. In literally every major report, school reform is considered to be the key corrective to America's failing economy, and a more productive U.S. worker is heralded as the "missing link" in recooping our global domination and supremacy.

But an important question needs to be dealt with: which segment of society would benefit the most from the proposed school reform agenda? In response to this central question, let us see how many of the proposals to reform the schools have essentially a social class bias that would, if implemented, only exacerbate the various social problems of poor and working-class people. I also argue that the concept of work in many of the national reform reports is based primarily on the realities of the current hierarchical U.S. social class system. And related to this, the reports are premised on the misleading idea that the current work force is no longer adequate to compete in the world's marketplace and therefore must be retrained. Likewise, the public school vocational training programs are thought to be inadequate to meet emerging international economic competition. Vocational education is sharply criticized and even condemned outright in a number of the recent reports. For example, Boyer (1983) doubts the value of traditional vocational education and criticizes it as "un unfulfilled promise," "irrelevant," and "inadequate." He cites recent studies that show the job prospects for vocationally trained students are not much better than for general education students (except for students in secretarial science). Thus Boyer concludes that "vocation students are often academically short-changed" (Boyer 1983, 121, 123).

Boyer's reform proposals for these discredited vocational programs center on his ideas for a "transition school." He calls for a single-track curriculum and for expanded guidance services. In a chapter titled "Transition: To Work and Learning," Boyer states, "Schooling should prepare all students for a life of work and learning. This means a solid grounding in the basic skills, a common core of learning, a cluster of elective courses, and student assessment and counseling to smooth the transition to jobs and higher education" (Boyer 1983, 118). For Boyer, the last two years of high school will become a "transition school," with student time divided between the common academic core and a small elective cluster. To aid in instruction, part-time lecturers from business and industry and from the professions are suggested for in-school instruction and training programs (Boyer 1983, 128–129). Business is called upon to aid students in their transition from school to work. Several examples of exemplary school/community relationships are cited (Boyer 1983, 130).

Boyer's proposals for a single-track curriculum call for the abolishment of the current three-track system—academic, vocational, and general (Boyer 1983, 126–127). Guidance services are recommended for significant expansion (Boyer 1983, 132). Both reforms would, Boyer says, "keep the career options open and ensure a smooth transition to work and further education . . . [and] would ensure that all young people realize their full potential. No goal is more important to the future of the nation" (Boyer 1983, 136).

But what would be the social and educational effects of Boyer's proposed reforms? Would a single-track curriculum and an expanded guidance program bring more fairness and equity to those suffering most under the present social and educational system, or would such proposed reforms only exacerbate their present condition? Certainly Boyer's proposal for a new Carnegie unit that would require all students to spend thirty hours per year working in the community has a democratic, even egalitarian potential. But such enlightened rhetoric will not help overcome structural inequities in the system.

Echoing Boyer's indictments of vocational education, John Goodlad's reform text, *A Place Called School*, criticizes tracking in the comprehensive high school and maintains that vocational education has placed "more emphasis on job training than on general education. Job-training programs . . . disproportionately enroll children from poor families . . . [especially] from racial minorities" (Goodlad 1984, 147). Describing "general education" as the best preparation for responsible citizenship and for productive, satisfying work, Goodlad wants the schools to stop training for specific vocational jobs (Goodlad 1984, 47, 344). Rather, career and vocational education are to be experienced-based in the workplace and accomplished via a cooperative school-business partnership program in the schools.

Many of the reform proposals, like those of Boyer's and Goodlad's, in spite of their rhetorical support given to the importance of individual cognitive skill development, still tend to be most concerned with the corporate demand for high school students with highly developed productivity skills and responsible work habits. In the same light, the school reformers seem to be more concerned with the expectation of producing a more highly disciplined work force built on the kind of "brain power" needed to serve the new information-based, high tech society than they are with providing a general education that would serve broad social, economic, and political purposes.

On the other hand, the reports appear (superficially, at least) to call for reform of the schools not only to meet the perceived present economic crisis but also to provide, at the same time, for the traditional "democratic spirit" of equal educational opportunity. For example, in the report *Action for Excellence* (Education Commission of the State 1983), while asserting absolute priority to making the U.S. economic system more competitive, nevertheless departs dramatically from its major focus by stating that schools have deeper purposes than merely to prepare people for entry-level jobs. The authors of *A Nation at Risk* also speak of the need for a "new civility" in addition to the goal of world economic supremacy. They wrote:

We do not believe that a public commitment to excellence and educational reform must be made at the expense of a strong public commitment to the equitable treatment of our diverse population . . . [and] in a world of ever-accelerating competition and change in the conditions of the workplace, of ever-greater danger, and of ever-larger opportunities for those prepared to meet them, educational reform should focus on the goal of creating a learning society. At the heart of such a society is the commitment to a set of values and to a system of education that affords all members the opportunity to stretch their minds to full capacity. . . . (NCEE 1983, 5)

An even more explicit reform statement in support of "equal opportunity" goals is found in the College Board's *Academic Preparation for College* report when it states:

Concern for educational equality should be expressed in ways that advance social justice. Educational quality must not lead to actions that limit the aspirations and opportunities of disadvantaged and minority youth, or that would reverse the progress that has already been made. Rather, concern for educational quality must be expressed in a commitment to quality for all students. Arbitrary standards must not be imposed without concern for enabling students to meet them. Expectations such as these learning outcomes should be used as criteria for designing educational efforts that will enable more students to succeed. (CEEB 1983, 33)

Is there an apparent conflict in the reports between the call for school reforms designed "to meet the current economic crisis" and, at the same time, provide for "educational equality," "equal opportunity," and "improving math, science, and technology education for all"? The National Science Board Commission on Precollege Education in Mathematics, Science, and Technology, in their report *Educating American's for the 21st Century*, expresses the typical "educational equity" reform goals:

Underlying every Commission recommendation is one basic objective: the improvement and support of elementary and secondary school systems throughout America so that, by the year 1995, they will provide *all* the nation's youth with a level of education in mathematics, science, technology, as measured by achievement scores and participation levels (as well as other nonsubjective criteria) that is not only the highest quality attained anywhere in the world but also reflects the particular and peculiar needs of our nation. (National Science Board 1983, 5)

But how can the challenge of "the crisis of world supremacy" be achieved via more select, high quality educational insitutions, at the same time, providing for the democratic ideology of "equal opportunity for all"? And what, correspondingly, will the role of the state be in the mediation of this glaring contradiction? One thing is clear—the reports are highly political documents signifying the central importance of the public school to those reformers. How is this "balancing act" between seemingly conflicting economic and social goals to be resolved?

Certainly "excellence" has become a key concept in the rhetoric of most school reform reports. The reform groups have generally interpreted "excellence" to mean such things as: raising academic standards; setting higher requirements for high school graduation and admission to college; eliminating "soft" subjects; mandating a common core curriculum for all students; increasing math, science, and foreign language requirements; testing achievement regularly; lengthening the school day and the school year; and generally getting tough with students, teachers, and administrators (Passow 1984, 674). Of course, any critic of the reform reports would have difficulty criticizing such "excellence" goals. Who could support anything less than school excellence? Yet is there a hidden curriculum in the excellence agenda? Does "excellence" become a liberal code word for the creation of a new class of technocratic elites? And how realistic, and desirable, is the proposal that all students pursue the rigors of such a highly technocratically oriented course of studies?

It is my view that many of the recent reform proposals are rooted in an elitist and class-biased corporate business perspective that, by its very structure, virtually dismisses an entire segment of the school population, most of whom linger as refuse at the bottom of the social system. I contend that if the proposed reforms were to become reality, most lower class students would face even greater academic failure, higher dropout rates, and further social decline. It may be, as Long (1983, 48) so cogently argues, that the reforms will benefit only the students who are already planning to attend college. In direct conflict with the rhetoric of "equal opportunity," the real consequences of the reform agenda seem to be that the disadvantaged would become instead an ever larger class of educationally and socially "deprived" citizens. In the new Goodlad-Boyer school system, most students would be forced out of school into dead-end, "entry-level" jobs as soon as they demonstrated bare minimal competency skills.

It becomes, therefore, an important political and ideological issue for the reformers to determine how the state system of public schools can be changed so that they better service the few highly qualified technocrats that will be needed in the new high tech society, at the same time, exposing the egalitarian rhetoric that educational institutions should "equally serve" *all* of its population. This is where the ideology of meritocracy becomes central to my analysis. The talented and the hard working (i.e., TAG kids—"Talented and Gifted") are to be rewarded according to meritocratic criteria. It is under the rubric of providing a meritocratically based notion of "equity" that the state apparatus through the public schools rather than implementing the ideals of real social equality and social justice plays so decisive a role in the imposition of real economic, cultural, and ideological hegemonic controls.

The reformers, many of whom represent the interests of the state, or indeed are leading members of the state apparatus, are divided in their assessment of what the role of the school should be. Two opposing views are inherent in the reform literature. Some proponents support the reform effort of the National Commission on Excellence that stresses higher quality education with a core curriculum. Chief among these proponents is a publication of the College Board, *Academic Preparation for College* (1983), which identifies the basic academic competencies for high school students preparing for college in reading, writing, speaking and listening, mathematics, reasoning, and studying. In addition to "computer competence," this report recommends the basic academic subjects of English, the arts, mathematics, science, social studies, and foreign language (CEEB 1983, 28). The core, it is assumed, would ensure equal educational opportunity for all, enabling all students to succeed in the work world. But some reform critics (Goldman 1983, 28) maintain that the disadvantaged lower classes would not likely experience positive academic achievement as a result of these goals, but, rather, are more likely to fail in the schools and later in the world of work.

On the other hand, attempts to rescue the underclass, and particularly minority children, through a nonacademic work study approach is also problematic. In one of the more thoughtful and enlightened reform reports, Lightfoot scrutinizes six selected secondary schools known for their "imperfections, uncertainties, and vulnerabilities" (Lightfoot 1983, 309). Her search for "good" schools focuses on Atlanta's George Washington Carver High School whose explicit educational goal is "to teach poor, outcast black students to become responsible workers, to move children from lives of poverty and chaos to futures of disciplined, steady hard work" (Lightfoot 1983, 39). Students come to Carver to prepare for jobs in industry, business, and the service occupations. About 150 students are in half-day work-study programs where they are paid $3.15 to $4.85 an hour. The work-study program culminates in a "free enterprise day." Students completing the program are paraded on stage and are praised for their discipline, perseverance, punctuality and civility in their work, which, it is assumed, fits into the principles of democracy, free enterprise, and capitalism. Another interesting program at Carver is the "Explorers Program" designed to provide an initial linkage to the world of work. All tenth-grade "Explorers" are bused to downtown Atlanta once a month for career orientations in local business establishments or social service agencies (Lightfoot 1983, 45–55).

Although Lightfoot provides an implicit criticism of how Carver High becomes the training ground of poor black students for largely subservient work in mostly white-dominated private service sector establishments, she does not examine the larger structural connections between Carver's vocational/career "educational" programs and the maintenance of a permanent racially based social class system in Atlanta. Lightfoot's limited emphasis on and over concern for the difficulties of inner-city school administrative decision making, particularly that of the school principal, precluded the kind of critical analysis that is so absent from all the reform reports. Thus, what amounts to a modern-day version of Booker T. Washington's ideology of "opportunity" taking place for Blacks at Carver High is transformed into a sanitized bureaucratic "Harvard policy problem" to be "solved" via administrative manipulations.

Perhaps the clearest assault on equality can be found in the Twentieth Century Fund Task Force's report *Making the Grade* (1983). The report begins with the usual lip service given to the "democratic ideals" of "equal educational opportunity." Yet how genuine is this commitment when later in the report the authors complain that affirmative action programs are being "hampered by excessive federal manipulation''? Such rhetorical game-playing (i.e., ''having your cake and eating it, too''—i.e., supporting the dual goals of social equality and technocratic elitism) can also be found in Sizer's (1984) *Horace's Compromise* and Adler's (1982) *The Paideia Proposal*. Both appear to recognize the unfair realities of the present American hierarchical class structure, to be concerned about social inequality, and both argue strongly for school reforms. Sizer's (1983, 84) emphasis on both ''education of the intellect'' and ''character education'' are matched by Adler's (1984, 15–17) call for a ''mental, moral and spiritual growth'' and ''the cultivation of appropriate civic virtues.''

In the end, the social effects of equal opportunity (or its lack thereof) are merely academic if Bowles and Gintis (1976, 100–101) are correct. They argue that inequality of opportunity (as it relates to one's chances in the social system) did not historically originate in the educational system but has its roots in the social and economic repression and inequality of a capitalist economy. Or, as Meyer (1983, 68) also argues, the curriculum changes resulting from the reform proposals would not create social equality because it is that very social inequality that is intrinsic to the very dynamics of a corporate capitalist economy—that is, social inequality is the driving force in perpetuating inequities both in the work force and in the schools.

THE CONCEPT OF WORK

The remainder of this chapter focuses more specifically on the concept of work as stated explicitly or implicitly in the reform reports. It is crucial to note that the idea of work, when included in the 1980 reports and linked to education, is most often treated from an elitist, nontraditional vocational perspective. This is in sharp contrast to the reform efforts of the 1970s, especially when compared to the concept of work contained in the literature supporting career education. It has been clearly established that career education was a direct reaction to the open, free school movements of the 1960s and early 1970s. Critics of open education claimed that it eroded the student's motivation to work.

In direct contrast to the child-centered themes of the open classroom pedagogy, a consistent theme of the 1970s reform reports was the development of an effective work study policy for all students. For example, the report of the U.S. Office of Education, *Youth: Transition to Adulthood* (1973), proposed a number of alternatives for mixing education and work. It advised that all youngsters be provided jobs programs that would emphasize specific job information and on-the-job training. During the same time, the National Manpower Institute rec-ommended that real work or service experience should become an integral part of all educational programs. Perhaps the most comprehensive 1970s reform report linking schools to work was the Carnegie Council on Policy Studies in Educa-tion's report, *Giving Youth a Better Chance: Options for Education, Work and Service* (1979), which argued that the schooling, employment, and community behavior of American youth was, in reality, an inseparable problem. That is, teenage difficulties over unemployment, dropping-out, lack of motivation, pregnancies, and other youth crises should seek community solutions as well as in-school remedies. The report shows how many of the new experimental school-work programs are seeking such a unified solution as in work experience programs, career education programs, magnet and alternative school programs, school/business partnerships, a variety of school financial reform plans (i.e., tuition tax credits, vouchers), the voluntary youth service projects, and a number of federal projects for "the deprived," including the Job Corps. This report represents the best example of the transition from the support for traditional in-school vocational education programs to a call for community-based alternatives. In a chapter titled "Vocational Education: Change Everything Including the Name," the Carnegie report on *Giving Youth a Better Chance* recommended the following changes: (1) eliminate tracking in high schools; (2) de-emphasize classroom vocational education in high schools in favor of community-based training programs; (3) increase the enrollment of high school students in occupational courses taught in community colleges and technical institutes; and (4) pool state and local funds in order to provide more effective combinations of education, training, and work experience programs for students (Carnegie Council 1980, 141–146).

Given the 1970s changes in vocational education programs, the 1980s educational reform movement, although a distinct product of the Reaganite conservative era, is also a continuing reaction against the free school, open education policies of the 1960s. As Shapiro has pointed out: "the basic 'skills' movement . . . with its demand for a 'return' to a clearly demarcated hierarchical epistemology and an authoritarian pedagogy, must be seen, in part, as a reaction to education change that gained momentum in the 1960s" (Shapiro 1983, 218). Career education in the 1970s sought to restore in the student a sense of the importance of the general world of work by developing a direct and positive link between the school and the workplace environments. Conversely, the reform reports of the 1980s generally shifted emphasis away from traditional vocationally oriented work roles to a more highly disciplined personality structure that could function with greater mobility in a more rapidly changing technological workplace. How else do we explain this general shift away from the workplace-oriented career education and vocational education reform of the 1970s to the "back-to-the-basics," minimal, common skills core curriculum of the 1980s? How do we account for this trend, especially in view of the growing imbalance between the present high technocratic requirements demanded by few students and the more basic core educational needs of the rest of the U.S. work force? As Randall Collins pointed out as early as 1977, "the educational level of the U.S. labor force has changed in excess of that which is necessary to keep up with the skill requirements of jobs" (Collins 1977, 121).

There appears to be a contradiction between the present educational demands of the workplace and the increasingly higher levels of education prescribed in the new school reform literature. For example, Rumberger (1984, 344) explains how the demands for highly educated labor in the U.S. economy has not kept pace with the rising educational levels of workers. In the past several decades, there has been a steady increase in the education of workers (especially in specific occupations), and the steady decline in their employment levels and salaries. In what social scientists refer to as the "certification gap," workers whose skills are underutilized find work less rewarding and less challenging than the jobs for which they were educated. This widening "gap" affects job performance and results in an overall decline in individual productivity (which ultimately contributes to the overall decline in the Gross National Product [GNP]). Moreover, these "overeducated" or unskilled semiskilled workers experience greater job turnovers and absenteeism (Berg 1970). This is the situation for many skilled and highly educated workers (including college professors and white collar corporate employees) who find themselves underemployed or, worse yet, totally unemployed.

If, then, there is a widening gap between the increased educational levels of workers and the lack of comparable educational demands of the workplace, why is it that most of the recent national school reform reports claim exactly the opposite—that a serious gap exists between the future skill demands of our high tech industries and the inferior quality of "human resources" now being provided by our schools? The reason, perhaps is because the reform reports do not intend to solve this "certification gap" problem at all. Rather, they seem more intent on responding to the "gaps" of a much more narrowly defined sector of the economy, that is, the technocratic education of a select, elite group of students who are to be educated primarily for a purportedly growing high tech, information based economy, and various related sepcializations. Accordingly, the "nonacademic" students (what Dewey earlier referred to as "the motor-minded"), mostly from minority groups and the lower classes, are, in effect, neglected in these reports, in spite of the conspicuous "democratic, equal opportunity" rhetoric. Much of the "equality" language in the reports, it would seem, is more of an afterthought, reluctantly inserted into the reports to ensure a broad-ranging social consensus from the liberal community. If the reform proposals in the national reports were operationalized, they would indeed enhance the academic preparation of a relatively small select student population for the future high tech military and commerce needs of the American economy. But the majority of students, especially those from the lower end of the social scale, would not become a part of this select group. Unfortunately, the "reform" proposals seem destined only to continue the widening gap between an elite, highly educated technocratic minority and a growing majority of low status, minimal competency able students.

The present reformers are clearly pinning their hopes for the restoration of American world supremacy on a revitalized high tech, information-based economy predicated on a lean educational system geared for the needs of the elite few. The 1980s school reformers are also pinning their meritocratic dream on the dubious claim that high technology will be a central source of new jobs in the United States in the closing decades of this century. However, what is the factual basis for their beliefs? What do some social forecasters say about these visions for America's future? Levin (1984, 32) warns us to avoid two fallacies reflected in the national reports. The first assumes that the fastest growing job categories (percentage-wise) are in high tech industries. The fact is, according to Levin's statistics, that no high tech occupations are included in the top eighteen job categories expected to grow most rapidly in the future decades. Levin writes,

Fast food workers, guards and doorkeepers, kitchen helpers, and janitors are among the top occupations. High tech occupations are far down the list. While it is expected that some 200,000 additional computer programmers will be needed by 1995, the increase in jobs for building custodians, fast food workers, and kitchen helpers is expected to be more than 1.3 million. It is obvious that most job growth will be in areas requiring at most a high school diploma or some community college training. Relatively few jobs will require the skills of a college graduate or any other post-graduate training. (Levin 1984, 33)

The second fallacy in this reform equation questioned by Levin equates high technology industries with jobs that require advanced education and highly complex job skills. Rather, the available evidence suggests just the opposite. Even now we are beginning to witness the displacement of high tech workers and the reduction in high tech worker skills due to the impact of microprocessors and robotics. Rumberger (1984, 345) points out that cashiers no longer need to have math skills because modern cash registers carry out all the necessary computations. Secretaries are being displaced by word processors and there is a reduction in the skills needed by computer programmers. Similar changes are occurring among workers in auto repair, industrial design, architectural drafting, and many other related occupations. Such changes in personnel needs may, in part, help to explain why the national reports place so much emphasis on "excellence" in academics for high tech and related occupations while de-emphasizing training for less skilled work.

The reform reports reflect what may well be a turning point in the history of public education that parallels a major shift in the world economic order. The types of employment currently found in local business and corporate industries can be divided into two major categories: (1) a continuation of the traditional past employment (with some modifications), plus a burgeoning service economy; and (2) a rapidly changing high tech and information-based economy requiring relatively few highly trained employees. According to labor force analysts, the former will still absorb the vast majority of workers in the foreseeable future, whereas the latter (although growing at a brisk pace) will only make up a relatively small percentage of the work force. The reform reports also reflect this changing economic reality. In effect, what the reports are calling for is a reformed school system that would more efficiently select the brightest and most capable for the traditional high status occupations in the emerging high tech, information-based industries, leaving behind the vast majority to compete for the remaining lower status jobs. Thus, in the name of "excellence," a new, even less observable tracking system would emerge. Although accommodating the changing international economic order, the public school system, as the mainstay of the ideological state apparatus, would more effectively legitimize and assist in the restoration and maintenance of a class-based hierarchical social system.

The school's image as an institution that promotes social mobility has suffered repeated setbacks throughout the 1960s and 1970s. The Coleman and Jencks studies, dealt this idea its severest blow. Massive federal educational funding, especially to vocational education programs, was the key to President Johnson's 1960s "war on poverty." However, his vast expenditures have had little lasting impact on the reduction of the root causes of widespread poverty. Career education and other forms of vocational education in the 1970s similarly failed to resolve the plight of the poor. Of course, there are still some vestiges of the reforms of the 1960s and 1970s in existence today, but their programmatic credibility and political popularity have been severely damaged. Whereas the present reform reports reflect a shift away from the discredited liberal reforms, they seem destined to contribute as little as the liberal reforms did to providing any significant alteration of America's well-entrenched class system. The reforms seem destined to only further reinforce alienation and resistance from lower and working-class students.

The most socially disturbing consequence might well be the resistance and challenge that lower class students give to this new round of school reforms. Such legitimate "resistance" might well express itself in academic failure or leaving school, which in all likelihood would ensure them a lifetime of reduced employment opportunities and a lifetime of lower social ranking. Only those students who comply with the new school requirements could count on moving up the social ladder, whereas those who resist will most likely find themselves in monotonous, low status employment.

CONCLUSION

Many of the national reform reports have been constructed from the fabric of a functionalist,[2] social efficiency ideology[3] that is intent on re-aligning the educational system in harmony with the future high tech and information needs of American industries. This ideology is grounded in the belief that schools should sort and select students based on individual merit. However, this form of a technocratic-meritocratic ideology masks the real intent of the reform reports, which is, in reality, selecting and sorting a small corps of technocratic elite for the new high tech workplace.

Yet the reports' implicit arguments about the need to reform the schools to ensure world economic supremacy do not cause them to overlook the need to address the problem of social inequality. To do so would be to violate and contradict the "democratic spirit" (usually conveyed in the rhetoric of "equal educational opportunity'') that we have become so accustomed to reading in our reform movement literature. It is evident that the reports are attempting to respond to competing political and economic interests. But there are no quick and easy resolutions to these complex, conflicting, and contradictory reform goals. As Shapiro has observed,

[the] potency of the reports has rested in their capacity to speak several languages; to represent separate, even divergent interests; to mobilize the concerns of a number of disparate groups. This capacity to articulate . . . the concerns and interests of divergent and even contradictory groups, all within the explicit framework of capitalist growth, illustrates precisely the process of hegemonic domination. (Shapiro 1983, 71)

Thus, whereas the 1980s school reform reports have not gone unchallenged, there must be more radical structural criticisms made by those who realize the devastating impact these proposed reforms will likely have on widening the gap between rich and poor children in the United States. What is most glaringly absent in all of the reform literature is any substantial body of new critical literature. Feinberg (1985) has perceptively noted how the school reform reports are a part of a larger trend in educational policy evaluation away from a more critical mode of educational analysis to one that seeks only to explain particular ethnographic mechanisms and social trends within their present context. The result is a static and largely unreflective framework of social evaluation.

Last, the reports claim that increasing school requirements and demanding higher standards will directly increase the level of talent and technical skills in the workplace and, at the same time, maintain equal educational opportunity. However, if these proposed reforms were to become a reality, students from culturally and economically ''superior'' backgrounds and higher quality academic schools would clearly have significant academic advantages over those from less academic schools and home environments. The social result would be an additional psychological and economic burden on the already disadvantaged, lower class student. Although this consequence is certainly not the explicitly stated intent of the reform reports (in fact, just the opposite rhetoric is expressed in many of the reports), the social and educational effects of the reforms would be as concluded here. Reduced opportunities for the poor and working classes and additional social advantages for the privileged (provided at state expense) has a long and inglorious history in America's past.

In conclusion, what is the scenario most likely to result from the reform proposals? What the reform proposals have done is to adopt the special interests of privileged groups in our society and elevated their occupational classifications to the status of universal social goals. Thus a few high tech positions are romanticized as idealized goals that should be met by all other American youth. In other words, the technocratic goals of few are presented as the ''pace rabbit'' to which we all must run and be judged. The interests of the few are misrepresented as being the goals for the many. If the disadvantaged fail to achieve these identified "excellences" (and I predict this would happen), this would further provide the social legitimization for the privileged position of the "new technocrats" in the emerging global high tech economy. The "American educational meritocracy" has once again provided the necessary social cement to ensure the perpetuation and legitimization of an emerging set of new social inequalities.

NOTES

1. One is often led to believe that it is the schools' fault that the U.S. economy has not kept pace with international competition. This is reminiscent of the arguments for vocational education in the early part of the century. Such criticism of the schools grossly oversimplifies the issues. From a very different perspective, Shaprio (1983) provides a sociological argument to explain why the schools have failed to produce students with traditional work values. Our society, he contends, has shifted to a "consumption culture," and yet the schools continue to operate as though we are still living in a "production culture."

2. Feinberg and Jonas Soltis (1985, 54) provide a good review of Randall Collins's critique of the functionalist position.

3. H. Levin (1978, 10–11) provides an excellent comparison of the "social efficiency model" and the "social growth model."

3

The State's Stake in Educational Reform

Edward H. Berman

Daniel Tanner has noted that, once again, American education is at a crossroads. "The road taken," he said, "will be determined not by the fantasies of crystal-ball gazing and futurology, but rather by what we do here and now in attacking our most pervasive problems through means that are consonant with the democratic ideal of optimizing educational opportunity for all" (Tanner 1984, 13). Tanner may well be assuming something that will not come to pass, at least if the structural reality rather than the legitimizing rhetoric of the reports calling for educational reform does indeed determine our educational policy for the next generation. Those reports most likely to do this include: *A Nation at Risk, Education Americans for the 21st Century, Making the Grade,* and *Education and Economic Progress.* Beyond the obligatory rhetoric paying lip service to the democratic ideal of optimizing educational opportunity for all, any real concern for the issues of "participatory democracy" are noticeably absent. This chapter suggests why this is the case and also notes a few concerns that we need to consider as we attempt to better understand the relationships linking our system of state capitalism to the current educational reform efforts.

STATE CAPITALISM AND EDUCATIONAL REFORM: THE MACRO VIEW

The relationships linking the state to the capitalist organization of society and both of these to the educational system have received considerable recent attention, a factor that precludes the necessity of an extended discussion here.[1] An overview of these relationships is in order, however, since the issue is of central importance in understanding the tone of the current discussions concerning educational reform.

Whereas there are indeed differences among the most influential of the several reports, the commonalities are more striking. The overarching concern is abundantly clear: the declining role of the U.S. economy in the world capitalist economy must be arrested and the nation's schools have a central role to play in accomplishing this. Several of the reports, implicitly or otherwise, go further and argue that the nation's schools are largely responsible for the long-term downward spiral. There is no dearth of suggestions for the remedial action required to reverse this trend and restore the United States to its rightful place as the unchallenged leader of the world capitalist economy. The suggestions most frequently made include: a greater emphasis on particular subject matter areas, an extended school day and year, and more attention to society's intellectually "gifted" youngsters.

The direct and repeated linkage of a reformed educational system to a more productive economy supports Svi Shapiro's contention that we need to understand the spate of reports as basically political and economic documents. More particularly, he is correct when noting that the main concern of the reports "is the long-term crisis of American capitalism" (Shapiro 1985, 58).

It has become increasingly obvious over the last decade or so that any meaningful discussion of American capitalism must include a consideration of the role of the state in the furtherance of capitalist expansion if it is to have even a modicum of explanatory potential. Richard Fagen addresses the state-capitalism linkage when noting how it has become "increasingly difficult in today's world to 'do business' nationally or internationally, without the active cooperation of the state" (Fagen 1979, 8). Manuel Castells elaborates on the linkages between the state and capitalism when observing how "the state subsidizes private capital directly or indirectly, particularly the hegemonic functions of monopoly capital." The state, he contends, has become "the center of the process of accumulation and realization in advanced capitalism" (Castells 1980, 70). This linkage—or perhaps "fusion" would be a more apt characterization of the relationship— between the state and the dominant mode of production and social relationships simply cannot be ignored as we attempt to unravel the implications of the educational reports. Nor is this linkage ignored in the national reports. One, *A Nation at Risk*, asserts that the state should marshall public and private resources and exert unambiguous leadership in the drive to reform the nation's school system. Such a concerted effort will, it is implied, help to better educate the nation's students in those areas crucial to increased productivity, which in turn will contribute to the alleviation of the larger crisis in American capitalism.

Obviously, capital's main concern is to maximize its profits, at the same time as it ensures the system's survival. Those who control capital will attempt to achieve this goal by whatever means are at hand. The U.S. public educational system, from its inception in its present form in the mid-nineteenth century, has regularly been utilized for this purpose (Nasaw 1979). There is no reason to expect that today's capitalists and state functionaries will not utilize this institution for their purposes, just as earlier generations did.

At this juncture a caveat might be entered to forestall the charge of positing an overly crude, functionalist correspondence between the state and the agents of capital. There are frequently real areas of disagreement and divergence between the representatives of the state on the one hand, and those of capital on the other. These differences are to be found as well among the several levels of the dominant class of capitalists. These conflicts are sometimes severe and their importance should not be minimized. At the same time, however, these disagreements are insignificant when compared to the shared interests that unite representatives of the state and of capital, the most important of which is the maintenance and furtherance of the capitalist system.

The system of state-supported capitalism has impressed its ideology on the current educational discussions in several ways. First, the majority of the reports have been initiated, sponsored, or guided by state agencies (e.g., the U.S. Office of Education, the National Science Board); representatives of capital (e.g., the report of the Committee on Economic Development, *Investing in Our Children*); or the major foundations (e.g., the Carnegie Corporation, the Carnegie Foundation for the Advancement of Teaching, the Twentieth Century Fund), whose structures, personnel, programs, and sources of support link them in particular ways to both the state and capitalist ideology (Berman 1984). The overarching ideology of the sponsoring agency determines the parameters within which discussions concerning educational reform will take place and is further reinforced by the fact that this agency selects and screens the personnel who will participate in the study. Sponsorship by one of these agencies ensures that the conclusions reached will fall within predetermined parameters, predetermined to the degree that they will be supportive of the existing capitalist organization of American society. Put more simply, the sponsoring agency sets the agenda, taps individuals whose ideological dispositions are "correct," guides the investigation, and presides over the compilation of a "balanced" final report.

A second way in which state capitalism has left its imprint on the education reports is by stressing particular curricular areas and simultaneously neglecting or minimizing the importance of others. A common theme throughout the reports is that the schools should give increased attention to their gifted students and should urge them to excel in those areas of science and technology that will help the corporate sector reestablish technological supremacy and economic predominance in the international economy. This emphasis on science and technology (today's "high status" knowledge) for a minority is augmented by a call for increased computer literacy for all. This proposal is posited on the belief that (1) the computer can be a valuable tool to facilitate the learning process; and (2) the changing American job market will require more individuals possessing basic computer skills. Neither supposition is sustainable by available data, however (Carnoy and Levin 1985). The reports also feature discussion about a return to the basic subjects for all, although there is less than total agreement on what constitutes these.

A third way in which capitalist interests are manifested in the reform documents is through the advocacy of a more direct corporate/financial sector involvement in the educational process. The recommendations contained in *Action for Excellence,* produced under the auspices of the Education Commission of the States, represent this trend. Business and industrial leaders should "help educators define the standards that the schools should meet." They should "share with school managers [sic] their expertise in planning, budgeting, and management," and establish "customized job-training efforts between business and schools." Finally, they should conduct "courses actually taught in offices and factories."[2] These suggestions, if implemented, would afford the interests of capital direct opportunities to establish educational policy and control the direction of school activities. The recommendations contained in *Action for Excellence,* which are not peculiar to this one report, clearly seek to mold school children to the specifications of the corporate state.

Fourth, capital seeks to privatize gain, not to distribute or share it for the public good. Yet, the education reform documents repeatedly encourage representatives of capital to get involved in school activities, to utilize *public* educational facilities to propagate and further individualistic capitalistic values. This they do with the compliance of, and frequently with active encouragement from, the state, acting through local school boards. Corporate-sponsored programs such as Adopt-a-School or Jobs for America's Graduates have grown out of capital's concern about the lack of suitably educated youngsters to assume entry-level positions in the job market. Since the school has failed to produce a reasonable pool of appropriately educated students from which the corporate/financial sector can draw, the response has been to seek direct access to the future labor pool through school-based programs. A primary purpose of these programs is to guarantee the minimal training of those formerly considered to be only marginally employable (Borman and Spring 1984).

School administrators and teachers regularly support these activities, probably for several reasons. Administrators frequently see the possiblity of corporate political support on such volatile issues as tax increases if they acquiesce in the penetration of their schools by the corporate and financial sectors. Other administrators agree that the corporate-sponsored approach has more positive benefits than negative consequences. Individual teachers feel that they can get additional material before their students, material that they would not otherwise be able to provide. The related field trips and incentives linked to the corporate-sponsored programs certainly look enticing to some. The ideological slant of the endeavor is inconsequential for most, since they may well share the ideology being propagated. Whatever the reasons might be, such activities represent a clear manifestation of the fusion of the state and capitalism and the direct penetration of the educational process.

The primary emphasis in the most influential of the educational reports is the necessity to utilize the schools to inculcate those competencies that can in turn meet the needs of American capital. Since economic growth is projected primarily in the areas of high technology, the curricular emphasis on science and technologically oriented subjects is understandable, as is the emphasis on providing this for a carefully selected few who will be absorbed into the middle and upper levels of the corporate structure and who will help to create capital.[3] The emphasis for the majority on the New Basics, coupled with the admonition to gain computer literacy, is also understandable in light of the necessity of increasing the minimal skill level of those who will perform the more routine jobs in the technologically oriented financial and corporate sectors, for example, as key punch operators, check sorters, and word-processing operators.

The attempt to increase the general educational level of the majority must be understood as well as part of the attempt to enlarge the existing pool of semiskilled labor. Failure to enlarge the labor pool will mean that wages among semiskilled workers will rise because of the shortage of appropriately trained personnel, a fact that will reduce capital's profitability. The successful attempt to increase the size of the labor pool will enable capital to keep wages low because there will be more qualified workers than job vacancies.

Now, if the above scenario is even close to being accurate, it helps to explain why the current reform proposals are not, and cannot be, "consonant with the democratic ideal of optimizing educational opportunity for all," as Daniel Tanner hoped might be the case. The main referent for a reformed educational system is economic productivity; the proposals advocated in the major reports are consonant with the achievement of that objective. Issues such as equity, social justice, the realization of individual potential, democratic empowerment, an appreciation of the arts and humanities, critical literacy, expanded educational opportunity—aside from the obligatory rhetoric concerning their importance in fostering "growth"—these concerns are obvious by their absence in the reports. This is not mere oversight, however, but is congruent with what Henry Giroux has called the "new public philosophy" (Giroux 1984). From the perspective of those who conceptualized and sponsored the reports, the provision of, say, critical literacy is not only irrelevant to the attempt to utilize the schools to help maximize capital, but it is also potentially detrimental to the realization of that goal. For the school to provide an education that enables the majority of its students to analyze society's current organization would perhaps encourage a possible reappraisal of—and perhaps revolt against—the existing arrangements that favor the few and disadvantage the majority. It is hardly surprising in this context, then, that none of the most influential of the current reform proposals offers even the possibility of an emancipatory or liberating education for America's students.[4] Attempts to optimize "educational opportunities for all" are equally irrelevant to today's reformers because this issue is totally unrelated to ensuring greater economic productivity. Indeed, such attempts might possibly impede the quest for greater economic productivity since valuable resources would have to be channelled away from "gifted" students and earmarked for those students whose contribution to the maximization of capital is at best questionable.

CAN THE PROPOSALS BE ENACTED?

There is little ambiguity about the major emphases in the national reports; the proposals flowing from these emphases are reasonably straightforward as well. In view of the singularity of purpose and approach that characterizes these documents, one needs to ask, quite simply: Can it be done? That is, can the proposed reforms be enacted in a significant proportion of the nation's schools? Or, are there too many impediments built into the fabric of American schooling and socioeconomic structure that will detour even the most dedicated attempts by the representatives of state capitalism to restructure the schools in a way that will minimize the formerly important political, democratic/socialization function of schooling while maximizing a narrowly defined economic, reproductive function?

The reformers have mounted a sophisticated public relations campaign to "sell" the importance of educational reform to the public. This campaign has in turn spawned numerous state and local initiatives, whose broad purpose has been to adapt recommendations contained in the national reports to the vagaries of local situations. If some of the proposed changes are not enacted, it will not stem from a lack of effort on the parts of the reformers.

The history of public education in this century clearly suggests how resistant the schools have been to structural change, although more receptive to curricular adaptation, what Carnoy and Levin term micro- or macro-technical modifications (Carnoy and Levin 1985, chapter 8). One need only recall the revised mathematics and science curricula that appeared in the 1950s, the widespread acceptance of the open-classroom concept in the 1960s, or the expansion of career education in the 1970s to appreciate just how malleable schools have been on the curricular issue. Given this propensity to alter the curriculum to meet the externally generated demands of the larger society (all the above examples were responses to externally generated stimuli), it is reasonable to surmise that the current emphasis on math, science, and technological subjects will be embraced as well, especially if school districts perceive continuing political pressure to do so *and* if they can garner external financial support to facilitate this.

It also seems reasonable to assume that efforts of the corporate/financial sector to influence what is taught in the schools will be sustained at least at present levels, and probably will increase. One of the reasons for this, noted above, is capital's need to ensure a pool of appropriately trained school leavers to enter the lower echelons of the corporate/financial enterprise. Another reason is the fact that money available for schooling is systematically being reduced. Part of the Reagan administration's campaign to reduce federal government presence has resulted in a reduction of various federally funded education programs. The administration's broader assault on social programs in general has meant that some of the burden to sustain these programs has been shifted to the states. State commitment to underwrite (even at a reduced level) some of these social programs has resulted in a reduction, or at least a leveling off, of state appropriations for education. These reductions are combined with the well-known resistance of taxpayers at the local level to support levies that would generate more income for education.[5] Local school districts, hoping to sustain their level of educational services in the face of budgetary uncertainties (at the least), may demonstrate little reluctance to accept external aid that can free the district's salaried teachers to staff potentially under- or unstaffed classrooms. If the administrator's ideological dispositions are consonant with that of the corporate-sponsored programs, then there is even greater likelihood that an externally funded program would be welcomed.

All this suggests that capital's penetration of the school will continue apace, and that the values undergirding the ideology of state capitalism will be impressed on the institution and on its students. But this mentions only one side of the ledger and ignores the various forms of resistance that possibly could impede the widespread introduction of the reforms into America's schools.

The recent work on various forms of student resistance to particular aspects of the schooling enterprise indicates the difficulty inherent in attempts to mandate educational reform.[6] Simply stated, this literature suggests that a significant proportion of a given student population, particularly poor and minority students, will act in a manner that impedes the realization of externally determined educational objectives. If these findings can be generalized, if students resist, in one way or another, any externally directed educational program, what does this portend for recommendations that stress the New Basics for these students, or for attempts by state capitalism to develop school-based skills commensurate with the requirements for entry-level positions in the labor market?

Many of the authors of this literature would argue that this resistance is embedded in the students' cultural particularities. This is surely an accurate interpretation. At the same time, however, we cannot neglect to link these cultural dynamics to the reality of the labor market, a reality that may also account for a certain degree of student resistance. That is, whereas students may resist schooling for reasons specific to their cultural backgrounds, they *may* also resist because they perceive that the school's education/training affords them the possibility of securing only the most meaningless and demeaning job in the labor market, one that offers scant opportunity for advancement, personal self-fulfillment, or even a decent wage.[7]

Teachers, both individually and working through their organizations, represent another potential impediment to the large-scale implementation of many of the recommended educational reforms. Teacher resistance will likely be passive, but this form of resistance thwarts recommended changes just as does a more active variety. The reasons for such resistance will be numerous, but the following can probably be included: the proposed reforms are seen as antithetical to the educational process, professionally threatening, irrelevant to the teachers' particular schools, or one more attempt to mandate change from outside while failing to seek the teachers' views or involve them in the change process.

It is also possible that various levels of the administrative bureaucracy in the educational system—for example, state and local boards of education—particularly within the administrative structures of local school districts, will resist the proposals. Here again, there will probably be numerous reasons for any resistance that may materialize. Some of the reasons might include: threats to professional autonomy, lack of clarity about the nature of the particular reforms, budgetary limitations, and inertial tendencies that are inherent to the educational bureaucracy.

Whereas some of the reform proposals may be implemented and others rejected (for reasons noted above or overlooked), there is also the possibility that reforms undertaken may have consequences unforeseen by those who advocate them. The school's location in the liberal democratic state means that it is not immune from the contradictions within the system of state capitalism. Carnoy and Levin address this issue, noting that

the challenge today is to explain how the public school can at one and the same time be an institution that reproduces the unequal class relations of capitalist society and an institution that is more democratic and equal than the workplace for which it prepares its students. . . . [T]he school is necessarily caught up in the larger conflicts inherent in the capitalist economy and a liberal capitalist state. These conflicts reside in the contradiction between the unequal relations underlying capitalist production and the democratic basis of the liberal capitalist state. (Carnoy and Levin 1985, 4–5)

By way of elaboration, note that purposeful actions, such as particular reforms in the educational system, do not guarantee predetermined outcomes. More specifically, it is possible to imagine that the efforts of the educational reformers to afford already advantaged students greater access to today's high status knowledge (in the form of a scientifically and technologically oriented curriculum) will be resisted by poor and minority groups, who recognize that their quite different educational fare is intended to reinforce their subordinate positions in the polity and economy.

This situation appears even more contradictory when we understand that the state is to be found on both sides in this struggle. That is, the state is inextricably an actor in the formulation and legitimation of the current reform movement. The school remains one of the most democratic institutions in American society and, as such, is a vehicle through which subordinate groups can redress particular grievances, such as social inequality and economic insecurity. Carnoy and Levin note how "in a politically democratic society, the State provides space for such struggles" (Carnoy and Levin 1985, 24). The manifestation of the state here is the school, which, as part of the state apparatus, is torn between several requisites. Again Carnoy and Levin express the dilemma most cogently. "In public education," they note, "the social conflict is expressed in the conflict between reforms aimed at reproducing the inequalities required for social efficiency under monopoly capitalism and reform aimed at equalizing opportunities in pursuit of democratic and constitutional ideals'' (Carnoy and Levin 1985, 24). The school is thus pulled in conflicting directions between the poles of democracy at the one extreme and inequality at the other. Such contradictory strains are, of course, rooted in the social conflicts in the society at large. In this situation, it is easy to understand that various forms of resistance by subordinate groups, augmented as they are by the states' contradictory position, might endanger the institutionalization of reforms initiated by those who represent state capitalism.

CONCLUSION

The state's role in both the accumulation process and in the legitimation of advanced capitalism is clear, as is the schools' relationship to the state. Analyses of current efforts to reform America's schools that neglect these equations will be seriously flawed. The interests of the state and of capital are clearly united at present in efforts to increase the school's reprodutive function, to ensure that appropriately trained youngsters can be marshalled in the effort to increase economic productivity. Managers of capital have turned to the schools in this effort because of their inability to stem the rate of profit decline. Attempts to discipline the labor force through layoffs and wage reductions have failed to arrest this decline, whereas the obsession with short-term profitability has sapped the ability of many capitalists to consider the implications of the longer term decline in profits, until it has become too late to take effective remedial action (Melman 1983, 27). In a situation like this that threatens the position of the United States in the world capitalist economy, the state's interest is at one with capital. The schools, as part of the state apparatus, understandably become part of the solution.

The situation gets murkier, however, when these interests diverge and when the state is called on to provide the means whereby disadvanted groups can improve their positions. Sometimes the state attempts to provide these means through various kinds of income transfers, for example, welfare payments of all sorts, or by incorporating large numbers of the formerly disadvantaged into government employment. More regularly, however, the state turns to the schools in its attempt to mediate social conflict and to provide the wherewithal to groups demanding more of their rights. In times of economic expansion, such a strategy usually works. In times of relative scarcity, however, such as the present, the social justice/welfare function that the school is called on to serve is challenged by those interests of capital that insist on the primacy of the school's reproductive/accumulation function. Whereas the current educational reform efforts clearly reflect this latter insistence, there is no guarantee that the disadvantaged will remain quiescent and will allow the representative of state capitalism to enact reforms that reinforce their already subordinate position.

NOTES

1. L. Althusser (1978), S. Bowles and H. Gintis (1976), and M. Carnoy and H. M. Levin (1985).

2. An elaboration of this perspective can be found in the report sponsored by the Committee on Economic Development (1985). The authors of the report note, on p. 12 that "we strongly encourage more businesses to share their management expertise with the public schools. We believe the business community needs to participate in the local policy-making process."

3. But numerous commentators have noted of late that the projections for jobs in the high technology sector are likely to be considerably below those numbers bandied about by the technocratic enthusiasts. See, for example, M. Castells (1980), and H. M. Levin and R. W. Rumberger (1983).

4. Two notable exceptions to this statement are E. Boyer (1983), and J. Goodlad (1983).

5. The dilemma in which the state finds itself because of these issues is the subject of James O'Connor (1973).

6. A representative sampling includes R. Everhart (1983), L. Weis (1985), and P. Willis (1977).

7. Philip Foster (1965) discovered this in his important, and frequently neglected, study of Ghanaian students some twenty years ago.

4

Where Computers Are Taking Us in the Education Field

Ernest Kahane and Andrew D. Oram

It is a principle among software programmers that a user's keyboard acrobatics should not stall the computer. Rather, the computer program should ignore a deviant response or should prompt the user to modify it. The selling of high tech works in a similar fashion. Those who set the agenda—in business, government, academia, and the mass media—turn debate about social and economic trends to the most effective restructuring of society around a vision of high tech growth. Critics are not expected to reexamine the evidence with a different set of values.

Educators have a special responsibility to examine high tech claims because of the pressure to accommodate these industries. Schools and universities are crucial to providing the skilled personnel upon which the technologies depend (Pearson 1985), and industry representatives want a large role in determining the goals, curricula, and techniques used (Alter 1986; Jain 1985; Pearson 1985). Attempts to accommodate such demands already include publicly funded technical training programs, business/university partnerships, and increasing purchases of computer equipment by schools. In particular, the desire of computer manufacturers for special academic dispensations has coalesced into a general drive to expand the pool of potential employees and buyers, which in the educational agenda is termed "computer literacy."

The authors, trained in philosophy of education and the social sciences, respectively, but who presently work for computer manufacturers, describe the rarely publicized world of high tech as a business operation: how hirings, promotions, and layoffs are planned, how work is organized, and how products are developed. Through some real-life observations on one central segment of high tech (computer manufacturing and software), we plan to clarify an educational debate marked by calls for more technically educated workers and computer-based programs (NCEE 1983; College Board 1984:7–8).

This chapter describes the day-to-day life of the computer industry, as well as the effects of computerization on work in other fields. The emphasis is on the social relations of employees to new technology and management. This chapter also analyzes what computer literacy means for computer companies and for schools.

It is not our purpose here to lay out or contrast the various concepts of computer-assisted instruction (CAI) in recent educational literature. Our contribution is to suggest a larger framework for judging claims, by providing background on the technology, the values of its makers, and the contexts where it is put to use. We place such evidence against the notions that computer companies are a humanistic model for educators and a force a priori for industrial and social progress.

CONSTELLATIONS IN THE MYTHOLOGY

As an ever-welcome guest on television and radio programs, government panels, at national conferences, and in newspaper columns, high tech is a popular focus for discussion, but not as we present it here. What appears instead is a mythological industry, judged by what it symbolizes or potentially could do rather than by what it is.

This mythmaking is evident in images like that of Apple Computer, which has promoted itself as the small individualist—an outgrowth of the 1960s counterculture—taking on monolithic big brother IBM. The Apple symbolism is entrepreneurial freedom versus corporate hegemony. What is not said is that Apple is now a large company, that it sees large corporations rather than individual buyers as its primary market, and that it practices coexistence ("tie-ins") with IBM (*Office Automation Reporting Service* 1985, 9–15).

As in advertising, the beliefs of popular and some academic discussion work best when they are not openly debated but form the tacit underlying perspective. One such belief is that high tech is the primary component of new industries that are transforming and transcending traditional hierarchies and antagonisms of work. In *Megatrends,* John Naisbett (1982, 10) writes: "An industrial society pits men against fabricated nature. In an information society for the first time in civilization—the game is people interacting with other people." Implicit in this statement is the latest version of an old-fashioned ideology: social advancement through technological growth.

The high tech promise is all the more powerful because of its intertwining and shared vision with influential forces across a spectrum from conservative (as the Heritage Foundation) to neoliberal (as Gary Hart's Center for a New Democracy).

The human resource requirements of new technologies are said to include attentiveness to new work styles, human diversity, "brain power," and participative management. Alvin Toffler (1983, 32, 34) suggests that technological growth will force a new respect for creativity and openness in the workplace: "Few if any of these new style occupations lend themselves to the kind of routine Taylorized labor that characterized most jobs in the past. . . . In the advanced de-massified industries, information and imagination are crucial and that changes everything."

At their most optimistic, management consultants claim that almost utopian conditions have already arrived in high tech and that the future looks even better: "What counts [in coordinating employees] is not so much form or structure as the pattern or networks of relationships. In satisfying this need, many successful high-technology organizations create very different and idiosyncratic organization designs. . . . Much will have to be learned on the job, as we 'develop' managers who can work with these new 'knowledge' people and within self-reliant teams" (Finkelstein and Newman 1984, 63, 64).

The educational side of the high tech myth decrees that academic excellence and preparation for the highly competitive job market of the future depend on redirecting the learning cycle through a layer of new technology. Thus the National Commission on Excellence in Education recommends computer training as one of the five New Basics, along with English and science, for instance (NCEE 1983). A national team presents to the Secretary of Education recommendations stating in part that traditional educational methods have not raised students to "maximum" levels—their position being that an investment in new technology will—and that more creative private-industry/school partnerships are needed (Charp 1985). Note the innovativeness and dynamism that, by implication, are attributed to the business sector while being denied to educational researchers and practitioners.

Thus, in a broad constellation of well-publicized accounts, computers symbolize egalitarianism, sharing, openness to change, constant growth and advancement, and a quest for excellence. Of course, negative connotations of authoritarianism, blind rationality, and so forth exist to counter the positive ones in the public mind. We try to take a route around both types of ideology by comparing the claims of high tech proponents to the reality of environments deeply penetrated by computer technology.

WORKING FOR THE COMPUTER INDUSTRY

Judgments of Employee Contributions

Since spokespersons portray high tech as promoting creativity and intelligence, industry success would seemingly depend on rewarding talent and encouraging the growth of individuals. The professional who enters high tech soon discovers a different (and disappointingly conventional) set of management concerns.

Even at initial job interviews, evidence of creativity and broad intelligence are brushed aside while the interviewer asks: "What's your background in Unix?" "Have you worked with local area networks?" In other words, intelligence and talent are defined as purely technical knowledge, preferably matching the hirer's immediate needs so that an employee can "hit the ground running from day one." Such values define a narrow career path for the employee.

Other qualities often associated with "entrepreneurship" (diligence, leadership, adventurousness) are also less important in real life than in promotional material. An internal study of management in a large computer company confirms traditional business biases in hiring and promotion. Engineering graduates are preferred for management ladders, whereas liberal arts graduates are suspect. Women and minorities may not advance as far as their abilities would permit. At review time, conformity to organizational culture far outweights competence or creativity. The strongest factors in promotion are "aggressiveness," "charisma," and "being a team player." These score much higher than "brilliance" (Leuchte 1985).

In most companies, salary structures and performance matrices ensure that most employees cannot become high achievers. A typical guideline used by managers for determining salary increases is the following performance distribution. All employees within a department must fit into this preset distribution, which is weighted by percentage for average performance (source is an internal document of a large computer company):

RATING	EMPLOYEE DISTRIBUTION
1. Far exceeds expectations	10%
2. Exceeds expectations at all times	25%
3. Meets expectations	55%
4. Meets expectations at times or fails to meet expectations	10%

In addition, since departments plan their budgets far in advance, salary decisions are made, for all practical purposes, a year before the performance they are supposed to reward. In short, the organizational framework for rewarding employees undermines the individual's drive toward excellence.

Individuality and Creativity

Very little corporate research in the computer field pursues an idea past its immediate marketability. Whatever resembles pure computer science research is conducted in universities and is, to a large extent, supported by the military for its own goals (Hayashi 1985; Thompson 1986).

Products are developed through group projects, along stringent guidelines designed to make different components compatible. Therefore, individual creativity often has no forum or is overlooked. Furthermore, few departments have free reign to develop something totally new. Most people's work builds on a previous release of the same product. Each release attempts to patch the problems of the prior release while simultaneously tacking on new features.

In the computer field, where deadlines are so important and software releases have a life of only a few months, the appearance of meeting a goal is rewarded more than the quality of the product. Those who advance give the appearance of supplying what the company needs and know how to shove responsibility for bugs onto some other organization.

For many, the only chance for quick advancement is to shift constantly between companies for a higher salary and more responsibility. However, since managers seek very specialized skills, personal advancement depends on becoming well versed in narrow technical points known only to a small group. This directly conflicts with broadening one's experience, and fosters an obsession with pure technique.

Classification of Work Force

Despite talk of open-minded attitudes toward employees and their career goals, computer companies have built an extremely traditional division of labor. The majority of employees are routine wage-earners, nonunionized of course, found on the assembly line or in clerical positions and support staff. These "hourly" employees are covered by totally different policies from the "salaried" employees and are the most vulnerable to layoffs and displacement through automation (Howard 1985; *Editorial* 1984).

Within professional ranks, to deal with an unstable market, computer companies have increasingly implemented a two-tier work force. A core group has a full range of employee benefits, whereas a temporary group is hired solely on a wage basis. Poor revenues can be handled either by letting the temporary group go, or conversely by expanding that group at the expense of the core group. The allocation of project tasks and narrow definition of skills required by this system impedes individual commitment and a sense of work continuity.

The economic instability behind cost-reducing strategies inflicts its own psychological costs on the "secure" work force. Talk of personal goals and attempting change within the organization recedes to concern about attaching oneself to safe projects and divisions. Under conditions where people seek economic survival as a paramount goal, the rhetoric of job advancement, creativity, and meritocracy strikes hollow tones. Fearing for their jobs, people realize that what really matters are economic forces, seemingly beyond their control, and that no single personal effort can belie or transcend that unhappy fact.

Effects of Computerization on Computer Users

The boasts of high tech companies about beneficient and innovative improvements that they make in the lives of their users can readily be seen as an attempt to spur employee effort and investor confidence. But this guise has a deeper purpose. Claims to perpetual innovation underlie the promises of social policy-makers that high tech will extend the bounds of human choices and control over our environment.

A subtle elision in logic, particularly significant for education, is the implication that the increased power given by computers to businessses and public agenices is also an empowerment of the individuals who do the computing. However, evidence accumulated by critical researchers increasingly shows that computerization fits the traditional model of automation, whereby workers' discretion is lessened or displaced (Howard 1985; Kuttner 1983; Geiser and Harrison 1985; *Editorial* 1985 [A]; NARMIC/American Friends Service Committee 1982).

In business, computerized systems often reduce risk-taking and individualization of tasks; workers cannot argue with the computer, cannot locate the source of authority, and worry about standardized measurements of their productivity (Zuboff 1982, 147–148). In local governments, computerized systems are usually installed where they reinforce social control or administrative efficiency (e.g., police departments, revenue collectors) rather than more equitable or wider distribution of resources (referral agencies, libraries) (Kraemer and Kling 1985).

Current business discussion about automating office activities illuminates the pressure of organizational priorities on technical development. Theoretically, the computerized office makes data more available, which in turn enhances the independence, productivity, and coordination of different parts of the organization (Johnson 1985). But as the networks of data bases and desktop computers spread, the companies have found that their proprietary needs propel a search for new and stronger forms of computer security, leading to a system that restricts information to certain departments and individuals (Rhodes 1985; Zimmerman 1985). The British Radical Science Collective (1985,7) perceptively calls this trend "centralization in the guise of devolution."

In short, the direction set by the computer industry is toward centralization rather than independence, tighter security rather than a new freedom, and a reinforcement of traditional automation. Those who exalt the changes wrought by computerization confuse production techniques, which are being upgraded rapidly, with fundamental relations among people, which are entrenched rather than elevated.

EDUCATING FOR THE COMPUTER INDUSTRY

As noted in the previous section, in the world of work, computers are part of an unspoken agenda. Educators should similarly initiate research into the hidden curriculum of computers in schools before encouraging investments that drain an educational system's resources. Notwithstanding the various definitions of computer literacy and arguments whether computer-assisted instruction (CAI) should be student- or teacher-based, the underlying authority relations of the school will inevitably structure the student's experience with computers, as with other media.

Justifications for computer literacy, especially in secondary schools, often state that these programs are vital to prepare students for the job market and that CAI can boost student performance (Douglas and Bryant 1985). Seizing on the techniques of television ads for personal computers, many schools offer computer training courses so that students can be prepared for the fierce competition over jobs. But as we have seen, predictions of a swelling job market for these skills have dubious validity.

Claims that computer instruction can boost achievement must also be viewed critically. Programs for developing courseware are pedagogically primitive. Students are tested through short answer, matching answer, and multiple choice questions. The fact is that most CAI is simply the old programmed instruction in a flashier package.

To justify purchases of computers as potent vehicles for old pedagogy and as preparation for skilled computer jobs is to play into the high tech myths: that is, continuous economic growth and solutions to social (and educational) problems through technology.

Computers are not transforming society into a community of programmers. Most of the created jobs have as little connection to programming as putting a bank card into a cash machine. Other than a small layer of specialists in systems work, computers for the most part generate a huge supply of low-paying unskilled jobs, often occupied by temporary female labor (Kuttner 1983).

Programming does not bring one into closer contact with or greater understanding of the world; it does not enable one to explain oneself to other people or to understand other people better; programming does not challenge assumptions or push one toward greater maturity. Computers, however, can help exercise logical skills and teach patience as problems are reduced to small decisions. Computers are also useful tools for typing, manipulating data, calculating, and playing.

Integrated into a curriculum with a concern for social and cultural impacts, the high tech disciplines could perhaps enrich students' understanding and mastery of the modern world. However, as the field now stands, the fascination with "computer literacy" becomes an excuse to ignore human interaction within classrooms and to subordinate education to the job-oriented demands of the business sector (Robins and Webster 1985).

CONCLUSION

This chapter has laid some groundwork for evaluating the role of computers in education by citing the actual expectations and conditions for individual achievement to be found in the companies that develop computers. In our experience, computer companies stress standardization of work and the technical implementation of immediate goals, while de-emphasizing the creative contributions of individuals and the evaluation of fundamental purposes. Such rein-forcement of technocratic values and centralization parallels the trend in other areas of society to use computers for the heightening of automation.

It would appear that the ideology of progress through computerization becomes part of a high tech vision of social policy: the promise that new freedoms and human abilities will somehow emerge from using new electronic tools, with no changes in social hierarchies or loci of power. The dangers of overestimating the benefits of computerization are very great in the field of education, potentially resulting in the abandonment of critical and interpersonal sensitivity for a narrow technical training. Educators, an important market for computer manufacturers, should be very careful and critical of the latent appeal of the "new machine."

5

The Corporate Community on the Ideal Business–School Alliance: A Historical and Ethical Critique

Peter Sola

The businessman dominates American civilization. His function is so to organize American society that he has the freest possible run of profitable adventure. To do this he must organize the symbolism of that society so that there are no vital obstacles to the performance of his function.

Harold J. Laski, *The American Democracy,* 1948

INTRODUCTION

"Those who fail to understand the past are condemned to repeat it" were the words that sprang to mind as I began to read through the literature for this chapter. The school reform literature, consisting of reports and articles, various commissioned papers from business and professional organizations, books and monographs issued by philanthropic foundations, all seem to echo the same rationales and arguments employed by business and educational reformers of the progressive era. This earlier reform movement wanted to reshape the public school curricula by introducing vocational education into American high schools and, in some cases, elementary schools. These reformers, led by the business community, offered to school administrators and teachers the promise of an enlightened business partnership. Together they would work for change based on "enlightened self interest." Education is again experiencing strong criticism, and both the business community and academics are calling for a new *civism* in American public schools, including a revised curriculum and close ties between schools and business.

The issues are clear. Do special interest groups, in this case the business community and the quasi-public philanthropic foundations that support them, have the right to define "the public interest"—especially if "the public interest" is one of self-interest?

The history of the relationship between education and the business community can be traced historically to the 1830s. In his *Fifth Annual Report,* Horace Mann argued that the educated worker was an economic necessity for the business community. According to Mann, the educated worker could be relied upon to be respectful of private property, be capable of following instructions, and in general would be a more efficient worker. Such an interweaving of business and government as well as educational interests seems always to have been part of the fabric of American society (Kolko 1967). The occupations of our founding fathers were not, in general, that of professional revolutionaries such as Tom Paine and Sam Adams, who were the exceptions. They were farmers and businessmen. The relationship between the federal government and business, at least through the Civil War, was one of government aid to the business community. The growing power of the business community from the 1840s through the 1890s was not only in the economic sector but the social and political sectors as well. And, as Gabriel Kolko concluded, this need to acquire power had one key purpose: "such domination was direct and indirect, but significant only in so far as it provided the means for achieving a greater end—political capitalism . . . [that is] the utilization of political outlets to attain conditions of *stability, predictability* and *security*" (Kolko 1979, 3). The need was for a society able to supply the necessary conditions for the business community to attain its goals—profits. An interesting illustration of this was noted by Clarence Karier, who pointed out that during the 1870s the textbooks began to portray businessmen as role models for American students, slowly replacing the soldier. We accepted that as well as the idea that our capitalist economic system was a natural outcome of a supposedly democratic political system. That is to say, these two institutions are mutually inclusive; criticism of capitalism became an attack on democracy. It is interesting to note that since China and the U.S.S.R. have begun experimenting with variations of capitalistic economic theories, there has been a conceptual change in the manner by which Americans refer to our economic institutions. They are no longer part of the capitalist system but are now part of the "free enterprise system," a phrase that links in our mind the terms "freedom-democracy-capitalism" in an almost subconscious manner. Americans believe wrongly that only in a democratic political system can capitalism exist. Since the turn of the century, we have been subjected to propaganda from the business community designed to shape proper attitudes toward economic programs and policies. It was during the 1930s that the business community launched a national media campaign to alter the American public's perception that business had caused the economic crash of 1929 and the subsequent economic depression (Church 1976). Utilizing the old adage that the best defense is a good offense, the business community attacked college professors and textbooks that criticized capitalism and any other group or individual that appeared to pose a threat to the business community. They began to wrap themselves in the flag, linking the interests of capitalism to the goals of democracy. Indeed, history not understood is repeated.

What struck me while researching the current school reform literature was a strong feeling of déjà vu. Fifteen years before, I had read the same general criticisms about education while researching for my doctoral dissertation. I reread my thesis with the man-the-barricades title of *Plutocrats, Pedagogues, Plebes: Business Influences on Vocational Education and Extra-curricular Activities in the Chicago High Schools 1899–1925* (Sola 1972). The educational reform criticisms of the 1890s and the 1980s are very similar. The critics are again raising many of the same issues: What is the purpose of education? What interest groups are defining that purpose? Who is drafting and implementing educational policy and law?

We know that the progressive era witnessed the end of the common high school curriculum and the introduction of the differentiated curriculum. This shift, justified on the basis of group differences as identified by the I.Q. tests, supported existing social, economic, sexual, and racial divisions in American society. These group differences also seemed to reinforce the need for different kinds of education, not based on individual choice or preference, but on how educational policy-makers and managers evaluated one's future potential based on seemingly objective measures. Remember, we were as a society deluged with southern and eastern European immigrants, speaking many languages, and believing in a non-Protestant God. In an age of intense, murderous racism, ethnic bigotry, and religious intolerance, it was not a coincidence that the schools were called upon to socialize and Americanize these groups to become right-thinking citizens. Businesspeople called for industrial and vocational education, the introduction of vocational guidance, and the need for students to develop the proper business and social skills as well as the right economic beliefs (Sola 1972).

Education was believed then, as now, to be the key for economic prosperity and productivity: the magic solution that would save U.S. industry from second-class status. The business community, then as now, believed that our weak worldwide economic position was the result of a poor or misdirected public school education that hampered rapid economic development and competitiveness. In the past, in order to promote internal social collusion and unity, nations or kings would often declare war on neighboring territories. Since the nineteenth century, we ideally prefer to shape our national social consensus via education. If education has come to hold such a crucial function in maintaining social cohesion in twentieth-century American society, it is not surprising that there would be a great deal of consistency between current and past reform movements.

RATIONALIZING EDUCATIONAL REFORM, 1890–1980

During the progressive era, the business community learned the functionality of pragmatic principles for their own self-interested goals. In short, the business community learned that in order to maintain a position of social power, authority, and wealth, one must be willing to be continually flexible: they learned that corporate success depended more and more on one's willingness to grant short-term concessions in order to obtain long-term profits. Similarly, the reasons the business community sought educational reform was similar in both eras, that is, for the long-term stability, predictability, and security of corporate capitalist institutions.

The progressive era business community claimed that a common academic curriculum was useless for the majority of students. Most students, they argued, would be better off economically enrolled in school programs that had a more practical curriculum. The business community also criticized the public schools for failing to inculcate the proper social, political, and work attitudes in American youth. During this era, therefore, there was an intense effort to ensure that school programs and curriculum fit the economic realities of the 1890s. Some of my basic assumptions clearly reflect a conviction that the business community today has demonstrated the same power to change school programs and structures to achieve similar self-interested, limited economic objectives. They achieved these aims in the 1890s and will probably do so again in the 1980s.

From the progressive era to the present, an analysis of who or what groups define the purpose and policy of education has not been systematically under-taken. Most of us simply assume that the public has control over education, that it is through this "public" that educational purpose and policy are formulated. Educators, so goes this common knowledge, merely implement this public man-date. The evidence we do have fails to confirm these commonly held beliefs (Cronin 1973; House 1974; Koerner 1968; Zeigler and Jennings 1974). Which group or groups actually make educational policy? During the era of local control, the school boards were at least reflective of the community (although how rep-resentative of the community is another issue). The past seventy years has seen a radical change in the social composition of school boards (Count 1927).

By the end of the progressive era, school boards consisted mainly of business persons and professionals and seldom of teachers, blue collar workers, or women. Citizens began to abrogate their responsibility not only in the arena of education but also in the economic and political spheres. We began to defer to the "experts" and to the technocrats who made both the school systems and the trains run on time (Karier 1975). Today these technocrats have even come to be relied upon to *make* school policy. School board members, believing that these technocrats are better equipped to develop more objective and effective school policies, routinely defer to the superintendent of education and her or his staff as au-thoritative educational experts. If Counts is correct, and the makeup of school boards represents largely business and professional classes, and if the school administrative staff largely keeps their collective eyes on "the bottom line," who is ensuring that the schools are performing their primary task—education? Maintaining fiscal soundness is a virtue and ensuring productive citizens is certainly in "the public interest," but not at the expense of treating people like objects and the school as a factory.

It would be reasonable to assume that we—the public—should have a major impact on setting the educational agenda. However, since we have deferred to the experts, the control of educational policy appears to have shifted to a "public" that is composed of philanthropic foundations, business organizations and associations, aspiring politicians, and teacher union leaders. The issue is one of power. Educational purpose as defined by "the REAL public" should be the real engineers of educational policy in American schools. Unfortunately, historically the business sector has always been able to shape educational policy. During the progressive era, this influence was criticized by both labor leaders and public schoolteachers. Although these groups were critical of some of the motives of the business community and in many cases actively opposed the reforms that the business community tried to implement, they were largely ineffective (Sola 1972, 1976, 1978). Today we need a similar critical examination of the motives determining the educational reforms of the 1980s. Are we moving toward the kind of national system of education that the authors of the Constitution tried to avoid? Aren't we currently creating a national agenda for education, including a federal curriculum, a national test for teachers, and a unified teacher education curriculum? I believe that rigorous teacher standards, a sound teacher education program, and curriculum revisions are worthwhile goals. I do not believe in a reform mandate that precludes a diversity of approaches to excellence in teacher education, or a curriculum that prescribes a unitary measure of student competency is necessary or desirable (Sola and DeVitis, Forthcoming).

SELECTED EXAMPLES OF EDUCATIONAL REFORMS 1890–1980

An analysis of the current educational reform literature when compared to progressive era school reform literature reveals some interesting parallels. Both reform movements call for curriculum improvement to help America regain world economic superiority. Both groups of social reformers blame education for falling behind in technological leadership. Both reform movements have as one of their key reform tenets that America is not at the forefront of technological innovation (*Nation at Risk* report of the National Commission on Excellence in Education 1983). Both reform movements seem to place the blame and the burden for maintaining economic leadership upon the schools. In the 1900s our rivals were the Germans and British, whereas in the 1980s we are in economic competition with the Japanese, Koreans, and Taiwanese. The business leaders of both eras believed that the solution to regaining economic superiority was to reform public education. Not many individuals are raising the question of how school reform will necessarily result in an improved economic position. What is the cause-effect relationship between improving/reforming education and the economic sector? If we are discussing increasing worker productivity by educating a person with more proficient skills, a reasonable argument may be made. However, why is education the focus of what is clearly a failure of business policy, that is, the decision to secure short-term gains in profit rather than long-term investment in the means of production?

Special interest group involvement in educational policy-making has been a topic of extended research by educational historians. The reform of education to serve business interests has been researched especially during the progressive era (Hays 1964; Filene 1970; Sola 1976). Some historians argued that educators were vulnerable to outside control because of poor administrative practices and were thus co-opted (Callahan 1962). Other historians argued that emerging values and ideology of school administrators were shaped largely by the new cost-effective administrative methods that were being applied to shape education (Karier 1973, 1975). Also historians have focused on the changing social com-position of school boards that became more and more dominated by the profes-sional and business classes (Counts 1927).

Cooperation between educators and businesspersons has been cyclical. During the progressive era, teachers and teacher unions were very skeptical of the intentions of the business community and, on some occasions, fought for a balance between the use of schools for business interests and for the common good (Sola 1972). Today, teachers and teacher union officials appear to be encouraging a renewed business/education partnership (McNett 1982).

One of the rationales used by the business community both during the 1890s and today is that educational reform must have social and civic benefits as well as "economic payoffs." Such business-guided educational reform does appear to have resulted in some social benefits. However, a closer reading of some of these "social benefits" raises some serious ethical questions. The social, civic, and economic purposes of education appear to be inextricably linked in the twentieth-century liberal school reform literature. For example, Russ Marks has shown that the Supreme Court's 1954 Brown decision was motivated as much by economic factors as by social considerations (Karier 1975). This complex intertwining of the economic and social spheres in educational decision making was also blatantly obvious in the progressive school reform. American progres-sive school reform included not only differentiated skill training, but also the inculcation of proper economic beliefs and civic virtues. Most important, the workers were taught the interdependence of social classes.

One troubling aspect resulted from the business community's rhetorical fusion of the civic, social, and economic purposes of education. Criticisms of business-led educational reforms are made to appear as attacks on the democratic way of life. What begins as rational criticism of private sector use of public institutions for self-interested purposes becomes entangled in a rhetorical fusion of the eco-nomic and the sociopolitical system spheres. Good citizenship is made to appear as the key ingredient in the school's efforts to train productive workers.

Why is the questioning of the business community involvement in the educational sector so muted? If religious leaders or left or right wing radicals tried to exercise even a fraction of the influence that the business community has on education, we would be vehemently arguing against them. Yet when the business community issues authoritative reform reports, we simply accept this as the way that educational policy ought to be formulated in American society. The purpose of education ought to be decided by the larger society, not just by those who have the hegemonic power. Thus in the current educational reform movement, the so-called public (that is, current commission members, task force members, influential educational reform figures, reform report authors, etc.) is not *my* definition of "the REAL public" (that is, those that are truly representative of the American populace). In sum, one does not need to involve oneself in any complex ethnographic probing to identify the nature of social control in twentieth-century American reform literature. The special interest group control over the public sector is visible, all-encompassing, monolithic, unapologetic. President Calvin Coolidge noted in the 1920s that the business of America is business. Today it seems one must add that the business of America is developing educational policy for business. The business of American education has really become inseparable from American business.

CONCLUSION/SOLUTION

If we examine the many education reports, keeping in mind their economic roots, one is struck by the degree of consensus regarding how to achieve social progress. Business leaders assume that if we can improve the quality of school programs and personnel, the American economy will improve. However, what if one argues the opposite position—that is, that our social institutions are not working because they are based on a flawed public philosophy? From this perspective, fine tuning institutional structures will not solve problems—social, political, or economic. What if we asked more searching questions regarding these institutions? For example, are the conceptual foundations that undergird our present society sound? Do these assumptions prove to be correct when we examine the consequences of implementing policy based upon them? If one holds a different set of assumptions about society—what would be the consequences? What if we assume American society is racist, materialistic, and using reward and punishment to cultivate a dehumanizing quest for status, power, and wealth (Karier 1973, xvii)? If such is the case, and many think so, then neither fine tuning nor laissez-faire responses would be appropriate. I believe the past century gives us a reasonable amount of evidence to support this opposing set of assumptions. In short, we ought to begin to raise basic issues directed at the causes of such problems as racism, classism, and sexism by asking the right questions. If we look at the past reform sequence, one can discern a rather depressing pattern of educational reform; from the initial production of reform rhetoric, to attempts to institutionalize the reform rhetoric, and finally to discussions as to the failure of school reform and the need for a new reform agenda. Social reformers of the 1830s, 1880s, and 1950s identified America's problems as poor housing, low wages, poor working conditions, inadequate education of the masses, and racism. These various reform efforts failed because the reformers assumed that present societal institutions needed only to be fine-tuned to solve social problems. With similar convictions, when these "reforms" failed in their aim, the working classes themselves became objects of scorn and ridicule. Thus the failure of educational reform was attributed to the very groups that were identified as needing help in the first place, or what William Ryan aptly referred to as "blaming the victim."

When a segment of society, one that is economically and politically powerful, imposes a specific view on the rest of us, I am concerned. Education was, education is, and education will continue to be used by the business community to further its own agenda.

Education is used by all modern industrial nations to generate a supply of trained individuals. From the floor sweeper with G.E.D. to the C.E.O. with an M.B.A., education performs a similar function. According to "the American dream," both individuals must be given "free choice" and "an equal educational opportunity" to succeed to the best of one's ability. Effective schools are those where each individual has been fairly sorted for an appropriate economic slot. This is the most commonly voiced purpose for American schooling. But what if the schools are structured to maintain class divisions, elitism, and vocationalism? What if schools reflect, enforce, and enhance racism, materialism, and special interest group activity in U.S. society? What if education functions more as a gate, limiting access to some while allowing others to pass through based on their "tested" ability? Does education really allow for "free choice" so that every individual is able to pursue self-chosen academic goals?

There is no doubt that special interest groups have the power to limit educational choices. In a democracy, a fine line must be drawn between social needs and individual interests. Schools should play a critical role in helping to articulate these educational prerequisites for life in a truly democratic community. Francisco Ferrer offers one insightful approach to this dilemma: "Education was not designed to make a person into a good citizen, a religious person or even a good person. . . . Education must bring the individual to the level of awareness . . . that there will be tyranny and slavery as long as one man depends upon another" (cited in Spring 1975, 45). As defined by Ferrer, such an education would be most threatening to those special interest business groups that have a specific reform agenda for American education. Until we ask these same, basic fundamental questions about the social aims and ethical explanations used to justify the United States' present social institutions, we have little chance to achieve real educational progress. Our failure is not a failure of technological expertise. Our failure is our unwillingness (and many point to our increasing philosophical incapacity) to examine the moral and ethical roots of our public philosophy. As Karier has succinctly stated:

If we had examined them, it [society] might have pondered the wisdom of consistently respecting and honoring those who, from Franklin on, found success in materialistic, competitive, cunning and self-seeking behavior. These are the Franklin virtues under-girding a capital-producing society. . . . These values were productive in the development of the wealthiest technological state in the world but counter-productive concerning the development of a moral culture based on humane considerations. . . . There might still be time and the possibility in the affluent cybernated age of the future to usher in the humane age that will enhance the dignity of man. (Karier 1973, 29)

PART III

EDUCATION REFORM AND "THE NEW EQUITY"

6

The Bootstrap Ideology of Educational Reform: What the Recent Reports Say about the Current and Future Status of Blacks in Higher Education

Beverly M. Gordon

INTRODUCTION

The experience of Blacks in the United States has been one of constant struggle against racist policies and procedures. Access to the highest levels of social, political, economic, cultural, and educational advancement, and self-sufficiency remains a dream unfulfilled. The paradox is that many times these racist policies were proposed in the name of social progress. The progressive era witnessed the transformation of local school control in rural and urban areas to a formal, modern American education system, emphasizing bureaucracy, centralization, and school consolidation, all under the watchword of efficiency. Educational policy and policy-makers played a key role in this process, particularly during times when the educational reform ferment was at its height. Decisions of particular interest for this discussion were those made for African-Americans, most times with little regard for their counsel, input, or consent and often in direct opposition to the best interests of their schools. History is replete with examples of attempts by educators and dominant power groups (such as philanthropists and northern industrialists) to control black institutions, at the public school level and higher education particularly, in an effort to control the kind (classical versus industrial) of education that African-Americans received. It appears that the thrust was to produce a class of African-American intellectuals who would endorse a conservative, accomodationist acceptance of a subordinate caste status in a racial hierarchy (Anderson 1978; Berry and Blassingame 1982; Dabney 1926; Franklin and Anderson 1978; Gordon 1985; Kliebard 1986; Mabee 1979).

Since the 1890s, American educators have focused on various reforms and evaluation in the hopes of guaranteeing youth, allegedly, a quality education.

One of the manifestations of this concern has been the periodic appearance of national committee reports that seek to reform existing programs. The reports of the Committee of Fifteen, Committee of Ten, Cardinal Principles, and others all have their historical roots in the issue of reform. Teacher training, administrative and curricular concerns, and calls to reform them were born of administrative managerial necessity in an effort to make schools more efficient and effective (Kliebard 1986; National Education Association 1893, 1895, 1916). Influenced by city planners, chambers of commerce, industrialists, and northern philanthropists, under the call for efficiency, bureaucracy, and school management, progressive educators began to make reforms in the hopes of guaranteeing youth a quality education to fit them into the world of work. Through consolidation and centralization, educators gained control over city urban school systems and brought with them standardization, efficiency in school management, and curriculum differentiation to meet the needs of a socially efficient society.

By the end of the nineteenth century, the Anglo-Saxons had risen to be the most powerful ethnic group in the struggle for control over developing urban centers. Whereas the use of consolidation and centralization as mechanisms for absolute control did bring order, continuity, and planned growth, this kind of organizational assemblages of the cities was produced by city planners for benefit of the industrial elites. The progressive era witnessed a power struggle between local ward leaders and the city manager. What this kind of empowering of the Anglo-Saxon meant is critical. The fight in urban centers was for control over school decentralization. Ward or community control meant that Blacks had power to influence the quality of education in their own schools. Consolidation eliminated the ward power base and put people outside of the community in control, which more often than not resulted in a quality change in the way schools were run.

At historically black institutions of higher education, the struggle for control during this same period was between control by Blacks and industrialists and philanthropic domination. According to James Anderson's (1978) work on the formulation of the black intelligentsia, the turn of the century from the 1890s to the early 1900s revealed the emergence of a young black radical intelligentsia. Encouraged and mentored by the black educational elite, who called on this "educated black vanguard to articulate the political and economic interests of the black masses and to keep the masses aware of points where their interests were at variance with those of the dominant society" (Anderson 1978, 97), this radical vanguard was seen as a threat to and in defiance of southern racism. In response to this increasing status and power of the radical black intelligentsia, the philanthropists sought to control these schools in order "to keep alive their efforts to win the ideological allegiance of influential black leaders" (Anderson 1978, 102). As a consequence many missionary black colleges lost their financial endowments, without which they could not operate. In turn, the industrial philanthropists through their financial support gained control and, consequently, political influence over the black colleges that were producing this critical mass of intellectuals during the period of 1910 to 1920 and achieved an "intellectual hegemony" over the black scholarly community.

Anglo-Americans, in essence, influenced the shape of the black intelligentsia and this new intelligentsia emerged with ideological perspectives detrimental to Blacks at that time and even today. Such perspectives defined mixing of the black and white races as advancement (accommodationist, integrationist, dependency) while criticizing any perspective that advocated black independency and autonomy. This ideology was very different from that of a Marcus Garvey, W.E.B. DuBois, Chandler Owen, or A. Philip Randolph (not that these men always agreed with one another, but they represented a genre of radical intelligentsia) and signified the production of a new conservative group who would embrace stands and positions to do anything to assist Anglo-Americans in order to become their designated authority, or spokesperson for the black community. It would be reasonable to say that the rise of the progressive era had negative overall effect on black community schools, specifically with regard to the question of education for what purpose, by what means, and to what ends.

As the twenty-first century is born, we are witnessing the restructuring of the societal and economic order at the national and international levels. With new urgency, we ask what such structural changes hold for African-Americans and other people of color. The intention of this chapter is to assess the current status and future projections of African-Americans in higher education, and assess the policy implications of such findings and what they mean for African-Americans.

The past thirty years have witnessed precipitous professional and economic reform within the American society. The decades of the 1950s through the 1980s, witnessed the doubling of technical and professional workers in the labor force to 14.5 percent (Karabel 1974) as well as changes in the relationships, negotiations, and tensions between workers and business management. The civil rights movement of the 1950s, coupled with the social protest movements of the 1960s and the push for equal access to higher education, assisted in increasing access to higher education for more people of color and precipitated the expansion among minority faculty and student populations in higher education during the 1960s and early 1970s. These students, part of the baby boomers, were coming of age at a time when changes at higher educational institutions occurred in response to the professions and economic changes that accompanied the rise of the technological era (Bell 1973).

The policy of Affirmative Action and its implementation procedure were prescribed in the 1965 Executive Order EO 11246. Such efforts were mandated not because people of color and other disenfranchised groups lacked the credentials to be hired, but because discrimination had been an integral part of the previous hiring procedures (Fleming 1978). The provisions of EO 11246 required federally funded projects or institutions to project a portion of set-aside minority positions and set numerical goals rather than quotas equivalent to their proportion in the national population. For African-Americans, for example, an equitable representation would be approximately 11.7 percent (Fleming 1978) based on the officially calculated percentage of the total represented by the African-American population as of 1980 (McNett 1983).

One outcome of mandated compliance of the Affirmative Action policies in education, in housing, and in employment is the pervasive belief within Anglo-American society that people of color, such as African-Americans, have made significant gains in their struggles for social justice in education, housing, and employment. In fact, the exact opposite is true. Particularly in higher education, the illusion of Affirmative Action policies cannot mask persistent reality. Harvey and Scott-Jones (1986), in their study of black faculty members at predominantly white colleges and universities, state the problem clearly: "By no reasonable, commonly understood interpretation of available data can it be said that Blacks as a group are succeeding as faculty members in predominantly white institutions of higher education" (Harvey and Scott-Jones 1986, 68).

Moreover, there is the erroneous belief that the Civil Rights movement has eradicated the existence and effects of racism. Reality suggests that Affirmative Action policy has taken the brunt of the Reagan administration's hostility toward civil rights. Reagan is the only one among Affirmative Action era presidents who has not made any positive administrative contribution to that policy (Schwartz 1984). Rather the Reagan administration has targeted the existing policy of Affirmative Action by dismantling civil rights gained over the last three decades by the disenfranchised, particularly people of color and women. An analysis of the demographic data suggests that the intention of this administration was to erode the blueprint for equity and parity crafted in the 1950s and 1960s and that it has done so within the last five years (Darling-Hammond 1985; Schwartz 1984; Gill 1980).

The effects of these policy changes have resulted in a multidimensional reaction and pernicious division within the black community. The middle class has benefited, although not to the extent generally believed, in education, jobs, and housing. Glasgow (1980) has shown that the working class, and particularly the underclass, is losing ground in economic status, employment, and education. This insidious (Machiavellian) schism between the middle, working, and underclass further alienates and physically separates the middle classes and the intelligentsia from the masses. There is a dawning awareness that the real issue is that there has been no effort to correct the structural factors that limit equal opportunity. In fact, the operating structural forces systematically attack any forms of collectivity based on a community effort. The history of consolidation or bureaucracy in the urban development of the late nineteenth and early twentieth centuries provides a salient example of how industry and business interests orchestrated such centralization of power and control over the disenfranchised ethnic communities. We are experiencing the end of the civil rights hiatus giving way to change that threatens erosion of the gains made.

Moreover, the sentiment at the federal level is to discontinue treating even the "deviancy" symptoms of underclass development. Again, there dawns on our understanding the tenuous nature of programs and policies that have not been translated into change within the existing social and economic structure.

Deficiencies in federal policy lead us to believe that programs created an illusion of the promise of upward mobility for all, primarily through education. Instead, deviancy theories, the culture of poverty, and no-skills arguments still reinforce the prevailing attitudes of the dominant society and policy-makers, who craft inadequate programs that perpetuate large-scale underachievement for the underclass.

THE EDUCATIONAL STATUS OF AFRICAN-AMERICANS: THE DARLING-HAMMOND REPORT

Access to postsecondary or higher education for Blacks provided the illusion of upward mobility through education without the dominant society having to actualize structural changes in the social and economic policy. In academia, for example, assessing the educational reforms and gains made provides a salient example of dreams deferred. By all accounts, the educational gains over the last several decades are in danger of erosion. Dr. Linda Darling-Hammond argues that "excellence" cannot be achieved until and unless African-Americans, other people of color, and the poor receive a litany of support services and systems we can repeat by memory: enriched curricula, remedial education, well-qualified teachers, and teaching methods that enhance the potential in all children instead of stunting their growth. Attention must be given to the content and substance of the curricula students receive to prevent a two-tracked system that determines who will receive a true education and [who] will merely be trained to assume a permanent role in the nation's underclasses" (Darling-Hammond 1985, 49). Interpersonal relationships and meaningful daily classroom interaction between student and teachers are also essential if the goal of quality educational opportunity and results is to be achieved.

There is also a critical need for more stimulation and the cultivation of interest in sciences and mathematics at the high school level, especially among black high school girls. Darling-Hammond noted that "advanced high school mathematics preparation was a significant determinant of college major for black females and for black students in white colleges" (Darling-Hammond 1985, 49).

Darling-Hammond (1985) also realizes that inadequate institutional services, rehabilitative programs, and school programs do not create clear paths to real achievement for ghetto youth. This occurs, in part, because those programs were not structured by people and scholars with a vested interest in the community and were not grounded in and informed by local cultural values and norms.

At the postsecondary level, there are problems of financial assistance for colleges and universities in regard to accessibility of funds, student scholarships, and loans, other funding opportunities (especially for graduate level research and teaching appointments). Additionally, the lack of a presence and availability of black faculty, the selection process, and per-student expenditure compound the problems (Darling-Hammond 1985; Hart 1984; Harvey and Scott-Jones 1986; Thomas 1984). Beyond these are the retention problems faced by black students who attend predominantly white institutions of higher education. One study discusses the possible methods needed to retain black students on campus. The author noted that:

Specific learned personality/attitudes, study skills, and behavioral strategies which encompass the variety of demands encountered on a college campus as well as a sense of support from the college environment are crucial in retention. It is speculated that patterns of social interaction on campus or in the school environment factors would be of even greater importance for black students on a predominantly white campus. Since these are learned attitudes and skills, intervention at the individual level coupled with campus factors can be implemented for the purposes of retaining black students. (Abatso 1982, 52)

For example, one Big Ten school, the largest in its state with more than 53,000 students, had the third lowest percentage of black students compared to all the public universities in the state. Its 4.4 percent of black students last year is low relative to the national average of 7 percent (Prentice 1985). It should also be noted that for the 1985–1986 academic year this same school, with a faculty of nearly 3,000 had only 61 Blacks on the faculty (43 men and 18 women). This further strengthens Harvey and Scott-Jones's (1986) contention that there is still a paucity of African-American faculty members in predominantly white institutions of higher education. Such an absence further serves to alienate students from positive role models and support systems essential for successful completion of graduate programs.

We should not be surprised with Darling-Hammond's findings or, for that matter, with any of the findings regarding the educational, social, and economic status of American Blacks. These persistent racial problems remain, in part, because of the underlying assumptions and realities of a capitalistic system, and, in part, due to the dominant society's analytical paradigms, beliefs, and assumptions about the black community. The paradigms employed underdevelop the black community and distort the nature of the black experience in the United States. This is due, in part, to the ethnocentric nature of the scientific community, and most importantly, the psychological and cultural struggles of people of color in resistance to the dominant society. The battle for the minds is the essence of ideological hegemony. Antonio Gramsci (1971) and Raymond Williams (1976) among others use the term of ideological hegemony when referring to models of social control, including specific social relationships and forms of social consciousness. They argue that society reproduces itself partly through the transmission of a system of values, attitudes, beliefs, social practices, and norms that function at once to convey and legitimate the ideological and social practices that serve the interests of the dominant class. The dominant world view of the society is thus perpetuated, in part, by schools and other agencies of socialization. Whereas the dominant world view in American society is far from monolithic, it nonetheless exercises a powerful influence in shaping and legitimating social structure and the normative social relationships of our society as a whole. This is, of course, the key point for African-Americans and other people of color in American society: the tension between competing and contradicting world views.

Unfortunately, Darling-Hammond ends where the real issues begin. She speaks to us about current status—tells us what we already know—but falls short of taking us to the next level. Clearly what she does not want to see emerge is a two-tiered educational system. Rather, importance must be given in the long-range planning and goals to a daily reality of classroom life in which students and teachers find opportunities, high status knowledge, and enriched environment. For Darling-Hammond "the quest is for education that will challenge, inspire, and stretch students while opening doors to new opportunities rather than screening them out with curriculum and tracking policies that constrain real learning growth" (Darling-Hammond 1985, 49).

To meet this challenge, she suggests reforms for the teaching profession that include some recommendations similar to those of the Holmes and Carnegie reports (discussed in the next section). What she does not speak to is the role of black intellectuals, scholars, and theorists in combating the ideological hegemony or the ethnocentric and bankrupt paradigms and conceptual handles used to depict, diagnose, and prognosticate black educational experience.

Darling-Hammond's report is the preface to the lingering history of issues and concerns that will confront and follow people of color into the twenty-first century and beyond. We know this. What we do not have a feel for is how to get beyond this. What will happen to these students with shrinking minority role models? Black institutions of higher education are faltering under complex problems. If these schools are lost, they will be difficult to replace. With the coming of the twenty-first century, what will happen to these historic schools that traditionally nurtured and graduated black students? We know, for example, that more black students need to become interested in science and mathematics, but what we do not know is how many Ron McNair's have already slipped through our fingers because we did not know what to look for, or because what we saw we misinterpreted or misconstrued. When we describe a child or the home environment of poor black families as "wild" and "chaotic" because of the high activity and sounds levels, is that "hyperactivity" or is it, as A. Wade Boykin, a black educational psychologist would contend, more of a "commentary on the psychological verve levels of the [researchers] who are used to a less exciting existence. It has been a practice for social scientists to view divergent customs and environments in a culturally egocentric way" (Boykin 1979, 354). Ultimately, African-Americans must articulate their own civilization through the building of institutions and the positing of alternative conceptual handles that represent the ideological, philosophical, economic, and scientific interests of the community. Whereas such issues would have gone far beyond the scope of the Darling-Hammond study, her acknowledgement of such concerns would have drawn attention to a vital issue.

REFORM IN TEACHER EDUCATION FOR THE TWENTY-FIRST CENTURY: THE HOLMES AND CARNEGIE REPORTS

A salient example of the threat that looms over the education of African-American educators and their students, as well as that of other people of color, can be seen in the new teacher education reforms for meeting the challenge of the twenty-first century. In essence, the Holmes Group and the Carnegie Task Force reports are the latest series of reforms in and for the teaching profession, and propose sweeping changes in the certification and the professionalization of educators. The proposed reforms would restructure the teaching force and the gate-keeping mechanisms that determine the standards for certification and develop specialized curricula in a select cadre of graduate schools to guide professional training programs.

African-Americans as well as other people of color need to take special interest in how these reports situate the overall status of people of color in the twenty-first century economic structure and the role of education in these reform plans "for" minority students and professional educators, teachers, and university faculty members. The word has already begun to trickle out. John E. Jacob, president of the National Urban League, along with other African-American and Hispanic organizations, have expressed serious reservations about the Carnegie Report, not about its goals or intentions, but about the potential unanticipated outcomes, which in essence could all but eliminate minority groups from becoming professional educators. As it stands, according to Shirley M. Malcom, program head of the Office of Opportunities in Science, of the American Association for the Advancement of Science in Washington, D.C., African-Americans "are projected to account for only 5 percent of the teaching force by 1990—a 'vanishing species' " (Jacobson 1986, 23). Gregory R. Anrig, president of the Educational Testing Service (ETS) was quoted as saying, "the [Carnegie Task Force] panel's hope of raising teaching standards without hurting minority groups was 'just not going to happen—[it is] going to have an adverse impact on minorities' " (Jacobsen 1986, 23).

When the Holmes Group names as a goal "To make education of teachers, intellectually more solid. . . . *To recognize differences in teachers' skill,* and commitment in their education, certification, and work: (Holmes 1986, 4, author's emphasis), what are the ramifications for educators whose differences are considered, labeled, identified, or discovered to be deficient or deviant? When the Task Force, speaking at length about people of color, pronounces, that "the problem of minority teachers can not possibly be solved without addressing the fundamental problems of minority educational preparation throughout the pipe-line'' (Task Force 1986, 40), what might this mean for black students in pre-dominantly white institutions, as well as for those in historically black institutions? This question becomes particularly urgent when we realize only one historically black institution of higher education was originally invited to join the Holmes Group.

The Task Force states that the lack of minority teachers is not due to a ''lack of ability [in these students] but [to the fact that] the schools have failed to provide and demand what was needed for success'' (Task Force 1986, 39). In response, the Task Force proposes a triad consisting of the proposed National Board for Professional Teaching Standards (NBPTS), those states that house predominantly black institutions, and the institutions themselves to ''assist'' in preparing students to meet the higher standards of the M.A. degree programs in teaching. What kind of assistance, and under what conditions will it be granted (or even denied)? Mary Hatwood Futrell, president of the National Education Association and one of three people of color[1] on the Task Force, has expressed grave reservations about its proposed development and application of the national certification standards and the ''potential for abuse'' in the proposed salary/pay scale differentiation. Such questions, among many others, deserve our attention.

We are also concerned about what such reform proposals do not say. Whereas the Task Force, and to a lesser extent the Holmes Group, discuss the future of minority education and teachers, the role of people of color in the education of their next generation is at best dubious. In the twenty-first century, the struggle will be for the hearts and minds of people of color. The real battle will be for control over who educates minorities and over the nature of that education. Clearly, the Task Force wants an educated work force in order to compete in the ''technological advancements [in] a changing world economy'' (Jacobson 1986, 23). Questions about the kinds of societal structures and assemblages, and the gradations of workers and work envisioned are directly linked to this author's major concerns: for what purposes might people of color be educated? What will their role be in the emerging technological society? What role will the black scientists and researchers play in its shaping and development? What are the societal, political, and economic stakes in true black participation, initiative, and leadership in guiding the black community for the next hundred years?

We are concerned lest societal and institutional reforms that have such pro-found implications for education remain unscrutinized by black and other mi-nority researchers. The questioning and dissenting voices must not be drowned out by the ground swell of accolades for raising standards and professionalizing the field.

One of the powerful points coming from the Carnegie and the Holmes reports is the power and influence of schooling institutions, particularly in higher edu-cation. Perhaps people of color need to ask about and gain an understanding of the value of black institutions. Perhaps we need to seriously question any potential threat, either to historically black institutions and the students they serve, or to the accessibility of African-Americans and other people of color to postsecondary institutions.

We need to speak out on the worth and value of black institutions. If people of color, and others among the disenfranchised, seek to be independent and self-sufficient and to actually pull themselves up by their own bootstraps, control over their own destinies is a prerequisite, as well as self-determination and an economic, political, and ideological basis upon which to build.

INSTITUTION, POWER, AND THE PRODUCTION OF KNOWLEDGE

The building, maintenance, survival, and development of institutions are a key in any society because they endorse, preserve, and pass on cultural artifacts of a civilization (Gordon 1986). For the purpose of this discussion, *institution* means a practice of a society, something that a society does as a habit of its functioning. The concept of institution building has at least four major components: (1) an evolving inner circle (collective) of scholars working together to solve a social problem or crisis; (2) the thought generated; (3) the life or longevity of these groups—that is, how they sustained their efforts; and (4) the physical location(s) of the work being done. This is important because such knowledge production usually occurs in locations such as research institutes, university research centers, public and private foundations, think tanks, community centers, churches, and schools.

The significance of institution building is in its potential to demystify and actualize an emancipatory practice. Institutions are cultural artifacts of civilization and generate cultural theory and artifacts. By their nature, then, the function of institutions, particularly those that generate social theory as well as instruct is as a normative structure. The questions that these institutions address can either perpetuate the societal status or challenge the prevailing trends by creating alternative scientific paradigms and normative structures.

The history of the Frankfurt School and the Institut für Sozialforschung in Frankfurt, Germany, is of particular interest. They take the broad approach to the problem of European racism, or, more precisely, anti-semitism or judeophobia, which is very similar to the racial hatred encountered by African-Americans in the United States. More importantly, their existence and work are better known than that of many black institutions (discussed later). They serve as a model since they bring an awareness of the evolutionary process by which schools of thought grow and by which social theory is informed by the creation, utilization, formulation, and legitimation of knowledge. This is important because it is through social, cultural, academic, and political institutions that cadres of scholars form alliances, develop their ideas, conduct research, and generate theory and praxis.

What is being discussed is the need to understand civilization and the role that culture plays in the making of civilization. Sekou Toure's (1969) discussion of the dialectical approach to culture seems to be most helpful. For Toure (who was president of the Republic of Guinea in Africa), culture is the sum total of material, ideological, and spiritual values created by people throughout their history. Culture encompasses "all the material and immaterial works of art and science, plus knowledge, manners, education, a mode of thought, behavior and attitudes accumulated by the people" (Toure 1969, 12). However, if used for the purpose of domination, culture can be a more effective weapon than guns: the initial step toward domination and oppression is to deny the oppressed their human attributes—their cultural activities.

In American historical educational literature, there is hardly any reference to the African-American intellectual scholarship or to institutions that address the issues of racism and capitalism; little reference to the kinds of educational ideology, knowledge, opportunities, and economic resources that would most benefit the black community. It is the very invisibility of these institutions and the scholarship produced in them when approached via the dominant academic literature that brings to the fore the broader questions of the relationship of institutional control to trends in scholarship, the content and focus of social and educational theory, and the determinants of "legitimate" activities of science production in American society.

The study of institution building is important for African-American scholars in order to articulate social theory reflective of the needs of their constituents. Even a cursory view of the literature suggests that the African-American community has a great history of building institutions: collectives of scholars, organizations, and societies. A careful study of the period during the late nineteenth and early twentieth centuries shows a full range of activities—periods of great movement in the formation and creation of a variety of institutions within the African-American community.

For example, Jamaican-born Marcus Garvey, probably one of the most provocative black men in U.S. and world history, inspired by B. T. Washington's *Up From Slavery* and the ultimate desire to reclaim Africa for the African race, launched the Universal Negro Improvement Association, which existed from 1914 to the 1920s. Its main purpose was race improvement: strengthening the pan-African movement, establishing economic and business programs and ventures, such as the Negro Factories Corporation and the Black Star shipping line. Its eventual downfall does not negate the fact that he created a type of global pan-African movement and built an institution in response to the racial tension and plight of the black masses who were responsive to him.[2]

In 1896 W.E.B. DuBois published the first of a sixteen-volume edited series, *Studies of Negro Problems,* published by Atlanta University Press, which marked the beginning of another example of institution building. As the director of publicity and research for the NAACP, DuBois's mission, as he described it, was to "[carry] out . . . the Atlanta University plan of social study of the Negro American, by means of an annual series of decennially recurring subjects covering, so far as practicable, every phase of human life" (DuBois 1911, 5).

DuBois' studies came almost three decades before Felix Weil also conceived the idea of pursuing a reexamination of the foundations of social theory (in this case Marxist theory) from an institutional viewpoint, which ultimately resulted in the formation of the Frankfurt School of Social Theory (Held 1980; Jay 1973; Schroyer 1973; Slater 1977). Although both efforts were successful in their own right, one gained prominence, whereas the other became invisible within educational history and social theorizing. African-Americans did not have the economic autonomy or control over their institutions, nor the university presses housed within them. This was the reason that DuBois ended the study series.

The key implications of African-Americans having economic control and autonomy over their own institutions were in the power and control over the production and dissemination of knowledge, and the freedom to support research and training deemed in the vested interest of the community. Unfortunately for DuBois, the reality was that the philanthropists and capitalists were not willing to contribute to, or to fund the acquisition of, that kind of knowledge and power (DuBois 1911).

Still another example of institution building can be found in the elite intellectual circles. On March 5, 1897, a cadre of black scholars met and organized themselves and by invitation, solicited, others to join their group with the specific goal of building an institution. The objectives of the American Negro Academy were: "The promotion of Literature, Science, and Art; The Culture of a Form of Intellectual Taste; The Fostering of Higher Education; The Publication of Scholarly Work; and, The Defense of the Negro Against Vicious Assaults" (American Negro Academy Occasional Papers 1–22 1969). For the duration of its lifetime from 1897 to 1928, the ANA was dedicated to the development and defense of African-American people. It produced and published twenty-two occasional papers on topics related to history, religion, culture, civil and social rights, "and the social institutions of black Americans." At the turn of the century, African-American scholars, including Alexander Crummell, W.E.B. DuBois, Archibald H. Grimke, Kelly Miller, Carter G. Woodson, Alain L. Locke, William S. Scarborough, and Arthur A. Schomburg (for whom the above New York City library was named), intellectually defended and justified themselves and challenged the ideas, attitudes, habits, and legal proscriptions that locked African-Americans into an inferior caste (Moss 1981).[3]

Other examples of the many and varying institutions that African-Americans created for their community included printed media, such as the socialist magazine, the *Messenger*, edited by A. Phillip Randolph and Chandler Owen (Kornweibel 1975), and numerous examples of schools, such as the "Colored Schools in Cincinnati," which existed from 1825 to 1887 as a series of schools established by the African-American community for the sole purpose of educating their young. Peter Clark, a charter member of ANA and considered to be Cincinnati's "most famous Colored Citizen" was superintendent of the "colored" schools (Dabney 1926).[4]

Facing extreme difficulties and setbacks, African-Americans have maintained their own institutions to combat racism and capitalism and the ideological/cultural hegemony of American society and culture that has viewed them in pejorative context. As Anderson's research has pointed out, the battle at the turn of the century was for the allegiance and the minds of black students. The philanthropists' and industrialists' struggle to control these black institutions demonstrates the critical nature of institutions and their power and importance in directing the communities that they serve: institutions not only serve to educate and encourage intellectual discussion and thought, they also socialize and cultivate, which are essential to the maintenance and survival of a people.

In this regard, when looking at Carnegie and Holmes projections toward the year 2000, the outlook is somewhat grim. If, in fact, the Holmes and Carnegie reports are actualized and certain institutions become the dominant gatekeepers to an alleged meritocracy of teaching certification and degree programs, students who cannot afford to stay out of the job market for more than four years in order to compete for the higher levels of the proposed differentiated teaching positions (career professionals, professionals, and instructors) will most assuredly be limited to the lower rung of the professional educator totem pole. Others will continue to be seduced away from historically black institutions to predominantly white institutions by the "promise" of a more rigorous undergraduate program. Those black institutions of higher education that manage to endure will have the task of preparing their students to pass highly subjective entrance exams, like the teacher tests. The reformers plan to work with the schools as indicated earlier. The question that comes to mind is whether this might evolve into a similar struggle for control and domination similar to what Anderson (1978) observed at the turn of the century.

THE BOOTSTRAP IDEOLOGY AND THE ROLE OF AFRICAN-AMERICAN SCHOLARS IN EDUCATIONAL REFORM FOR THE TWENTY-FIRST CENTURY

Whereas the bootstrap ideology is part of the American dream, African-Americans and other people of color as a group have had a difficult time in realizing it. What we are witnessing is not simply racism—the picture is far more complex. It is a picture of an evolved culture that combines racism with elitism, an inherited, empirically bounded Spencerian rationale, and capitalism. What does this say about equity, fairness, and justice in society? If there is incongruency, how can fairness, equity, and justice be brought about? As we have implied, part of the success of any group is in the members' ability to reproduce themselves and their culture and adapt to the existing conditions. Another part of the success formula must also rely on the willingness of the dominant society to provide opportunities of access and safeguards to ensure positive results. African-Americans have made significant strides in American society because of their work in law, commerce, medicine, arts, and such, all of which revolve around the hub of education. Through these strides, historically speaking, black scholars have paved the way, not just for their people but for all people. DuBois' influence on the NAACP publication *Crisis* developed it into an influential journal that today is still a forceful cultural artifact. Edward H. Jones founded the Urban League; Edmund Haynes founded the Department of Sociology at Fisk University. Another salient example of the power of education was the transformation of the Howard University Law School into an institution of thought that revolutionized the legal approach of the NAACP. In the early 1930s, the NAACP had no legal committee to speak of and randomly attacked legal issues principally with white lawyers. When Charles Houston and William Hastings joined with the NAACP in the mid–1930s to establish its legal arm, they brought in a cadre of black lawyers. Led by Thurgood Marshall, they gave new contours to the struggle for equal rights by identifying segregated "separate but equal" schools as Jim Crow. The social knowledge and legal interpretations of constitutional law treated by these black scholars gave birth to civil rights law. One year after the 1954 Civil Rights Supreme Court decision, Martin Luther King began the Montgomery boycott. All this hinges on the notion of what schools do and the role played in the production of knowledge and the advancement of African-Americans.

It behooves minority educational researchers and scientists to come forward with their agenda for the twenty-first century and to plan their course of action. Obviously, they can not do this alone, but they must put forward their own research and sociopolitical agenda. In part, the African-American agenda and, for that matter, the minority agenda for the future in education must be focused around active, consistent participation in decision making at every level from the individual school to the state and federally funded institutions of higher education. There are new opportunities to respond to the old problems. Such responses are neither new nor provocative. They encompass community-empowering participation in the control of the institutions that serve their communities, such as public schools, and political power, community involvement, and activitism.

At the public school level, not only must the basic and academic content, analysis, and critique be taught to children of color as well as in preservice and inservice teacher preparation, but the relatedness of what they are learning to live must also be emphasized. Students must know about power and the uses of power, that is, political and economic forces. They must acquire an understanding of their communities with a view toward how to improve their functioning. Students must develop the will to be active participants in the society all of their lives—so that the society, in fact, lives up to its democratic ideals. Moreover, parents and educators must supplement school learning with after school or weekend programs focused on their specific needs and cultures.

At the postsecondary level, particularly at historically black institutions of higher education, the real issue is that teaching and learning cannot stop, even if the dominant society and its attendant gatekeepers employ the legitimacy criterion of a license to practice in order to exclude people of color. Dependency and seeking approval are powerful psychological and cultural weapons. Black educators must avoid being seduced by this form of social hegemony. What would be the agenda of black intellectuals and educators even if no one would help? This is not a rationale for separatism, but one for self-narcotic-detoxification. Perhaps community remedial history lessons are in order, lest the black institutions be threatened with economic uncertainty and academic mediocracy. Such lessons would also serve black students at predominantly white institutions to understand and work through their own alienation and isolation so that they can successfully complete their work in adverse and even hostile situations.

True democracy will be achieved only when all citizens have the knowledge and the motivation to live up to society's highest values and when economic and political opportunities are made equally available to all its constituents.

NOTES

1. The other people of color on the Carnegie Task Force are Shirley M. Malcom, program head of the Office of Opportunities in Science at the American Association for the Advancement of Science in Washington, D.C., and Arturo Madrid, president of the Tomas Rivera Center in Claremont, California. For the Holmes Group, the people of color who participated in the development of the reform agenda are: Frank Brown, dean of the School of Education of the University of North Carolina; Bernard Gifford, dean of the School of Education, University of California at Berkeley; and Richard A. Navarro, assistant professor, College of Education at Michigan State University.

2. This brief paragraph does not begin to do justice to Garvey and all of his work. For an in-depth look, see: M. Garvey, and A. Jacques (eds.) (1925), and E. D. Cronon (1968).

3. The American Negro Academy is perhaps the most provocative group of black nationalists unearthed thus far in this research. From its beginnings on March 5, 1897 to its demise in 1928, the ANA, with its exclusive list of 99 men who at various times were members and its collection of 22 Occasional Papers, has been described as the "voice of the talented tenth." The statement of its principles here does not begin to scratch the surface of this incredible organization. For a comprehensive study of the ANA, see: *The American Negro Academy Occasional Papers 1–22* (1969) and A. Moss (1981).

4. For an in-depth discussion of Peter Clark and a history of the "colored schools" of Cincinnati, Ohio, see: W. Dabney 1926 (1970).

7

More of the Same: Reforms of American Public Schooling and the Minority Language Student

Timothy Reagan

Calls for reforming the American public educational system are nothing new. Indeed, a number of educators have suggested that the phenomenon of the "crisis of schooling" literature is actually cyclical in nature (Keesbury 1984). This view, which we might call the "locust theory" (Reagan 1985), has critics of American public schooling periodically descending on educators, filled with short-term (but nevertheless righteous) wrath and indignation, nearly all of which can be expected to dissipate and be forgotten as some new national crisis or fad emerges to occupy their, and the general public's, attention. Often the cycle is presented as representing conflicting approaches to "excellence" and "equity" in education—with the reforms of the 1950s being seen as concerned primarily with "excellence," those of the 1960s and 1970s with "equity," and the recent calls for reform (as embodied, for instance, in the National Commission on Excellence in Education's *A Nation at Risk,* Mortimer Adler's *The Paideia Proposal,* and Bill Honig's *Last Chance for Our Children*) as exemplifying a return to concern with "excellence."

The distinction between reforms concerned with ensuring "excellence" and those committed to "equity" is an important one, especially if we are interested in the impact of educational reform on the minority language student. However, much of the current debate on the issue of school reform may not actually be on target in this regard. It seems that virtually everyone—regardless of ideological or political orientation—is agreed that we can and should have *both* "excellence *and* "equity" in American public education. In *A Nation at Risk,* for example, one reads that:

We do not believe that a public commitment to excellence and educational reform must be made at the expense of a strong public commitment to the equitable treatment of our diverse population. The twin goals of equity and high-quality schooling have profound and practical meaning for our economy and society, and we cannot permit one to yield to the other either in principle or in practice. (National Commission on Excellence in Education 1983, 13)

The linkage of "excellence" and "equity" here (as "twin goals" no less) is, a shared and commonly held aspect of the school reform debate currently underway. It is a linkage taken as a starting point in both the recent calls for educational reform and in the responses of the educational community to those calls. Obviously we wish to provide excellent education to *all* of our society's children—the debate rather centers on how we can accomplish this end.

However, this is the point at which some serious concerns and doubts arise. Whereas both "excellence" and "equity" are seen as desirable goals, and, no doubt, it is logically possible for American public schools to meet the social and educational goals of both "excellence" and "equity," we, as a society, are not actually committed to doing so. The most accurate measure of our public commitment to and support for public education is, after all, not what national commissions and the like say, nor how much politicians and other public figures discuss the schools and their problems, but rather our willingness to become actively involved in the schools (both as parents and as citizens), and our readiness to provide additional financial support for the schools.

One interesting aspect of the debate on "excellence" in American public education is the commonly held, albeit often implicit, assumption that we are trying to regain something that we have lost. There is a popular, mythical view of past schooling in our society: the one-room schoolhouse, staffed by the dedicated, ultracompetent (and inexpensive) schoolmarm, in which—without benefit of fancy AV equipment, expensive textbooks, and so on—children learned vast amounts thoroughly and were taught appropriate moral and spiritual values as well. Such an outlook, for better or worse, rests on a most distorted view of the past. American public schooling now does not provide most students with either equitable or excellent education, and in fact never has. Rather, we provide all too many students with a schooling experience that is both inequitable in a variety of ways and that seldom rises above mediocrity. In this, at least, the recent spate of school reform reports are unfortunately correct.

The fault, however, has not been placed entirely properly or appropriately. Certainly as teachers and educationalists we need to recognize our own shortcomings and failures—but we are most surely not the only ones who have *mea culpas* to say and penances to serve. The financial constraints under which the public schools have been expected to function make the achievement of *either* equity *or* excellence, let alone both, virtually an impossibility. As noted earlier, meaningful public support for the schools is in large measure missing in contemporary American society, and there are few, if any, signs of change in the immediate future. At the same time, social expectations of the school are higher now than they have ever been. Educating children is no longer enough (if, indeed, it ever really was); now we are expected to provide daycare, vocational training, sex education, family training, driver's education, and so on—and even to promote and engender various kinds of social and economic change. I do not mean to suggest that these are not or may not be valuable and worthwhile activities— but we, and our critics, *do* need to understand that they place a further burden on an already considerably overburdened profession.

In short, I would argue that whereas in principle "equity" and "excellence" are in no way mutually exclusive, in practice we are unlikely to be able to achieve both. Indeed, I have grave doubts about whether we can achieve *either* of these goals on its own, and my doubts on this point arise in large part out of our past efforts to deal with minority language students in the public schools.

ANGLO CONFORMITY AND THE SCHOOLS

Although there have been notable exceptions, such as German-language public schooling in many parts of the country throughout the nineteenth century (Kloss 1977), a central focus of American public schooling through much of our history has been on ensuring that children from non-English-speaking backgrounds acquire competence in English (Weiss 1982). Americanization played a role in the Common School Movement (Nasaw 1979, 66–79), and became increasingly important as the "new immigration" of the late nineteenth and early twentieth centuries brought both more immigrants, and immigrants from southern and eastern Europe rather than from northern and western Europe, to America's shores—and, of even greater significance, to its schools and classrooms (Violas 1978, 37–66). Americanization, of course, meant far more than just the acquisition of English, but the acquisition of English was one of the more important signs that the immigrant was being "brought into complete harmony with our ideals and aspirations" as a people (Brandeis 1954, 340–341). As Louis Brandeis commented, Americanization:

manifests itself, in a superficial way, when the immigrant adopts the clothes, the manners, and the customs generally prevailing here. Far more important is the manifestation presented when he substitutes for his mother tongue the English language as the common medium of speech. (Brandeis 1954, 340–341)

The Americanization Movement was, in essence, a reform movement directed at minority language students and had as its goal the acquisition of Anglo-American cultural and linguistic norms. Perhaps every bit as significant, though, was the need for the child to actively reject all ties to the "old country." As the superintendent of the New York City Schools explained in 1918,

Americanization is a spiritual thing difficult of determination in mere language. Broadly speaking we mean by it an appreciation of the institutions of this country, (and) absolute forgetfulness of all obligations or connections with other countries because of descent or birth. (Quoted in Berkson 1920, 59)

In short, what was commonly termed "hyphenated Americanism," as manifested in such labels as Irish-American, Polish-American, and so on, was simply not acceptable. Students were to be anglicized and Americanized, and cultural and linguistic diversity would play no part in their futures.

The public schools remained committed to this sort of assimilationist ideology (Pratte 1979) well into the twentieth century. Indeed, whereas there had been calls for "cultural pluralism" in the early decades of this century, for the most part the social and educational objective of Anglo conformity went largely unchallenged until the 1960s.

THE RISE OF BILINGUAL EDUCATION

As a consequence of various social and political changes in American society, not the least of which was the Civil Rights Movement, the 1960s saw the rise of bilingual eduation programs in many parts of the nation. Such programs were, from their inception, highly controversial. Advocates saw bilingual education as a long-overdue rejection of Anglo conformity, and perceived in such programs a commitment to the ideology of cultural pluralism (Pratte 1979). Opponents, on the other hand, feared that the schools had abandoned necessary, perhaps essential, efforts to ensure national unity and predicted the development of ethnic separatist movements. Both sides in the debate, however, failed to understand the real nature and goals of contemporary bilingual education in the United States (Reagan 1980).

Although much of the rhetoric surrounding bilingual education in the United States does in fact reflect the ideology of cultural diversity (Pratte 1979, 236–280), the actual practice—by which I mean not only what takes place in the classroom, but also the supportive legislation, program proposals and designs, and so on—is clearly transitional in both orientation and nature (Kjolseth 1973). What this means is that bilingual education programs, as they are currently conceived and implemented in the United States, have as their primary objective the preparation of non-English speakers for English-medium classrooms. This has led to an interesting development in public school jargon: students who are unable to function in English are labeled "bilingual." Once they are competent in English, they are no longer considered to be "bilingual" and are moved into "regular" (that is, English-medium) classes. I would suggest that such a usage is most probably uniquely American.

Bilingual education programs need not, of course, be transitional in nature. Many of the more compelling and forceful arguments in favor of bilingual education generally tacitly reject such a transitional approach (Reagan 1984), and the empirical evidence suggests that such programs are likely to be considerably less effective *at teaching English* than other types of bilingual education programs (for instance, maintenance programs) (Reagan 1984; Troike 1978). However, these more effective types of bilingual education programs are not the sort that the law now requires, nor are they likely to prove particularly popular with most local school boards at this time.

We are left, then, with programs that are basically assimilatory in nature and orientation. To be sure, contemporary bilingual education programs differ from Americanization as it has traditionally been manifested in methodology, and perhaps also in that such programs tend to favor and encourage a somewhat more tolerant approach to cultural and linguistic diversity in the public schools, but the fundamental objectives remain constant. The fact that bilingual education continues to be seen as basically compensatory in nature (both academically and economically), as well as its increasingly close ties to vocational/technical education, provide further reason to wonder about how much has really changed in our treatment of minority language students.

The recent debate about bilingual education programs, which was ignited by the efforts of Secretary of Education Bennett to, in essence, deregulate the education of limited and non–English-speaking children, similarly mistakes the nature of contemporary bilingual education in the United States. The position of the present administration has stressed the political, social and economic need for linguistic unity and has emphasized that the primary function of the school for the linguistic minority student must be the acquisition of English—in whatever sort of program the local educational authorities deem most suitable. There has been a clear preference for E.S.L. and immersion programs, and a tendency to minimize the use of the child's language.

Opponents of such a change in approach to the education of minority language students, many of whom represent minority constituencies, have argued that bilingual education programs are committed not only to the valuable and worthwhile goal of meaningful bilingualism (which includes, of course, functional fluency in English), but also to helping minority language children develop positive self-esteem, pride in their cultural and linguisitic heritage, worthwhile economic skills, and so on (see, e.g., Fernandez 1985). One is left with the impression that the debate is basically one between assimilationists and cultural pluralists—whereas in actual fact both the types of programs preferred by Secretary Bennett and the administration and contemporary bilingual education programs are fundamentally transitional (and hence assimilationist) in nature.

THE CASE FOR BILINGUAL EDUCATION

Does this, then, mean that there is no case to be made for contemporary bilingual education programs? Certainly not—whatever limitations and problems bilingual education programs may have as they are currently constructed, their benefits can, and generally do, far outweigh the arguments against them. There are four distinct kinds of arguments that can be used to justify bilingual education programs in the United States: pedagogic, sociopolitical, economic, and cognitive. It should be noted that whereas these are, in fact, very distinct arguments, they are commonly conflated in debates about bilingual education. By clearly identifying and explicating each of these arguments at this point, the nature of the current debate on bilingual education programs in the United States may be made somewhat clearer.

Pedagogic arguments are those that seek to demonstrate that in actual classroom practice, the most effective way of teaching the socially dominant language to minority language children is often through the medium of the mother tongue. The principle of vernacular language instruction has long had international support (Bamgbose 1976; UNESCO 1953) and has played a formative role in the development of primary education programs in many parts of the world. Beyond this, however, the idea is simply good common sense: anyone is likely to learn *anything* better if they understand what is going on. With regard to the education of linguistic minorities in the United States, there are two important aspects of this idea (see Troike 1978, 1981). First, a non–English-speaking child is likely to learn English more rapidly if some instruction can be done through the native language—the same educational procedure that is used in much foreign language teaching in the United States. Second, and far more important, if subject matter instruction (math, social studies, science, etc.) can be provided in the child's native language while he or she is acquiring English, this will prevent the child from falling behind in subject matter areas while English is being learned.

Sociopolitical arguments for bilingual education are concerned mainly with the rights of ethnic groups to maintain their languages and cultures, and will usually advocate the development (or, on some accounts, the maintenance) of a pluralistic society in the United States. Arguments of this sort are basically normative in nature, and a clear articulation of the normative bases for such arguments would take considerably more space than is available here (see Pratte 1983).

It is nevertheless both possible and desirable for us to make a few observations about such sociopolitical arguments at this point. The notion of the desirability of a pluralistic (rather than simply a diverse) society is hardly a new one (see Pratte 1977). Indeed, a strong case could be argued for a logical need for the acceptance of pluralism as a component of an acceptance of democracy (without going into detail here, this would entail relating cultural/linguistic pluralism to political/ideological pluralism as necessary conditions for democratic life; see Appleton 1983). However, sociopolitical arguments for bilingual education are perhaps most useful in their emphasis on the fact that there is no such thing as a nonethnic curriculum; it is simply a question of *whose* language and ethnicity (or cultural heritage) is to be valued and taught in the public schools. That is, at the moment Anglo-American cultural and linguistic norms are being inculcated in students in spite of the fact that these norms are, at least historically (and often more than that), alien to a significant proportion of the school-age population.

A common criticism of bilingual education programs has been that such efforts are far more political than educational in nature. This critique has two sides: on the one hand, it asserts that such programs are actually little more than attempts to appease various minority groups; on the other hand, fears of social divisiveness and separatism are raised. With respect to the former, Troike and Saville-Troike (1982, 200–201) have commented that:

It is important to realize that all education is political, and no matter how much researchers, philosophers, and technicians may focus on other aspects, the political "bottom line" ... is inescapable. ... [Further,] the provision of bilingual education for the upper classes is rarely seen as political, unless control of the society by the upper classes itself comes to be challenged and the opportunity for education in a second language is viewed as elitism.

Fears that bilingual education programs will promote ethnic consciousness and inspire social division are often voiced, with Belgium and Canada used as examples of such an outcome. These are interesting cases for critics to employ, since in both cases the problem is not so much the presence of diversity as it is the historical oppression of one group at the hands of another (see Swing 1980). It might, in fact, be argued that the lesson to be learned from such cases is the value and importance of cultural and linguistic toleration as a way of *preventing* such interethnic tensions.

The third type of argument that can be offered in support of bilingual education programs are those labeled "economic arguments." These arguments have received a great deal of attention in recent years and are likely to have a significant impact on policy-makers. There are two distinct aspects of such arguments. First, as was stressed in a relatively recent Presidential Commission report on the status of foreign language education in the United States (The President's Commission on Foreign Language and International Studies), foreign language skills is costing the United States dearly in business, diplomacy, and a number of other areas. Bilingual education, properly constructed and implemented, can provide a way of making use of our tremendous national linguistic resources.

There is a second aspect of the economic arguments entailed as well, which is concerned more directly with the minority language student's own socioeconomic status and "life chances." Most minority language children are also from the lower SES levels of American society; bilingual education programs provide a way of giving them the necessary cultural, social, and linguistic skills to "make it" in the dominant society.

Last, cognitive arguments for bilingual education are concerned primarily with the cognitive benefits of certain types of bilingualism. It is interesting to note that until Peal and Lambert's (1962) landmark study, the bulk of research on bilingualism seemed to suggest that bilinguals suffered from linguistic handicaps when measured with verbal intelligence tests (Cummins 1976). However, the studies that suggested these negative effects of bilingualism on the individual were methodologically flawed on a number of counts. Most seriously, they had "failed to control for confounding variables such as socioeconomic status (SES), sex, and the degree of the bilingual's knowledge of his two languages" (Cummins 1976). Recent research has presented a much more positive picture, showing that bilingualism in children can, at least in some instances, accelerate the development of both verbal and nonverbal abilities (Bain 1974), facilitate aspects of cognitive flexibility (Balkan 1970; Ianco-Worrall 1972), and help in the development of divergent thinking skills (Landry 1974).

In short, there are a number of reasons to suspect that bilingual education programs, properly staffed and designed, can be not only viable but desirable as a way of helping the minority language child cope with the dominant society. Indeed, there may well be justifications for involving Anglo-American children in such programs as well, although support for such an innovation is likely to be hard to come by.

THE RECENT REFORM LITERATURE

Both Americanization and bilingual education programs had as their pincipal target population the minority language student. For the most part, the recent educational reform literature has provided an interesting contrast to this emphasis. Concern with minority students in general, and minority language students in particular, has been tangential at best. Reading *A Nation at Risk,* for example, one might well think that the population of the United States was virtually entirely English-speaking; one certainly gets no sense whatever that there are some 3.5 million school-age children with a primary language other than English (Heisner 1980), nor that this section of the population is growing considerably faster than is the English-speaking section. In fact, not one of the more than forty papers commissioned by the National Commission was specifically concerned with the problems of minority language students.

Even more troubling than the ignorance of the status of the minority language student found in *A Nation at Risk* is the tendency to fall prey to what has been called the "blame the victim" syndrome (Gollnick and Chinn 1983, 55–56). Given the Commission's whole-hearted commitment to meritocracy (Spring 1986), as manifested in its glowing view of "the persistent and authentic American dream that superior performance can raise one's state in life and shape one's future" (National Commission on Excellence in Education 1983, 15), one is left with an implicit but nonetheless powerful condemnation of those in our society who have been unable to "pull themselves up by their bootstraps." This rejection of any clear analysis of the structure of contemporary American society, and of the role and function of the school in social and class reproduction, does a grave disservice to all minority and oppressed students, and especially so, I believe, to the minority language student.

The Paideia Proposal contains within it a somewhat similar view of the minority language students. This view is made quite clear in the section of the book devoted to "Overcoming Initial Impediments," in which we read that:

The sooner a democratic society intervenes to remedy the cultural inequality of homes and environments, the sooner it will succeed in fulfilling the democratic mandate of equal educational opportunity for all. (Adler 1983, 39)

This is in no way different from the rhetoric of the cultural and linguistic deprivation theorists of the 1960s (Cooper 1978; Edwards 1979). Not only has this position been widely condemned in recent years on political grounds, but it has been demonstrated to be quite problematic empirically (Keddie 1973) and also all too often racist and class-biased as well (Valentine 1971). Many if not most educators in the United States today have serious doubts about their ability to build worthwhile educational experiences for *any* children, let alone minority language children, if we assume the theory of cultural inequality as their point of departure.

In fact, the view of cultural diversity found in many of the recent educational reform reports is problematic. Where cultural diversity is dealt with at all, it is most commonly either identified simply as a problem or vague assurances about the value of living in a pluralistic society are given, generally in the context of the need for minority students to adopt the cultural and linguistic norms of the dominant society. To respond to the challenges and opportunities presented by the presence in our society of a variety of cultural and linguistic groups in such ways is not simply to disregard many of the positive changes that have occurred in American public schooling since the Civil Rights movements, but to actively return to educational policies that in fact reject the language and culture of a sizable number of students.

Pratte (1979, 51–85) has distinguished between cultural diversity and cultural pluralism in a way that is especially enlightening in this regard. Pratte believes that cultural diversity refers to the presence of a variety of different cultural groups in a community. It is a nonnormative concept, in that it takes no position about the presence of multiple cultures; in short, its use is solely descriptive. Cultural pluralism, on the other hand, is one of a number of possible ideological responses to the presence of cultural diversity. It is most clearly normative, since it sees the presence of cultural diversity in a society as a desirable condition and goal. It is clear that whereas the recent reform reports have taken cognizance of the cultural diversity in contemporary American society (albeit briefly and without, in general, great sensitivity to the actual complexity of the situation), they have for the most part rejected cultural pluralism.

It is interesting to note that this tendency to support, whether implicitly or explicitly, a more assimilationist approach to minority language populations in the schools is in many ways a major challenge to the development of multicultural education (see Banks 1981; Tiedt and Tiedt 1986). The approach seemingly advocated by many of the reform reports demonstrates a number of serious weaknesses, including:

1. ignorance of the problems and nature of contemporary urban American society;
2. lack of understanding of and sensitivity to the needs, expectations, and desires of minority teachers, students, and parents;
3. the presence of an appalling degree of ethnocentrism in American society; and
4. the rejection of the development or even toleration of any meaningful degree of bilingualism in American society.

Taken together, what we find is that the reform reports all too often share a distorted, myopic view of American society that is based in Anglo, middle-class mythology rather than in reality. The focus and concern of the reports have been on the middle-class white student, and the consequences have been potentially devastating for the minority language student.

In conclusion, it seems that minority language students have been the victims of educational reformers fairly often throughout the course of American educational history. Methods and approaches have differed, but the core concern with assimilation into Anglo-American society has remained fairly constant. I see no change in the recent reform reports in this regard, save perhaps a more blatant and offensive emphasis on assimilation; indeed, what I see is simply "more of the same."

NOTE

I am grateful to the graduate students in my spring and summer 1986 Contemporary Educational Issues classes at Central Connecticut State University for many helpful (and lively) discussions of *A Nation at Risk* and *The Paideia Proposal*. I am also grateful to several of my colleagues for their help; most especially, I want to thank Bonnie Handler and Larry Klein.

8

The Eighties Image of Girls and Women in the Educational Reform Literature: A Review of the Issues

Kathryn M. Borman and Patricia O'Reilly

In their zeal to address matters of educational excellence, the authors of the national reports have ignored or slighted a number of issues related to social equity. For example, the special needs of at-risk youth in areas such as mental health, substance abuse, dropout prevention, reclamation, and the transition from school to work are overlooked (National Coalition of Advocates for Students 1985). The institutional context (with respect to social and demographic issues such as the differential needs of schools and youth during periods of school population boom and bust) is apparently considered irrelevant in the face of an unremitting commitment to excellence, a concept tied primarily to a narrow credentialing orientation. Schoolchildren and their teachers, those most affected by the proposals, are those most systematically ignored (Berman 1985).

Given their general lack of concern with social equity, the excellence reports and commissions have virtually ignored issues specifically related to sex equity. This is hardly surprising given the narrow focus on the "productive" purposes of education, that highly restricted set of means-ends relationships schools have with institutions located in the labor market and in higher education. In examining the image of girls and women in the educational reform literature, this chapter has several purposes. First, to provide a context for the discussion, we review the position taken by the national reports on sex equity issues. This does not take very long as these issues are addressed tangentially if at all by the reports. Next, we review policies currently being put in place by state-level commissions to indicate the directions being taken in educational reform, which have been, for the most part, established by these groups. Third, we suggest areas where problems remain for girls and young women who are students in public elementary and secondary schools today. Finally, we speak to issues directly affecting classroom teachers today for they have also been slighted by the reports to the extent that matters pertaining to credentialing and certification have been exaggerated in contrast to issues surrounding classroom and school organization and the status of teaching as an occupation and semiprofession.

At the outset, it is noteworthy to examine the composition and activities of those groups that are likely to have the most pronounced effect on educational change over the next decade. We are speaking of the task forces and commissions operating in individual states. These were formed within months after the National Commission on Excellence in Education had issued its report. By February 1984, forty-seven of the states had organized at least one statewide body to analyze some aspect of education. Most of these commissions were established by governors directly or with the chief state executive's approval and encouragement. Membership was generally made by appointment with the greatest representation (close to 40 percent) from people associated with education. However, this group for the most part was not representative of the interests of the classroom teachers. Smaller percentages serving on these bodies represented private citizens, public agencies, and elected officials. An evaluation study of the state commissions' activities concludes that, overall, women were seriously underrepresented, comprising less than one-third of the memberships of these commissions (Cook 1984).

The reports acknowledge the importance of civic education and the development of personal awareness, although the language used by the authors is vague and rhetorical. According to Cook's (1984) review of the reports,

In the list of goals he recommends for schools, Goodlad (1983) includes emotional and physical well being, emotional sensitivity and the realistic acceptance of self and other. Boyer (1983) similarly speaks of the importance of students' learning about themselves and their roles in the world. Also, *A Nation at Risk* describes social studies as ideally enabling students to "fix their places and possibilities within the larger social and cultural structure." (Cook 1984, 7)

However, Cook concludes that the reports are ambivalent on matters related to socialization and citizenship issues. Although the authors of the reports point to the central role of the school in transmitting values and the need for students to be aware of the social groups and institutions that shape their lives, they balk at considering what the National Coalition of Advocates for Children has termed the "barriers to excellence": class discrimination, racial discrimination, cultural discrimination, and sex discrimination. In its conclusion, *A Nation at Risk* admonishes students "to work to your full capacities to obtain the knowledge and skills that will enable you to create your future and control your destiny. If you do not," the report warns, "you will have your future thrust upon you by others." Cook concludes, and we agree, that this statement "ignores how women's achievement in education and work may be more parsimoniously explained by women's relative status in society than by an individual woman's own striving . . . " (Cook 1984, 9).

We are now seeing recommendations emerging from state-level and national task forces that reinforce this focus on educational productive functions. All of them, according to surveys conducted by both the Education Commission of the States and MDC, an independent evaluation firm, are concerned with five major issues: curricular reform; professional development of teachers and administrators; student evaluation and testing; graduation requirements; and teacher certification preparation. According to MDC's report, the major initiatives generated by these state-based agencies call for the establishment of the following programs:

1. a variety of new state-developed curricula or curriculum guides, often focusing on basic skills, but also covering many other academic areas;

2. a range of new school accreditation standards designed to address quality, requirements for local district and individual school site-planning, and expanded state review of local instructional programs;

3. numerous broad-based and comprehensive school improvement programs, sometimes specifically including an effective-schools program in which the characteristics of the most effective schools are identified and attempts are made to replicate those characteristics in other school settings;

4. many state-initiated dissemination and adoption assistance programs, local capacity-building and problem-solving initiatives, and a wide array of new technical assistance services;

5. a variety of strategies related to the testing of students, including state-developed and administered competency tests;

6. an array of activities focused on improving the capabilities of the education work force, including new types of teacher proficiency examinations, and teacher and administrator professional development training programs; and

7. a host of initiatives aimed specifically at improving mathematics, science, and technology instruction and programs in the schools, and including efforts to recruit and retain mathematics and science teachers. (Cook 1984, 8–9)

Although there are programmatic and curricular reforms proposed here, the list is chiefly concerned with credentialing and certification issues with respect to students and teachers. Overlooked by this agenda are the day-to-day experiences and issues confronting students, particularly girls and young women in elementary and secondary schools, and their teachers, most of whom, particularly in the elementary grades, continue to be women. These daily difficulties constitute major barriers to achieving excellence with respect to sex equity.

The image of girls and women projected not only by the states' agendas but also by the reports before them is devoid of a concern for educational equity that we wish to raise here. Specifically, the reports and recommendations overlook the questions raised by Title IX legislation more than ten years ago and now swept aside in the push for excellence, a push that really translates to constructing policy in the areas of credentialing and certification as we have seen. There are a number of abiding concerns with respect to fairness questions, but the ones we wish to discuss here include, for girls and young women, differential access to rewards and opportunities in both elementary and secondary school classrooms and student life and for teachers, especially at the elementary level, matters related to staffing and classroom practice.

ISSUES FOR STUDENTS: GENDER INEQUITIES IN THE SCHOOL AND CLASSROOM

Girls and young women in elementary and secondary school classrooms are subject to a number of inequities that are both subtle and pervasive. Lockheed and Klein (1985) have defined a sex equitable classroom as "one in which both the overt and the hidden curriculum treat boys and girls so that they receive equal benefits from instruction." Major categories of treatment include role models, teacher-student interaction, peer interaction, school rules, and the physical location of resources (Lockheed and Klein 1985, 190).

In their review of the related literature on questions of gender-related inequities in the school, Lockheed and Klein are at pains not only to describe the several types of interpersonal and structural inequities present in classrooms but also to identify areas of classroom organization and climate that can be altered by the teacher to allow the development of equal benefits. The areas in which inequities are most visible are sex segregation in the classroom and in the context of informal interaction, inequities in teacher-student interaction, and sex inequities in peer interaction.

First, Lockheed and Klein suggest in their findings that although sex segregation is voluntarily initiated by children, it can be minimized by the sensitive teacher who takes care to provide opportunities for cross-sex cooperative interaction. The wages paid by both sexes as a result of their exclusion from cross-sex interaction are high indeed. By the time they are in high school, both hold a very narrow view of what it means to be masculine and what it means to be feminine. Even girls and boys who engage in a similar activity or play on varsity soccer teams (sex segregated, of course) hold very different views of their reasons for participation. Girls emphasize the rewards received by affiliation with other team members, whereas boys emphasize the importance of competition and the individual development of athletic skill (Borman and Kurdek 1984). Linda Valli's (1985) ethnographic account of rituals, extracurricular activities, and student life in high school reveals how traditional gender relations are portrayed in what Basil Bernstein has called the "expressive order of the school." The expressive order regulates the transmission of the beliefs and the moral system of the students. Thus student rituals such as senior assemblies, interscholastic athletic competitions, pep rallies, and skits are powerful vehicles for passing on the culture in a manner that does not allow it to be questioned but rather conveys the message that this is the way things are.

Students in the large midwestern comprehensive high school in which Valli carried out her observations orchestrated an assembly at the time of graduation in June that, in Valli's terms, served to identify "women on the basis of their sexuality at the very moment of high school graduation, at the time when academic achievement is foremost while senior boys asserted their superiority and dominance by dramatizing girls' social identities" (Valli 1985, 42). The skits that formed the assembly's program were organized and performed for the class as a whole and featured senior boys dressed as girls. Valli's description of one of the performances follows:

The first skit, a parody of "The Twelve Days of Christmas," was called "The Twelve Years of School." As the curtain went up, twelve boys stood with their backs to the audience singing:
    In my first year of schooling my father said to me, "Don't. . . . " As they went through the 12 years, the boys turned around one by one, adding the specific line written for their year. Some of the don'ts were: pick your nose, suck your thumb, fight with boys, stuff your bra, lift your dress up, drink and drive, get pregnant.
    Audience laughter was loudest when the "7th grade girl" turned, displaying balloons stuffed in his shirt to form voluptuous breasts; and when the "12th grade girl" turned to reveal his pregnant appearance, created with the help of a pillow. (Valli 1985, 42)

Rituals such as this assembly reinforce the instrumental learning and curricular structures of the school. As in all high schools where young women overall constitute 92 percent of those planning to be secretaries and cosmetologists, the young women Valli observed uniformly "enter office jobs not because of aspirations and motivations but because, given culturally accepted standards and the availability of jobs, office work is regarded as respectable employment for women" (Valli 1985, 39).

Patterns of sex segregation such as those documented by Valli with their enormously negative social consequences by high school have their beginnings in the early elementary school years. Highly sex integrated classroom arrangements in elementary school allow children the opportunity to confront and minimize sex stereotypes, if children's experiences are well monitored by sensitive teachers.

The second set of findings concerning gender inequities in the school are related to inequities in teacher-student interaction and inequities in school policies based on gender. Teachers appear to interact more frequently with boys than girls, bestowing both more praise and more blame on their male students in the elementary grades and beyond. These general findings do not necessarily reflect teachers' unfair treatment or neglect of girls but rather appear to be based on sex differences in student behavior. Boys, no matter what the grade level, are more active and more inclined to act out in class than girls, and as a result gain more attention, both positive and negative, from their teachers.

A recent study of second- and sixth-grade classrooms noted variations in girls' and boys' behavior depending on the type of classroom activity under observation, but did not note differential types of response based on student gender by their teachers. Classroom activities included recitation, small group work, and seat work: "In small group settings, boys talked more, whereas girls sought help more: in seat work, boys engaged in more social comparison than girls. In general, girls seemed more conforming, behaving more appropriately than boys in recitation and small group settings" (Lockheed and Klein 1985). Most of the research investigating patterns of teacher-student interaction related to sex equity suggests that teachers on the whole respond to their students in ways that are consistent with their students' behaviors. Although girls are less likely to receive encouragement than boys and are more frequently the target of sexual harrassment, it is also likely that "after a decade of exposure to Title IX and to the Civil Rights and Women's Movements, those teachers who have always wanted to treat their students fairly have become more aware of how to do so" (ibid.).

However, it is not so clear that school administrative structures have been inclined to move in this positive direction. In fact, the National Coalition of Advocates for Students concluded that "Title IX . . . which specifically prohibits sex discrimination against pregnant teenagers in schools and colleges receiving federal money, has not been adequately enforced" (National Coalition 1985, 25). Although schools cannot be held responsible for soaring rates of teenage pregnancy, traditional school programs and facilities are likely to diminish rather than enhance the likelihood of a young mother's completing her education. According to the National Coalition's Report, lack of day care is a major reason why adolescent parents have difficulty returning to school. When child care is unavailable, the young mother must stay at home, miss school, and risk suspension. Even while pregnant or newly a mother, there are few institutional supports to enable these adolescents to retain a commitment to school. One witness who spoke to the Coalition's Advisory Board stated, "Even if she is granted medical maternity leave, she will probably fall behind in her studies . . . because home tutoring is not readily accessible and schools for pregnant girls do not have a full curriculum" (National Coalition 1985, 23). *Barriers to Excellence* concludes that the substantial proportion of female dropouts, pregnant school-aged females, have in effect been all but written off by the schools. Having allocated few resources designed to prevent pregnancy, schools offer little help once a student becomes a young parent. Inflexible institutional procedures, stigmatizing attitudes, and a lack of support services all represent barriers for thousands of young parents who might complete their education if the school reached out to them (National Coalition 1985, 23–24).

A third area in which inequities persist in school and one in which teachers can effectively promote change is peer classroom interaction. In summarizing the related research in this area, Lockheed and Klein conclude that in most classrooms studied there is infrequent or no spontaneous cross-sex "academic helping behavior." Whereas girls respond equally to requests for help from either sex, boys ignore girls' requests, responding only to other males. With respect to leadership and initiative in classroom interaction in carrying out instructional tasks, research indicates no differences when learning styles, age, height, and social class are controlled in experimental conditions. However, in the classroom boys generally display more influence in ongoing students' activities. These findings spell negative consequences for girls and young women to the extent that their bids for recognition are ignored or discounted (Lockheed and Klein 1985). It is in just this area, however, that teachers can have the greatest impact, depending on how they orchestrate classroom interaction in the elementary school and how roles that gain recognition are parceled out in high school. For example, when classroom activities are structured to reflect student interests and promote cooperative activity on the part of participating students, girls with special talents can be identified to lead and coordinate the group's work. In high school, plays and projects that promote student recognition can similarly be structured to actively engage the participation of young women. Yet few schools are likely to recognize the extent to which girls are stigmatized, ignored, and stereotyped. The roots of this problem are embedded in the nature and content of teacher education programs to which we turn next.

ISSUES FOR TEACHER EDUCATORS: THE CONTEXT AND CONTENT OF TEACHER EDUCATION

Among the responses to the education reform reports is *A Call for Change in Teacher Education* (1985) by the National Commission for Excellence in Teacher Education. This commission was proposed and initiated by the American Association of Colleges for Teacher Education and is comprised of educators, college and university presidents and deans, politicians, and union leaders. Of the seventeen members of the commission, only five were women.

The reform proposal put together by the commission was explicitly in response to *A Nation at Risk*. It examines and makes recommendations in five areas: (1) supply and demand for quality teachers; (2) content of teacher education; (3) accountability for teacher education; (4) resource requirements for teacher education programs; and (5) conditions necessary to support the highest quality of teaching. The Commission for Excellence in Teacher Education sees this report filling the gap left by other reform reports that did not focus on "how prospective teachers are recruited, educated, employed and assigned or on how new teachers develop into fully competent professionals" (NCETE 1985, 1). Like the education reform proposals that preceded it, this one also does not treat issues of sex equity as an important component either of the problems inherent in teacher education or the solutions necessary for change.

In examining the issues of sex equity in teacher education, it seems advisable to begin with the campus environment for both women and men students who enter any program in higher education. In their report *Out of the Classroom: A Chilly Campus Climate for Women*, Hall and Sandler (1984) find that all too often colleges and universities fail to meet the challenges of providing the co-curricular activities and experiences that constitute the expressive order in these institutions, that involve all of the campus community—faculty, staff, and students. These authors believe that "the college environment as a whole should help students acquire knowledge, build skills and confidence, learn how to make informed choices, and how to handle differences—including those of race, class and gender" (Hall and Sandler 1984, 1).

Astin (1977) in his longitudinal study of student development concludes that "even though men and women are presumably exposed to common liberal arts curriculum and other educational programs during the undergraduate years, it would seem that these programs serve more to preserve, rather than reduce stereotypic differences between men and women in behavior, personality, aspiration and achievement" (Astin 1977, 217).

Despite Title IX of the Education Amendments of 1972, which guarantees women and minorities access to higher education, women undergraduates and graduate students frequently do not enjoy full educational opportunities on campus. Many women and minority students report that both attitudinal and institutional factors relegate them to second-class status (*Report of the Select Committee on the Quality of Undergraduate Life, Amherst College* 1980, 4).

Hall and Sandler (1984) list the following as examples of overt behavior that women meet in higher education that negatively single them out because of their sex:

—disparaging women in general, women's intellectual abilities, or women's professional potential;

—focusing attention on women's appearance or women's personal or family life as opposed to their performance;

—using sexist humor;

—grouping students by sex in a way that implies that women are not as competent or do not have status equal to men (as in campus employment, lab, or field work);

—counseling women to lower their academic and career goals;

—engaging in verbal or physical sexual harrassment; and,

—making disparaging comments about lesbians, or using lesbianism as a label by which to accuse or threaten women. (Hall and Sandler 1984, 4)

These same authors also list behaviors that contribute to the social construction of the "invisible" woman in higher education, including giving women less quality time both in and out of class, and through a series of demeaning interaction patterns that only seek to further erode their public credibility. For example, they cite the following commonplace behaviors:

—frequently interrupting women;

—giving minimal responses to, or ignoring entirely, women's questions and comments, but responding at length to and developing statements contributed by men;

—seeking abstract problem-solving opinions, comments, and suggestions from men, while seeking didactic, simplistic factual information from women;

—crediting comments and ideas to men, and emotional reactions to women; and,

—adopting a posture of bored inattentiveness when talking with women but a posture of focused concentration when talking with men. (Hall and Sandler 1984, 4)

The effects of a "chilly campus climate" can have negative results for women. They may be discouraged from seeking help with academic concerns, they may not make the best use of student services, and they may not participate fully in campus life. Women students may miss out on guidance and other opportunities that are available to all students, but that may in reality be much more available to and supportive to men. Universities and colleges, in many instances, may continue to reinforce the values of middle and upper middle class males for which they were founded, perpetuating the divisions of race and gender rather than reducing them (Hall and Sandler 1984).

Turning to schools, colleges, and departments of education, we can begin to examine their contributions to maintaining the status quo. Elementary school teaching is considered to be an especially appropriate career choice for women since it requires the societally approved behaviors for women: passivity, dependency, and nurturance. Most teacher education students are women; however, they received their training in male-dominant colleges and universities. One-third of the education faculty members are women, but less than 15 percent of education chairs or deans are women (Gollnick 1979). The women faculty in education are found in human development and curriculum, whereas male faculty are located in research, administration, and philosophy. As in the university at large, women faculty in education are less visible at higher faculty ranks. Staffing patterns in teacher education send the same message to women that they have received since elementary school and will receive through graduate school: education is directed, managed, and led by men (Sadker and Sadker 1985, 147).

Another phenomenon unique to colleges of education is the lack of awareness among both women and men faculty about the cost of sex bias in the classroom. Teacher educators, for the most part, remain convinced that they are preparing teachers to teach "everyone" regardless of race and gender, apparently unaware that differential treatment of students based on gender and race is institutionalized in higher education. Lather (1981) found that in most schools and colleges of education the overwhelming perception is that sexism is of peripheral concern.

Little research can be found that is conducted by teacher education faculty on sex equity issues and education. A woman faculty member who does dare to look at sex equity issues in her research risks having her male colleagues question the relevance of that research. In addition, little curriculum development is done on sex equity issues. It is also unlikely according to Lather (1981) that information concerning sex bias is integrated in any coherent or systematic manner in the core courses of teacher education, that is, into foundations, psychology, or methods of teaching in the content areas.

The structure and content of teacher education texts provide insight into the nature of teacher education programs. These texts provide valuable data as to which topics, issues, and skills are emphasized as well as those that are ignored. Sadker and Sadker (1980) found in a comprehensive line-by-line analysis of twenty-five of the best-selling teacher education texts in foundations of education, psychology of education, and methods texts in math, science, language arts, reading, and social studies, that twenty-three of these texts allocated less than 1 percent of their space to the issues of sexism.

It is also important to note that education students are not as politically active on campus as students from other disciplines and therefore do not find themselves embroiled in the political issues related to race and gender. Lather (1981) found limited political awareness and low social aspirations in education students and placed the responsibility for promoting sex equity "squarely on the shoulders of teacher education faculty" (Lather 1981, 3), who, the researcher concluded, tend not to be on the forefront of the struggle for sex and race equality.

State certification requirements tend to be constricting in allowing education students to take electives that would widen their knowledge of women's contributions in literature, history, and such, and other women's studies courses in which they might be interested. This restrictive stance lessens the likelihood that students will encounter ideas that allow them to question the status quo. Not surprisingly, in 1979 Florence Howe surveyed women's studies programs and courses nationally and concluded that schools of education "were among the most resistant to the impact of the women's movement."

CONCLUSION

Whereas the image of girls and women in the reform literature is hazy or nonexistent, the issues confronting classroom teachers, their students, and those who work in departments and colleges of education are very apparent. In all quarters we face the continuing practice of policies and expectations that conspire to keep girls and women resolutely "in their place."

The educational reform literature is sadly lacking in any serious concern for matters of social equity, stridently calling for eduational excellence that translates into narrow standards for teacher certification and credentialing requirements for students at all grade levels, ignoring the susbstantive issues raised here. In our view, a concern with social equity and especially a concern with sex equity issues must be strongly voiced by faculty in colleges of education. The gaps and inadequacies of the reports and state commissions must be addressed by those who work directly with students and their teachers. Education faculty are in a unique position to assume leadership on the issues we have raised here.

9

The New Equity: Competing Visions

William T. Pink

The 1983 publication of *A Nation At Risk,* prepared by the National Commission on Excellence in Education, was an important event in the history of American education. The report was not only the first of a flood of commission and foundation reports that attempted to take stock of the condition of education and outline reforms, but it also managed to generate sufficient media attention to bring education back to the center of the political stage. Thus, *A Nation At Risk* has become an important document because it (1) reawakened the public interest in education in general and the importance of educational reform in particular, as it (2) set the agenda for subsequent reforms at the state and district levels.

The report has been widely praised for grabbing the national spotlight by using dramatic language to describe the current condition of America's schools.

Our Nation is at risk. . . . We report to the American people that while we can take justifiable pride in what our schools and colleges have historically accomplished and contributed to the United States and the well-being of its people, the educational foundations of our society are presently being eroded by a rising tide of mediocrity that threatens our very future as a Nation and a people. If an unfriendly foreign power had attempted to impose on America the mediocre educational performance that exists today, we might well have viewed it as an act of war. (National Commission on Excellence in Education 1983, 5)

The report has also been criticized, however, for a number of limitations. It has been criticized most frequently for: (1) presenting no new solutions for school reform; (2) proposing reforms insensitive to life-in-schools; (3) assuming that schools can be improved through state and district mandates, top-down legislative reform; (4) reproducing the capitalist status quo; (5) ignoring the costs of the proposed reforms; (6) failing to incorporate existing knowledge about effective instruction and organizational change; and (7) failing to address the integration of reforms at the secondary and elementary levels (Berman 1985; Darling-Hammond 1984; Feinberg 1985; Hawley 1985; Kirst 1986; Pink 1986).

Whereas each of these limitations is important and needs to be considered when assessing the efficacy of the reforms proposed in the report, the purpose of this chapter is not to examine these issues. Rather, this chapter argues that a much more fundamental limitation, namely the conceptualization of educational excellence and equity, seriously undermines the potential of the proposed reforms to stem the "rising tide of mediocrity that threatens our very future as a Nation and a people."

EXCELLENCE AND EQUITY IN EDUCATIONAL REFORM

A review of the various commission and foundation reports reveals that there is both a considerable difference in the perceived problems with education and the proposed reforms (e.g., Boyer 1983; Carnegie Corporation of New York 1983; Committee on Economic Development 1985; Goodlad 1984; National Commission on Excellence in Education 1983; Sizer 1984; Taskforce on Elementary and Secondary Education Policy 1983). In short, because different factors are seen as contributing to the current state of education, different remedies are proposed to remediate education. Thus, whereas the National Commission on Excellence in Education focuses on declining student SAT test scores as a primary indicator of the failings of the current educational system, both Boyer and the Twentieth-Century Fund point up the increased numbers taking the test, which makes the changes in scores far less dramatic. Whereas the Commission on Excellence suggests raising academic standards for academic subjects as the means to elevate SAT scores, Boyer points to the need to restore the support for education from middle-class whites as a remedy for improving schools and student test scores.

These substantive differences among the reports are important, if only because they indicate a lack of concensus about what should be done to reform schools, but the vast majority of the reports focus on the concept of excellence as the means of improving schools. A focus on excellence is, of course, nothing new to American education (remember the call to upgrade math and science education following the Sputnik launch), but this time around the focus on excellence comes at a time of general fiscal restraint. The problem now becomes how to distribute limited resources among students with different needs (e.g., students in gifted and talented programs and students in Chapter 1 remedial classrooms).

The recent focus on equality of opportunity, begun with the *Brown* decision in 1954 and reinforced by the 1964 Civil Rights Act, was an attempt to provide the widest possible distribution of resources to all students. Issues of access to learning opportunities and equal facilities, for example, have been the primary targets of the subsequent desegregation litigation. This present appeal for excellence, however, has spurred some to call into question the wisdom of equalizing expenditures if the result makes excellence unattainable (Gardner 1985).

The reports signal a shift from a primary concern with issues of social justice so important since the mid–1970s (e.g., the various entitlement programs) to concerns with economic productivity, international competition, and national security. As excellence has become the new goal of education, with it we must acknowledge a diminished concern for educational equity. The reforms proposed in the majority of reports favor not only the development of student achievement in the basic subject areas, but also an increased focus on those students judged to be most capable of assisting America to regain a leadership role in the economic marketplace. In short, the reforms tend to suggest only minor modifications to existing schooling practices and to further limit the opportunity of low-achieving youth to achieve at the level of their high-achieving peers. Missing almost completely from the majority of the reports is a recognition that low-achieving youth, prime candidates for long-term unemployment or underemployment and dependency on the social welfare and criminal justice systems, are helped very little by continuing "business as usual" in schools. Also missing are reform proposals that would sufficiently restructure schools to create a different learning environment to overcome the existing inequities in schooling based on factors such as social class, race, and gender. Only the work of Boyer (1983), Goodlad (1984), and Sizer (1984), for example, three reports based on extended research in schools, addresses the connection between student achievement and such commonplace practices as tracking, differentiated curricula, and uninspiring or "flat" classroom teaching. However, even these three reports offer few reforms to sufficiently restructure schools in ways that would eliminate such inequities.

A central issue is the meaning of exellence, equality, and equity. Definitions, however, tend to vary from report to report. Equality, as suggested above, has most frequently been defined as providing students equal opportunities to learn: facilities, per pupil expenditures, teacher experience, and the like are the usual indicators. Equity, however, goes beyond this to include the notions of (1) providing disproportionate effort and resources for students experiencing difficulties succeeding in school, and (2) removing school practices that work against the best interests of students. Defining equity in this way raises a set of questions about the possibility of attaining excellence as it is outlined in the majority of the reports. The reports suggest that excellence, that is, the production of individuals capable of regaining for America a competitive edge in the international marketplace, can be achieved by focusing attention on those students presumed to be the "best and brightest." Not only is such a position exclusionary and elitist, but it also suggests a disinvestment in the education of those students presumed *not* to be the "best and brightest." This tension between equity and excellence, a tension that I suggest cannot be relieved without first ensuring equity, is brought sharply into focus by the fact that those students traditionally thought *not* to be prime candidates for the "best and brightest" label—minority

and low socioeconomic students—are increasing disproportionately in the nation's schools. To reduce our effort to educate an ever increasing proportion of
the student population moves the nation away from rather than closer to implementing equity.

To discuss this issue in detail, namely a shift from a concern with equity to
a concern with economic competition and national security, requires that we
focus on a single report. To attempt an analysis of all the reports would simply
detract from the position being developed here. In recognition of its political
and educational importance, *A Nation At Risk* is used to illustrate the argument
that the present focus on educational excellence not only signals but requires a
retreat from equity.

A NATION AT RISK: EXCELLENCE OVER EQUITY

Despite the attention drawn to excellence by the publication of *A Nation At
Risk,* the report defines excellence in rather vague terms:

We define ''excellence'' to mean several related things. At the level of the individual
learner, it means performing on the boundary of individual ability in ways that test and
push back personal limits, in school and in the workplace. Excellence characterizes a
school or college that sets high expectations and goals for all learners, then tries in every
way possible to help students reach them. Excellence characterizes a society that has
adopted these policies, for it will then be prepared through the education and skill of its
people to respond to the challenges of a rapidly changing world. (National Commission
on Excellence in Education 1983, 12)

Whereas it is difficult to argue with this philosophic position, the central issues
here are: (1) What is individual ability and who defines personal limits? and (2)
How will current school practices be altered to permit *all* students to reach the
high expectations they are encouraged to hold? The report unfortunately addresses
neither of these critical questions. By implication, however, it suggests that
student performance will continue to be assessed in the same way as in the past,
that is, grade point average and standardized test scores, and that schools will
not alter ''standard operating practices'' sufficiently to permit currently lower
achieving or at-risk students to realize their high expectations. In other words,
equity is not well served by this report.

This is not to say that a sensitivity to equity is totally missing from the report.
Rather, we should note that there is a wide discrepancy between the language
in the body of the report and the focus and substance of the proposed reforms.
In noting that America is presently in danger because the educational system is
failing to produce sufficiently competent citizens, the report contains several
passages that suggest a sensitivity to making the American dream a reality for
all the citizens:

Part of what is at risk is the promise first made on this continent: All, regardless of race or class or economic status, are entitled to a fair chance and to the tools for developing their individual powers of mind and spirit to the utmost. This promise means that all children by virtue of their own efforts, competently guided, can hope to attain the mature and informed judgment needed to secure gainful employment and to manage their own lives, thereby serving not only their own interests but also the progress of society itself. (National Commission on Excellence in Education 1983, 8)

The report also states:

We do not believe that a public commitment to excellence and educational reform must be made at the expense of a strong public commitment to the equitable treatment of our diverse population. The twin goals of equity and high-quality schooling have profound and practical meaning for our economy and society, and we cannot permit one to yield to the other either in principle or in practice. To do so would deny young people their chance to learn and live according to their aspirations and abilities.

Our goal must be to develop the talents of all to their fullest. Attaining that goal requires that we expect and assist all students to work to the limits of their capabilities. (National Commission on Excellence in Education 1983, 13)

Missing from this discussion is the recognition that providing equal access to opportunities to learn (a practice not yet routine in schools and thus the prime focus of the recent desegregation litigation) is insufficient to overcome the inequities currently found in many schools that are based on factors such as presumed ability, race, social class, and gender. The concept of equity has little practical significance in the life of low-achieving, at-risk students, unless it involves providing additional resources to assist them to succeed in school and realize their high expectations. This is more than a restatement of the argument for compensatory education as typified by Chapter 1 programs, which have traditionally focused on basic skills remediation in reading, mathematics, and language arts for students scoring lowest on standardized tests. In practice this has focused the resources of schools on assisting students reach rather modest educational goals. By contrast, the position being developed here would require schools to provide a sufficient range of educational experiences that would assist *all* students to succeed in mastering *all* of the materials offered by the school (excluding, of course, students with some learning disability). In other words, schools should be about *maintaining* the widest possible life and career options for all youth, by assisting them learn *all* the curriculum, rather than restricting learning options because of factors such as presumed ability, race, social class, and gender (Pink 1984; Pink and Leibert 1986; Weis 1985).

WILL THE REFORMS IN *A NATION AT RISK* REFORM SCHOOLS?

Simply stated, the proposed reforms in *A Nation At Risk* not only ignore the most important component of schools, namely students, but also fail to address the issue of equity. It should also be noted that the report confines its remarks to high schools; elementary and junior high schools receive no attention. Put bluntly, the reforms proposed in the report, even if implemented, would not change life in schools sufficiently to be called a reform; a modification perhaps, but certainly not a reform. This assessment is best illustrated by a close examination of the five primary reforms proposed in the report.

The first recommendation concerns graduation requirements:

We recommend that State and local high school graduation requirements be strengthened and that, at a minimum, all students seeking a diploma be required to lay the foundations in the Five New Basics by taking the following curriculum during their 4 years of high school: (a) 4 years of English; (b) 3 years of mathematics; (c) 3 years of science; (d) 3 years of social studies; and (e) one-half year of computer science. For the collegebound, 2 years of foreign language in high school are strongly recommended in addition to those taken earlier. (National Commission on Excellence in Education 1983, 24)

This recommendation completely misses the fact that large numbers of students experience difficulties graduating under the existing requirements (those students coming disproportionately from minority and low socioeconomic status groups) and that stiffening the requirements is likely to make things that much more difficult for an even greater number of students. Implementing the "New Basics" *without* increasing alternative (not repeat) experiences that can effectively remediate the learning deficiencies of students will result in the continued frustration, failure, and perhaps dropout of lower achieving and alienated students (Oakes 1985; Ogbu 1978; Rist 1970). To promote equity the recommendation must address the kind of treatment needed to educate those groups presently experiencing difficulty in schools (e.g., Blacks and Hispanics, low-achieving students, poor students, limited English-speaking students) and detail ways in which schools might implement such effective practices (Pink 1986).

Not only is the report silent on what schools should do to assist students currently experiencing difficulties succeeding in school, but it offers little guidance to schools concerning either the content of the courses in the proposed New Basics, or the most effective instructional strategies to use when teaching these proposed courses. The net result is that schools are encouraged to do little else but change their graduation requirements. Left unexamined are the more important questions about what is taught in classrooms, what instructional strategies are effective for which students, which range of remedial programs facilitate learning for all students, and how schools should be reorganized to maximize the success of all students. The report suggests that:

We must emphasize that the variety of student aspirations, abilities, and preparation requires that appropriate content be available to satisfy diverse needs. Attention must be directed to both the nature of the content available and to the needs of particular learners. The most gifted students, for example, may need a curriculum enriched and accelerated beyond even the needs of other students of high ability. Similarly, educationally disadvantaged students may require special curriculum materials, smaller classes, or individual tutoring to help them master the material presented. (National Commission on Excellence in Education 1983, 24)

In so doing, the report merely reaffirms the widely held belief in immutable individual differences that is institutionalized by commonplace practices such as tracking and ability grouping. The report also assumes that grouping by ability is the best way to teach *and* that students in these different groups should be taught using different teaching materials. Testing a student to demonstrate that they are eligible for placement in the lowest (basic) academic track works against equity if the outcome is that basic track students experience a curriculum that prepares them inadequately for academic success in school, college entry, or occupations requiring anything beyond basic entry level skills (Oakes 1985; Ogbu 1978; Pink and Sweeney 1978). Again, raising the graduation requirements as a means of attaining academic exellence misses the importance of creating a range of learning environments and curricula that provides for the success of all students, not just the select few who currently enjoy the rewards attached to placement in the high-achieving (college preparatory) tracks.

The second recommendation in the report concerns standards and expectations at several different levels:

We recommend that schools, colleges, and universities adopt more rigorous and measurable standards, and higher expectations, for academic performance and student conduct, and that 4–year colleges and universities raise their requirements for admission. This will help students do their best educationally with challenging materials in an environment that supports learning and authentic accomplishment. (National Commission on Excellence in Education 1983, 27)

The problem here is similar to that detailed for the first recommendation. Raising standards and expectations will exclude greater numbers of students from achieving academic excellence *unless* some provision is made to give *additional* support to students currently deficient. The report says nothing about such a support structure. Again, then, implementation of this recommendation will make life-in-school that much more difficult for those students currently experiencing difficulties, perhaps causing higher dropout rates, as well as ensuring that fewer of these students have the qualifications to enter and remain in college. By suggesting that grades be used as "indicators of academic achievement" without a discussion of the relationship between grades, track location, and previous academic history does little but further disadvantage low-achieving students (Hargreaves 1967; Pink 1984.)

Whereas, this recommendation does single out textbooks as an area for improvement, suggesting that they should be evaluated "on their ability to present rigorous and challenging material clearly," it also reaffirms the position that students in different tracks need different material:

Because no textbook in any subject can be geared to the needs of all students, funds should be made available to support text development in "thin-market" areas, such as those for disadvantaged students, the learning disabled, and the gifted and talented. (National Commission on Excellence in Education 1983, 28)

Missing is a discussion of important issues such as the content and bias of textbooks, the simplification of textbooks for students of presumed different ability, and the way in which teachers use textbooks to drive the curriculum in classrooms containing students presumed to have limited ability. Without addressing these issues, equity does not seem well served in this recommendation concerning standards and expectations.

The third recommendation in the report concerns the use of school time:

We recommend that significantly more time be devoted to learning the New Basics. This will require more effective use of the existing school day, a longer school day, or a lengthened school year. (National Commission on Excellence in Education 1983, 29)

Here the emphasis is on doing more of what is currently done in schools—more homework, more hours in school, stronger discipline and attendance policies. There is no discussion of the effect these proposed changes might have on the lives of students or teachers. Missing, for example, is a discussion of the notion of changing schools to make them more attractive to students and teachers as a means to making schools more effective within the existing time frame. Similarly, the report proposes that employing harsher discipline and attendance codes is the route to raising academic achievement, at the same time giving no heed to data suggesting that it is these very practices that predict both student alienation and suspension from school (Gold and Mann 1984; Newman 1981; Wehlege 1983; Wu et al., 1982). Finally, whereas the report contains a suggestion to find additional instructional time to meet the special needs of different kinds of students (e.g., "slow learners, the gifted, and others who need instructional diversity"), there is no concern about the inequities in a system that sorts students into such distinct groups and systematically educates them differently. Again, treating students equally in terms of the time allocated to instruction misses the importance of how that time is used to keep educational and occupational options open for all the students in every school. Time is not the issue. The content and quality of instruction are the issue, yet these remain unaddressed by the report.

The fourth recommendation concerns teachers and teacher education:

This recommendation consists of seven parts. Each is intended to improve the preparation of teachers or to make teaching a more rewarding and respected profession. Each of the seven stands on its own and should not be considered solely as an implementing recommendation. (National Commission on Excellence in Education 1983, 30)

Each of the seven parts ignores both life-in-schools and the factors that teachers repeatedly note as important to the quality of their lives. Also ignored are factors such as the recruitment of minority and bilingual teachers, which affects the ability of the schools to operationalize equity. The seven recommendations involve (1) raising the entry and exit standards for preservice teachers; (2) raising teacher salaries that are performanced-based; (3) providing an eleven-month teacher contract; (4) the development of career ladders for teachers; (5) recruiting nonschool personnel to teach in "shortage areas"; (6) providing grants or loans to "attract outstanding students" into teaching; and (7) including master teachers in program design and the supervision of teachers. The emphasis, yet again, is on raising standards in colleges and universities, without a discussion of the need to provide additional assistance to students unable to compete because of inadequate preparation in schools, and on raising the monetary return to teaching. Missing is a discussion of critical issues such as the content of teacher education programs, how teachers should be evaluated, how schools should be reorganized to improve the quality of life for teachers and students, and how nonteaching personnel might be used to restructure teacher time to permit adequate time each day to engage in planning and professional development. Also missing is a discussion of the need to recruit and retain minority teachers and administrators. Again, concerns for equity are absent in the fourth recommendation.

The fifth and final recommendation concerns leadership and the fiscal support needed to sustain the proposed reforms:

We recommend that citizens across the Nation hold educators and elected officials responsible for providing the leadership necessary to achieve these reforms, and that citizens provide for fiscal support and stability required to bring about the reforms we propose. (National Commision on Excellence in Education 1983, 32)

This recommendation calls on principals, superintendents, and school boards to exert leadership in gaining community support to implement the proposed reforms. State and local officials, including governors and legislators, are urged to finance the proposed reforms. The federal government is charged to continue (1) meeting the needs of special students (e.g., "gifted and talented . . . disadvantaged, handicapped, and minority students"); (2) protecting constitutional and civil rights, collecting data, improving curricula, and the like; and (3) exercising the "primary responsibility" for maintaining the national interest in education and marshaling the public and private resources to implement the proposed reforms. Finally, the report "calls upon educators, parents, and public officials at all levels to assist in bringing about the educational reform proposed in this report."

Without belaboring the point, the problem is that the four proposed reforms champion the pursuit of excellence at the expense of equity. Thus implementing the reforms will further damage rather than assist the realization of equity.

WHY THESE REFORMS?

As a policy statement, the substance of *A Nation At Risk* is disappointing. It lacks a clear statement of the problems confronting schools, a thorough synthesis of existing data, a discussion of policy alternatives, and a reasoned rationale for an integrated set of reform proposals. Whereas the report was much heralded by the media, it is not only silent on several critical issues (such as equity), but offers a set of poorly integrated reforms that are, in many cases, too ill-defined to be implemented. Because these reforms are largely cosmetic and favor actions that are both easy to manipulate through state or district level mandates (e.g., changes in graduation requirements) as well as simple to document, it is important to ask what factors work to influence the substance of the report. Six factors seem worthy of note.

The first factor affecting the substance of the report concerns the charge to the members of the commission. The then Secretary of Education T. H. Bell charged the commission to do several things. Perhaps most important was "To report and make practical recommendations for action to be taken by educators, public officials, governing boards, parents and others having a vital interest in American education and a capacity to influence it for the better." The result was not bold ideas aimed at fundamental reform of the American system of education. Rather, the commission chose to produce a document that contained strident language but reforms that emphasized fairly simple-minded changes that could be controlled by those most influential in the existing power structure, that is, governors and state legislators.

The second factor concerns the diversity and expertise of the members comprising the commission. A diverse membership, bringing with it a wide range of individual interests and concerns, works against the production of detailed proposals for reform. The Commission on Educational Excellence was no exception. The reforms remain at the level of generalities. Moreover, we must acknowledge that it is politically dangerous to propose fundamental reforms for a system that historically has been so resistant to change.

A third factor is the political climate in which the report was produced. The commission was working during a time when the Reagan administration was working hard to elevate the importance of the military and national security while retreating from issues such as civil rights and equal employment enforcement, and full-funding for educational entitlement programs like Chapter 1. Thus we should not be surprised that the report also stresses themes of economic leadership in the world markets and national security while retreating from issues like civil rights and educational equity. In this respect the report mirrors the political climate in which it was prepared.

The fourth factor affecting the substance of the report is the time-frame and format for the commission. The commission met for a short time (eighteen months) and gathered information largely through expert testimony at open meetings. Such working conditions are far from optimal for systematically pursuing answers to difficult questions. Much time is spent in the ceremony of a national commission; too little time is spent analyzing competing ideas and generating a carefully crafted plan for school reform.

The fifth critical factor is the inability of a commission to engage in additional research that might illuminate areas where little data presently exist. The result is a report that remains at the level of generalities and stays clear of highly controversial areas. Also, given the typically wide range of expertise in research displayed by members of national commissions, a thorough synthesis of existing research is never attempted. The reforms presented in *A Nation At Risk* carry no citations to educational research and are not grounded in what we know about effective instruction and management, or organizational change.

The sixth factor is that the reforms in the report do not reflect life in schools (no visits were made to schools), or the major concerns of teachers (e.g., concerns for fewer students each day, increased professional autonomy, and a work setting that supports greater collegiality). By ignoring student and teacher concerns, the proposed reforms talk past critical issues in school reform such as equity.

In sum, these six factors work against the production of a report that presents an integrated set of reforms to serve as an agenda for significant change in the way schools educate students in general, *and* further open up the opportunity structure for minority and low socioeconomic status students in particular.

WHAT'S MISSING? A FOCUS ON EQUITY

Without an emphasis on equity as outlined above, it is evident that the reforms proposed in *A Nation At Risk* will do little to improve the educational experience of a large number of students. In fact, there is every reason to believe that a majority of students attending urban schools (e.g., minority and low socioeconomic status students in urban centers such as New York, Los Angeles, Boston, and Chicago) may well be further disadvantaged by the implementation of the reforms proposed in the report.

In order to successfully include equity in the push for academic excellence, reform proposals must focus, at the very least, on the following issues:

1. How can schools be restructured to create an educational setting and ambiance that facilitates rather than prevents
   (a) success in school for *all* students, and
   (b) the development of a supportive work culture for teachers? (Little 1986). This would require proposals to reform such practices as tracking, ability grouping, and the overreliance on standardized test scores for student selection, placement, and promotion (Oakes 1985; Pink and Leibert 1986; Rosenbaum 1976). It would also require proposing reforms that will alter commonplace school practices that result in the development and support of oppositional student cultures (Hargreaves 1967; Weis 1985; Willis 1977). Reforms should also talk to changing the work context of teachers and to involving teachers more directly in the governance of schools. To expect gains in student achievement without addressing these issues is to invite disappointment.

2. How can the content of the curriculum be revised to remove bias and encourage critical and reflective thinking (Apple 1972; Bowers 1974)? Reform proposals are needed that would address the practice of using textbooks to shape the curriculum and defining

success in school as the ability to master the material in the texts. Such practices work to the disadvantage of students given limited access to this material because of beliefs about their ability to master the material. Thus education cannot be improved without an examination of what constitutes knowledge and the opening up of access to that knowledge base for *all* students.

3. What instructional strategies are effective under what conditions for which students? Equity cannot be achieved until teachers can make a better match between how instruction is delivered and how students learn. *A Nation At Risk* says nothing about instructional practices, yet we know that students learn in different ways (Brophy 1982; Leinhart and Palley 1982; Pink and Leibert 1986). Reform proposals must address how teachers teach, as well as the resources needed to teach *all* students effectively.

4. How are teachers best prepared to be effective? Reform proposals must address the efficacy of (a) teacher education models, (b) instruction models, and (c) professional development models. Equity cannot be advanced, for example, if teachers can be certified without demonstrating skills working with racially, linguistically, and culturally diverse students. Similarly, proposals for reform need to address the content of teacher education programs (e.g., what areas of study are essential and how might mastery be measured?), the induction years, and life-long professional development. *A Nation At Risk* is silent on these issues. They are fundamental, however, to the improvement of schools.

5. How does the substance and the process of schooling fit with the occupational structure? Equity cannot be advanced if minority and low socioeconomic students continue to be poorly prepared by schools to succeed in the world of work. Proposals for reform must address ways to open up the world of work to *all* students. *A Nation At Risk* offers no insight into the ways the opportunity structure might be changed to give all students access to social mobility.

It is clear that a retreat from equity as illustrated in this analysis of the proposals presented in *A Nation At Risk* suggests that the attainment of excellence might well be impossible. The attainment of educational excellence, it would seem, is dependent upon a parallel commitment to the full implementation of educational equity.

PART IV

SCHOOL REFORM PROPOSALS FOR "THE NEW CURRICULUM"

10

Civic Education Reform and the Quest for a Unified Society: A Critique of R. Freeman Butts's Agenda for Civic Learning

Stuart A. McAninch

R. Freeman Butts has developed a rationale for American public schooling that stresses its civic functions. Concerned with what he believes to be the corrosive effects on the body politic of a growing sense of political privatism and of the increasingly pluralistic nature of education, Butts argues that the most important objective for schooling is the preservation of a cohesive democratic political community through the preparation of the young for citizenship. Whereas not dismissing the importance of those objectives of schooling that are vocational or are related to social and cognitive development of the individual, Butts emphasizes that such objectives should not distract the American public and professional educators from the critical civic mission of the schools.

The need for constructing methods of civic education capable of cementing national unity in a time of growing divisiveness, civic illiteracy, and loss of public spirit is, in fact, a theme that is common to much of the reform literature and discussion of the 1970s and 1980s and that transcends conventional political divisions. Both political conservatives and liberals have looked to educational reform as a means to combat what they interpret as the largely negative civic legacy of an era in recent American history characterized by widespread public questioning of U.S. policy in Vietnam, overt hostility toward governmental authority by many members of ethnic minority groups, a considerable degree of student radicalism on college and high school campuses, and the considerable public disgust triggered by the scandals of the Nixon administration. Believing such phenomena have promoted dysfunctional civic attributes like cynicism or apathy, reformers representing a number of different political perspectives have looked in recent years to educational reform as a vital instrument for restoring the people's faith in common values, sympathetic understanding of republican institutions, and commitment to social cooperation and unity.

Butts's particular expression of this theme might well be described as having its roots in the old political liberalism of the 1930s. Prescribing major roles for governmental planning and action in the preservation of social welfare and insisting upon a common civic education provided by strong public school systems, Butts demonstrates an abiding attachment to elements of the social reconstructionist viewpoint that influenced his development as a young scholar at Teachers College, Columbia University during that decade. In his view, restoration of public confidence in the rectitude and efficacy of the central institutions of the federal government and establishment of consensus on civic values are essential for the stability of democratic government in the United States.

On the other hand, political conservatives who are strongly critical of energetic federal intervention in social matters and who often favor stimulation of competition among public and private schools have also energetically expressed the need for civic education to re-establish social and ideological unity. In October 1985, *The Christian Science Monitor* reported that dismay at the U.S. Department of Education "over the moral and ethical condition of our society" has prompted the search for methods to build "a more cohesive society around a commonly shared vision of the American democracy and its traditional ideals" through a revised history curriculum (Editorial 1985 B). William Bennett has identified the teaching of the humanities, use by educators of "*the quiet power of moral example*," and the environment provided by the disciplined and efficient school as important means for developing among students those particular social and moral understandings and those particular traits of character that he identifies as necessary for this more cohesive society (Bennett 1985, 453–454).

The point to be made is not that conservative and liberal educational reformers possess the same conceptions of what constitutes a properly unified and cohesive society. Their conceptions obviously differ in certain important respects. What is significant, however, is the fact that authors representing a variety of political positions have called upon civic education to stabilize the nation in the aftermath of the social crises of the 1960s and 1970s by educating youths to respect one set or another of purportedly traditional democratic values and by further educating them to distrust those critical political and social perspectives that deviate from such values. Such educational reformers frequently couple a desire for a reformed civic education capable of reinforcing a weakened sense of national unity and responsibility among Americans with a strong warning regarding the dangers of excessive individualism and of divisive social inquiry on the part of individuals.

In her essay for Connaught Marshner's *A Blueprint for Education Reform*, Linda Chavez argues that in civics classes during recent years "[d]oubt seems to have replaced patriotism as a virtue to be inculated" (Chavez 1984, 131). Although hardly denying that rationality is a necessary component of civic consciousness, Chavez argues that the civic educator needs to channel the individual's exercise of reason by intensively cultivating his or her loyalty to the national community and to the values that underlie it. She also makes clear the dire consequences of allowing youths to develop social ideas not informed by a deep sense of loyalty to dominant American political institutions and values: confusion, selfishness, apathy, and alienation.

In *The Reconstruction of Patriotism: Education for Civic Consciousness*, Morris Janowitz cites as a major task for civic educators the redressing of that overemphasis on individual rights that has been, he believes, characteristic of American political life since the end of World War II and that was exacerbated during the 1960s and 1970s by such factors as strengthened ethnic/racial group consciousness and anti–Vietnam protest. Perceiving individual rights and thought not counterbalanced by a strong sense of obligation to the American political system as being antithetical to a cohesive democracy, Janowitz argues that civic education programs in the schools since 1945 have largely failed to develop a sense of obligation. By priding themselves on "myth smashing" and "their critical stance," many programs have unintentionally promoted such consequences of excessive individualism as "negativism" and "near nihilism" (Janowitz 1983, 146).

R. Freeman Butts's work on civic learning provides a particularly promising vantage point for studying the view of civic education as a means to counteract the social crises of the 1960s and 1970s and to restore national unity. Butts's agenda for civic education reform is currently one of the most systematically developed articulations of this position. Moreover, Butts's reputation as an honored elder statesman in educational history and philosophy and his close ties to a variety of foundations and professional organizations sponsoring educational dialogue and research have enabled him to enjoy wide circulation for his ideas among educators and educational policy-makers. Finally, at a time when this view of civic education most commonly finds its way into newspaper headlines through coverage of the conservative leadership at the U.S. Department of Education, it is good to keep in mind that it is also expounded by a prominent educational theorist with deep ties to political liberalism. The quest for a unified society characterized by a common frame of political values and rejection of individualism judged excessive is as much a goal for advocates of the liberal political community like Butts as it is for architects of the Reagan revolution like William Bennett.

REKINDLING THE SENSE OF COMMUNITY

Butts's writings on civic learning generally highlight the need for strong public school civic education programs by selectively stressing the negative effects of public reactions to the political and social conflicts of the Vietnam era. In a 1973 article for *The Nation*, he observes that "[o]ur people are badly divided and dispirited, if not demoralized, by trials they underwent in the late 1960s and early 1970s" (Butts 1973, 559). Four years later, Butts describes the results of these "trials" at some length. Referring to survey data that suggested a growing political skepticism and lack of respect for constituted authority among American youth, Butts warns that a "whole generation believes that our political institutions do not practice what we preach." Such skepticism is related, in Butts's view, to a widespread feeling among college students that they have little obligation to participate in the political system. Again referring to opinion poll results, he describes the "dominant mood" of large numbers of American adults as "widespread disillusionment, disenchantment, discontent, distrust of public men in public institutions, with corresponding paucity of public knowledge of political affairs, apathy, cynicism, and lack of participation" (1977B, 9–10; Butts 1977a, 21–22). Whether looking at youths or adults, Butts draws a clear connection between deep-seated skepticism and disillusionment with public institutions, on the one hand, and undesirable political attributes (ignorance, apathy, cynicism, etc.), on the other.

Butts's prescription for remedying various forms of political alienation is to use the public schools to "rekindle the sense of community" (Butts 1973, 559). The idea of the American people constituting a liberal political community is a central one for Butts and is ultimately the foundation upon which he justifies public school civic education. He argues that, even though they have somewhat lost sight of the fact, Americans constitute a political community because they are a people unified by "a common frame of political values" and "common participation in shared governing processes" (Butts 1980, 124). The American political community is liberal for several reasons. First, it is not afraid to resort to state action in order to maintain its cohesion, achieve its aims, or accomplish needed reforms. Second, it is deeply concerned with individual liberties and, in order to assure the freedom and well-being of all the people, swears its allegiance to democratic values and constitutional processes of government.[1] Butts does not claim that the liberal political community always acts in accordance with its democratic values. He nevertheless concludes that there is a close enough correlation between democratic values and the actions of liberal institutions to clearly illustrate the superiority of that community over any alternatives put forward by opponents of liberalism, whom he characterizes as neo-conservatives when on the political right, and neo-radicals, radical leftists, radical revisionists, and such when on the political left.

Butts argues that the public school is a vital institution for disseminating among the citizenry the values, knowledge, and will to participate in liberal political processes necessary for achieving the aims of liberalism: "I would argue that if the teaching profession of two or three million persons took seriously the authority of the enduring ideals, sentiments, and moral commitments of our historic political community at its best, as embodied in the constitutional regime and especially in the Bill of Rights, the schools and colleges of this country *could* mobilize the majority of people on behalf of putting into practice our professed democratic ideals" (Butts 1976, 14; 1980, 117). To weaken the public schools and a common civic education oriented toward all children is to virtually undermine the liberal state itself by removing the best means for achieving common allegiance to democratic values and liberal political processes.

As the above quotation indicates, a key function of civic education is to facilitate students' realization of the "authority" of the enduring ideals and traditional values that underlie the constitutional order and bind together the liberal political community. Student acceptance of enduring ideals and traditional values is, however, to be selective since only those standards embodied in the historic community *at its best* are to be chosen. Butts attempts to safeguard what he considers healthy forms of political diversity and stable forms of pluralism by advocating a balance between those values that contribute to unity and those that contribute to pluralism. He attempts to avoid inculcation by advocating that study of values be "based upon realistic, scholarly knowledge and searching criticism" (Butts 1980, 132).

Besides advocating study of what he refers to as the "decalogue" of traditional democratic values (that is, justice, equality, authority, participation, personal obligation for the public good, freedom, diversity, privacy, due process, and international human rights), Butts also argues that acquisition of political knowledge and skills of participation are an essential part of any vital civic education program (Butts 1980, Chapter 5). He thereby attempts to provide for a balanced development of the normative, cognitive, affective, and practical attributes of citizenship in a liberal political community.

A CRITIQUE OF BUTTS'S SENSE OF COMMUNITY

An opportune place to begin a critique of Butts's conception of civic learning is his depiction of the United States as a liberal political community bound together by shared political values. Perhaps the reason why Butts is able to envision a national community united by a common framework of political values lies in the manner in which he defines those values: they are "the sets of attitudes, sentiments, feelings, beliefs, commitments, and obligations *that contribute to the support of the political system*" (Butts 1976, 12, emphasis added). Hence, the utility and legitimacy of political values are judged by Butts from the perspective of the political system as a whole rather than from the perspective of the valuing individual or of the concrete and immediate social circumstances that influence the individual's formation of values. Only when the values of the individual are reconcilable with the requirements of the liberal political community are they legitimate; otherwise, they fall within the realm of what he designates the "corrupted forms" of democratic values or are attributed, as in his response to the widespread public disillusionment with liberal institutions during the 1960s and early 1970s, to apathy, cynicism, ignorance, or other negative civic attributes.[2]

Whereas Butts stresses the acquisition by individuals of civic knowledge and thinking skills during the course of civic education, such objectives must in actual practice conflict frequently with what for him are the even more fundamental objectives of building "positive commitments in thought and action to the democratic values of the liberal political community and to the liberal political processes of the democratic constitutional order" (Butts 1976, 14; 1980, 118). By paying homage to what he alludes to as "realistic, scholarly knowledge and searching criticism," Butts works to reconcile the ideal of informed and intelligent citizenship with the objective of achieving through schooling a considerable measure of consensus on political values. Yet, for me at least, it is difficult to see how the public school can possibly incorporate searching criticism into its curricula and instruction at the same time that it provides the spark to rekindle the sense of community. Is it conceivable, for instance, that a thoughtful high school social studies unit on the history of U.S. relations with Nicaragua would be an effective means for engendering within a group of students positive commitments to liberal democratic values? If the unit presented a variety of perspectives—ranging, perhaps, from Jeane Kirkpatrick to Noam Chomsky—might it not actually lead some students to conclude that the evidence indicates deep, systemic problems in American values, institutions, and society that liberal political processes as presently structured do not seem equipped to address?

Is, in fact, the possibility of school stimulating in some students fundamental doubts regarding the viability of liberal values and institutions necessarily a bad thing for a participatory democracy? The deep-seated skepticism and disillusionment that Butts refers to in order to impress upon his audiences the need for a vigorous civic education aimed at social cohesion may not be the dangers he makes them appear to be. It would be interesting, for instance, to poll how many citizens had their political and social consciousness significantly sharpened by the militant protests and radical currents of thought that abounded in U.S. colleges and other environs during the late 1960s and early 1970s. For many Americans, elements of radical skepticism developed during that period and maintained during the Reagan years have stimulated political thinking and public action.

Even if one accepts the argument that negative attributes such as cynicism, apathy, lack of political knowledge, and withdrawal from political participation are widespread problems impeding participatory democracy in the United States, he or she is not obliged to accept Butts's remedies. Ira Shor explains how, in his teaching at Staten Island Community College, New York, he sought to stimulate political consciousness and activism among alienated students by having them initially study the chairs in their classrooms. Using their observations and understandings of such familiar commodities as graphic illustrations, Shor helped them to develop working understandings of how political power relationships and ideology are manifested in even the most routine activities of their daily lives and mundane objects of their environments. Shor then made these understandings, drawn directly from students' experiences, the basis for construction of social critiques and visions of alternatives to the political-economic status quo (Shor 1978). Whereas Butts seeks to eliminate political alienation by shaping the consciousness of the alienated individual to fit a decalogue of traditional democratic values, Shor suggests a means for combatting alienation by addressing its roots in the concrete experience of the individual and helping him or her to extract normative standards from analysis of that experience.

CONCLUSION

In summary, by studying Butts's conception of the liberal political community and the type of civic learning that he sees as essential for its welfare, one is able to get a sense of a theme that runs through much of the reform literature. Positing turmoil of one sort or another that keeps substantial numbers of Americans from realizing their full potentials as citizens, educational reform documents from both politically liberal and conservative sources have proposed as remedies various measures to teach students the virture of the unified, cooperative society in which teamwork, respect for political and economic institutions, and common ideals predominate. When skills of social thinking are stressed in such documents, they are stressed in such a manner as to not lead to fundamental challenges of that type of society by individuals. I would argue that we need to ask ourselves as educators two questions when we come upon the theme of the unified, cooperative society in reform literature. First, what price in terms of diminished capacities of the citizen to arrive at truly individual social understandings and values must be paid if civic education is to be reformed in accordance with that particular social vision? Second, how much diminution of such capacities can a society tolerate before it ceases to be democratic?

NOTES

1. For a typical statement by Butts on what constitutes the liberal political community, see F. R. Butts (1976).

2. For a listing of the "corrupted forms" of the democratic values, see Butts (1980, 128; 1982, 392ff).

11

An Evaluation of the Aims and Curriculum Proposals in Sizer's *Horace's Compromise*

John Martin Rich and Joseph L. DeVitis

Theodore R. Sizer, former headmaster of Phillips Academy and former dean of the Harvard Graduate School of Education, has completed a study titled *Horace's Compromise*, which is cosponsored by the National Association of Secondary School Principals and the Commission on Educational Issues of the National Association of Independent Schools (Sizer 1984). Our purpose is to examine and evaluate two vital areas of the study: aims and curriculum proposals. First, some comparisons are made with two earlier Carnegie reports that shaped educational reform; next, aims and curriculum proposals in *Horace's Compromise* are evaluated; finally, the study is compared to other contemporary national surveys.

A COMPARISON OF CARNEGIE REPORTS

A two-year study completed in 1959 that attracted national attention was James B. Conant's *The American High School Today*, a study of fifty comprehensive high schools in seventeen states (Conant 1959). Conant found that the comprehensive high school could provide adequate programs of citizenship education, vocational education, and challenging studies for the more able student. He identified the more gifted students as about 15 percent of the high school population; he recommended that each of these students study three or four years in the basic disciplines and take at least five subjects each year with homework of fifteen hours or more each week. Placement tests would determine the appropriate sections for the academically talented, and effective guidance programs would be needed to assist this group and the rest of the student population, who would take a more limited number of advanced courses in the basic disciplines. Conant, for example, wanted to trim the number of pupils for which English teachers would be responsible (100 in all) in order to allow more time for thematic writing. Similar to Sizer, he also advocated "blocks" of time for English and social studies classes as early as junior high school.

The Conant Report was likely influenced by the Cold War, the launching of Sputnik, and the National Defense Education Act; its publication aroused a greater national consciousness about the status of American education. Tying into the space race with the Soviet Union, it called attention to the need for more academically talented girls to enter science and mathematics programs, the neglect of foreign languages, and a more complete education for all students attending comprehensive high schools. Conant, according to one observer, was a Jeffersonian meritocrat who sought to integrate democratic schooling for scientific and technically competent personnel and help strengthen and expand the economy's industrial base (Grissom 1973).

In sharp contrast, Charles Silberman's *Crisis in the Classroom*, a Carnegie-sponsored study published in 1970, emerged during the upheavals of the Civil Rights movement, the Vietnam War, and student militancy on campuses (Silberman 1970). Not surprisingly, the tone and content differed markedly from the Conant Report.

Silberman deplored the school's preoccupation with order and control. This preoccupation could be found in a focus on time and the clock (though time frequently was not used productively) and on the demand for silence. The repressiveness he observed was reinforced by parental attitudes that viewed discipline as more important than student self-inquiry. At the root of the problem is "mindlessness," the failure "to think seriously or deeply about the purposes or consequences of education" (Silberman 1970, 11). Silberman's curricular solution was to promote the growth of open classrooms.

Sizer's study is generally more similar to Silberman's findings than to the Conant Report. Even stylistically, there are certain ostensible similarities. Silberman writes in an idiosyncratic, digressive style; he is fond of injecting items and case studies and is given to waxing passionately over his favorite nostrums. Sizer's style is simple and direct; his numerous case studies are usually longer than those of Silberman. However, Sizer's interesting yet confounding use of "nonfiction fiction," which combines actual situations and characters with contrived dialogue and artificial persona, can be disconcerting to read, digest, and evaluate. (Parenthetically, his reliance on the research literature is paltry at best.) In brief, such techniques are more apropos an intuitionistic humanist base than a genuine science of pedagogy. But, substantively, just as Silberman found too much emphasis on order and control in prevailing school environments, Sizer observes that students are often docile and lacking initiative (though such traits curiously do not carry over to the students' part-time jobs). In this regard, Sizer does not see larger possibilities for a nexus between work and community service as does, for example, Ernest Boyer in his *High School*. In Sizer's survey of

American secondary education, he observes that a high premium is placed on punctuality and a low premium on reflection and repose. Both Silberman and Sizer value flexibility and innovativeness in their school design; they also reject a conventional subject curriculum.

AIMS AND CURRICULUM

Over the past decade Sizer visited over 100 schools; and during the 2 years of field work, he visited over 40 American secondary schools. His study is especially addressed to the lay reader. The title of the book is drawn from Sizer's observations of the daily activities of Horace Smith, an English teacher whose situation is similar to that of many public school teachers. Effectively, Sizer dramatizes the dilemma of *all* public school teachers via the individual plight of Horace: meager salaries, oppressive school climate, and the inability to control one's professional destiny due to a maze of bureaucratization. Smith teaches five classes daily, a total of 120 students, and he also handles extracurricular activities. Smith believes that students should have a written assignment twice each week, but, because of time constraints, he has them write once a week and assigns but 1 or 2 paragraphs. He finds that he can give only 5 minutes to each student's assignment and an average of 10 minutes of planning for each 50-minute class. It is both with Smith's plight and student's docility and lack of initiative that Sizer is spurred to search for solutions.

Sizer's solutions are structured in terms of aims and curriculum proposals. Sizer lists four goals: literacy, numeracy, civic understanding, and sound character. The first three goals are essential for responsible citizenship and government. Literacy means the ability to understand ideas and arguments to the extent that they can be used. Numeracy refers to the ability to use numbers and to understand concepts, relationships, and logic in mathematical thought. Civic understanding involves a comprehension of democratic government, a respect for its processes, and an acceptance of its obligations.

The state, beyond expecting rudimentary civility, has no right to shape the citizen's personality. As for character education, Sizer asserts that it would be "impossible" and "repugnant" for schools to attempt to produce philosopher kings or moral revolutionaries (though he does not explain the basis for his conviction). Character education should focus on decency, which consists of fairness, generosity, and tolerance. These values would be taught by example and the influence of school itself; the values themselves, however, would need to be made explicit. Ironically, for example, Sizer stresses "a political philosophy [which is] essentially associated with American constitutionalism" at the same time he denounces the principle of church-state separation as an artificial abridgment on socialization (Sizer tends to mix Jeffersonian meritocracy and Judeo-Christian credo; Sizer 1984, 133). In this light, Sizer's argument, though couched in more general, sophisticated language, seems not too far removed from some recent neo-conservative recommendations (*vide* William Bennett) for a return to a "Boy Scout bag" of virtues in character education.

Sizer's curriculum would be divided into four areas or large departments:

1. inquiry and expression
2. mathematics and science
3. literature and the arts
4. philosophy and history

By "inquiry and expression," Sizer means all kinds of communication, including writing, visual communication, gesture, and physical nuance. "Literature and the arts" would seek common ground among literature, music, and art. The departments of mathematics and science would be merged and computer science would help by serving as an adhesive. History can be approached through biography and autobiography to make it less abstract; then, in order better to understand events, concepts from geography, sociology, and economics can be introduced. The study of political philosophy promotes enlightened citizenship, and inquiry in elementary ethics develops intellectual skills and promotes students' interests.

But why so few subjects? The reason pertains to Whitehead's dictum not to teach too many subjects and that whatever you teach, teach thoroughly. Sizer would like to see students learn more while being taught less. Information is plentiful, but learning how to use it is more demanding. Compulsory schooling should end upon demonstration of a "mastery of the minima"; and since most students can do so before senior high school, schooling at that level will be voluntary. Secondary schools, then, would award diplomas upon demonstrated mastery rather than after four years of study or the collection of a stipulated number of credits.

The curriculum in the secondary schools studied equates disparate courses on the basis of hours taken (e.g., physical education and physics), a rationale is lacking for most subjects, a coherent sequence across subjects is missing (e.g., reading skills as a precondition for reading history), and the curriculum lacks a coherent whole. A standardized curriculum based on master plans of cities, states, or the nation is insufficient; the curriculum should arise out of the conditions peculiar to each school.

Sizer believes that his curriculum will avoid this fragmentation and the other problems enumerated, that is, electives will be accommodated within each of the four broad areas, vocational education will be learned on the job, foreign language study would not be encouraged until students mastered their own language, there would be no tracking (in the form of honors, college preparatory, and the like) because students would be expected to progress at their own pace.

Motivation to pursue the curriculum successfully would be based on developing a more positive self-concept and stronger learning incentives. This means that students will need someone whom they respect that believes in them and gives them responsibility. This assumes that students will respond to a challenge and that schooling can be personalized so that teachers can know students as individuals. Each student needs to succeed at something and from that success move on to other important things. Students are also better motivated to learn in good schools: these are schools that are challenging rather than threatening, have standards, are stable, clear about their mission; in sum—fair and decent places that deserve loyalty.

In appraising the Sizer study, one is struck by the numerous and vivid examples that, although sometimes unnecessarily lengthy, afford fruitful suggestions for implementing instruction. The aims are clear and distinct and relate closely to citizenship responsibility. The curriculum exhibits flexibility, ferrets out essentials, and avoids the fragmentation in the traditional subject curriculum. Sizer's conviction that students should learn more while being taught less provides a basic principle to undergird the curriculum, and his ideas about motivation may facilitate mastery of the material.

However, Sizer predicates goals primarily on fulfilling the requirements of the state for citizenship responsibilities. The relationship of numeracy to citizenship is not developed; undoubtedly, a stronger case could be made for its relation to occupations. More importantly, why the state should be given precedence over individual and group interests is not shown. The individual needs not only to develop skills to assess and criticize state policies and programs but afforded an education that promotes self-realization and actualization. Whereas one might assent to Sizer's goal of character education, his treatment is woefully lacking and ignores research in moral education for the past several decades.

The call for a simpler, more unified program is admirable when juxtaposed with the traditional subject curriculum, but Sizer fails to make clear why the structure of the disciplines approach is not a satisfactory alternative to the traditional curriculum. His own curricular proposals are a mere bare-bones sketch and vital matters of sequence, articulation, and integration remain untreated. He produces no research to demonstrate that the attractive Whiteheadian principle is pedagogically sound. Nor is Sizer's curriculum as rich and resplendent with open possibilities as is that envisioned by Whitehead. After all, as Sizer well knows, Whitehead chastised "the fatal disconnection of subjects which kills the vitality of our modern curriculum" and argued that "there is only one subject-matter for education, and that is Life in all of its manifestations."[1]

Thus, despite their modern humanistic trappings, Sizer's curricular aims take on a kind of "perennialist" or "essentialist" edge and appearance. Their focus might seem narrowly academic to contemporary scholars and practitioners who have long ago abandoned such doctrines as "mental discipline" and "transfer of learning" (at least since the turn of the twentieth century and the discoveries of more rigorous researchers). With the Paideia Group, Sizer explicitly resuscitates such schoolroom ghosts and goblins as "intellectual training" and "developing mental powers"—and even aiding pupils to "exercise their minds" (as if such processes were largely akin to "muscular" exercise).

COMPARISON OF CURRENT REPORTS

Sizer's study can be placed in clearer perspective by briefly comparing it to three other influential nationally sponsored reports. These reports are *A Nation at Risk*, undertaken by a commission created by former Secretary of Education T. H. Bell (National Commission on Excellence in Education 1983), Mortimer Adler's *The Paideia Proposal* (Adler 1982), and Ernest Boyer's Carnegie Report titled *High School* (Boyer 1983). Although each of the three reports refers either directly or indirectly to goals, none of them provides a sufficiently adequate justification for the goals chosen; therefore, our attention will be given to brief comparisons of their curricular proposals with *Horace's Compromise*. An adequate justification of goals should include relating goal choices to value statements and a delineation of the linkage between the goals and the curriculum.

A Nation at Risk is written in a strident, urgent style employing military metaphors reminiscent of the Sputnik era. Warning that the nation stands on the verge of losing its pre-eminence as a world leader in industry and commerce because of its education failures, the commission recommends a high school curriculum for all students consisting of three years each of English, mathematics, science, and social studies, and one-half year of computer science. The college-bound student would be required to take two years of a foreign language. The commission generally believes that more is better—more homework, a longer school day and school year—though research supporting this claim is not presented.

Sizer eloquently tries to dispute the "more is better" syndrome. His curriculum is more innovative and offers a more flexible, unified approach than *A Nation at Risk*.

The Paideia Proposal attempts to provide a liberal and general education for every student and is a required curriculum that provides no electives or specialized courses. Electives, Adler holds, are appropriate for different forms of preparation for the professions or technical careers at the postsecondary level. Adler's curriculum is subject not only to the usual criticisms of required curriculums, but is probably also inconsistent with Adler's goal of preparation for good citizenship if it is held that students, at least in part, become good citizens by learning to make intelligent choices, in proportion to their maturity and judgment, about critical decisions that affect their lives, which would include some responsibility for curriculum choice. However, Sizer agrees with—and emphasizes—Adler's commitment to the importance of teacher (1) questioning and (2) "coaching" as essential vehicles for pedagogical practice in habituating students to cognitive skill development.

Boyer's Carnegie Report studies fifteen divergent high schools in all sections of the country. The report advocates a core curriculum to be structured around those ideas, experiences, and traditions that are significant at a particular time in history. These shared experiences include history, use of symbols, group and institutional membership, need for well-being, relation to nature, and our dependence on technology. The required courses of the core would constitute two-thirds of the total units needed for graduation. The last two years of high school would be considered a "transition school" where half the time is devoted to the core and the other half to elective clusters.

The two strongest features of the Boyer Report are clearly stated goals and the exceptional balance of the curriculum as a whole. The principal weaknesses are the lack of a rationale for goal selection, a failure to use unifying themes in the curriculum, and problems in mandating a required curriculum.

In conclusion, certain similarities were identified between *Horace's Compromise* and Silberman's *Crisis in the Classroom*. In comparison with the three recent national reports under review, Boyer's *High School* would seem to offer the most reasonable alternative to *Horace's Compromise* because it provides the greatest curriculum balance; yet it still is afflicted with problems besetting a subject curriculum. Thus those seeking the virtues of simplicity and adaptability to divergent student populations in a broad fields approach will turn eagerly to *Horace's Compromise*. At the same time, Sizer's study will also remind others of a romantic return to a more "princely" form of education, which may be more attuned to a laissez-faire classical liberalism and attendant "enlightened elites" of the nineteenth century than it is to any modern-day vision of participatory democracy. In this sense, Sizer's puzzling humanism bespeaks both challenge and threat to public secondary education as it might exist in future democratic societies:

Compulsory attendance in an educational instituion should cease when a young citizen demonstrates mastery of the minima, and most young citizens should master these minima before senior high school. As a result, schooling for most adolescents would be voluntary. Few would be compelled to attend high school, though a prudent state would vigorously encourage it. High school would be an opportunity, not an obligation. (Sizer 1984, 88)

NOTE

1. A. N. Whitehead. 1929, as cited in Sizer (1984, 114).

12

Is Continuing Education Anything More than a Yuppie Phenomenon?

Paul C. Violas

The issue of equity surfaces whenever Americans conduct any large-scale activity. Continuing education—for the purpose of this chapter defined as including all organized learning activities participated in on a part-time basis—enrolled 21,252,000 Americans in 1981 (National Center 1982, 9). This represented 12.8 percent of the total adult U.S. population. Computations based on Wagner's estimates indicate direct costs for continuing education exceeded $14.8 billion in 1980 (1982, 277–278). Continuing education is a large-scale endeavor in the United States. Not surprisingly, issues concerning the distribution of continuing education services have troubled writers in the field for several decades. Recent works that address the question generally cite the National Center for Educational Statistic's *Participation in Adult Education, 1981* (1982) as the authoritative source for participation data.

Thus let us first turn to some selected demographic data from this report concerning participants in continuing education. The most significant data involve the age, sex, educational background, ethnicity, family income, occupation, geographic region of the participants, the participants' sources of funding, and the type of courses taken.

In 1981 the 21.25 million total participants in continuing education represented a 17 percent increase over 1978 participation. The majority (54 percent) were under 35 years old and only 12 percent were 55 years old or over. Not only were young adults the majority of participants but they were overrepresented as a percent of their age group. In contrast, older adults were significantly under-represented (National Center 1982, 3).

Figure 1
Age-Group Participation Rates in Adult Education, by Sex

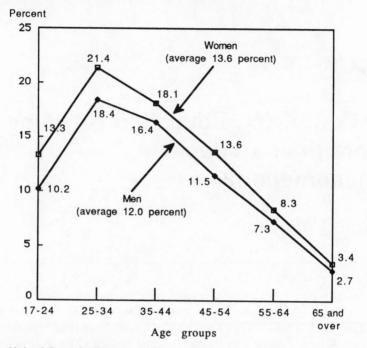

Source: National Center for Educational Statistics 1982, 4.

Female participants were 56 percent of the total in continuing education. They also participated at higher rates than males in every age category. Furthermore, white, black, and Hispanic females all participated in higher numbers than their male counterparts (National Center 1982, 4). Figure 1 illustrates the age and gender of participants.

The racial and ethnic breakdown of participants shows white non–Hispanics at 88 percent, black non–Hispanics at 6 percent, and Hispanics at 3.6 percent of the total. Only white non–Hispanics were overrepresented. Thus the racial and ethnic inequities displayed in secondary and higher education are replicated in continuing education (National Center 1982, 4–5).

The pattern of participation according to educational background shows that the most well educated were the most highly represented. Over 44 percent of the participants had at least one year of college. As summarized by the Center: "The level of participation in adult education is directly related to the level of education: as educational levels increase, the rate of participation increases" (National Center 1982, 5). The following chart indicates the educational background of participants. Participation rates showed a similar pattern when annual family income rather than previous education was the criteria. Rates ranged from

Table 1

Educational background	% of the total participants in continuing education
0-8 years of school	2.2
9-11 years	5.6
12 years	11.1
13-15 years	19.6
16 years	26.1
17 or more years	31.1

Source: National Center for Educational Statistics 1982, 5.

6.3 percent with family income of less than $9,000 to 18.8 percent over $50,000. About 58 percent of the participants had family income of more than $20,000. Only 23.3 percent had family incomes of less than $15,000 (National Center 1982, 8). Clearly, continuing education has its greatest constituency among the more affluent.

An overwhelming majority of the male (90.1 percent) and female (70.3 percent) participants were employed; 70 percent of the participants were in white-collar jobs and only 30 percent in blue-collar occupations. Among the male participants, 30.4 percent were from professional jobs, 18.4 percent from the crafts, and 17.1 percent were managers or administrators. Of the female participants, 31.8 percent were clerical workers, 12.8 percent service workers, 11.4 percent teachers, 10.7 percent health workers, and 10 percent were "other professionals" (National Center 1982, 9–10).

In geographic terms, urban areas were overrepresented when compared to rural, and the western states topped the list, followed by the north-central, northeast, and south. These data reflect, in part, relative cost and ease of access to continuing education (National Center 1982, 8).

Perhaps the most suggestive data presented by the National Center report related to reasons cited by participants for taking courses. Job-related reasons were most frequently cited. Interestingly, 69 percent of the courses taken by men were reported as job-related, whereas women reported only 54 percent. Moreover, the men's percentages of job-related courses is higher at every age with the gap increasing as age increases (National Center 1982, 11–15). Figure 2 shows this relationship.

These data take on added significance when it is revealed that 54 percent of the courses taken by women are paid for by themselves or family compared to 39 percent for men. Moreover, 41 percent of the courses taken by men are paid

Figure 2
Proportion of Courses Taken by Men and Women for Job-Related Reasons, by Age Group

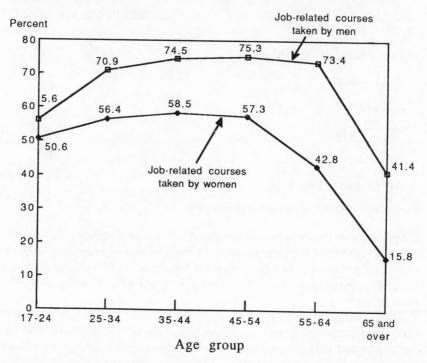

Source: National Center for Educational Statistics 1982, 15.

for by employers compared to 26 percent for women. The relative proportion of women taking courses for job-related reasons, the distribution of occupations of participants, and the percent of courses paid for by employers—when analyzed on a gender basis—collectively indicate that, in terms of economic and occupational status outcomes, males are better served by continuing education. These patterns undoubtedly reflect historical biases embedded in the American occupational structure. It can be expected that if, and/or when, the discriminatory patterns against women are eliminated in the professional and managerial occupations, the percentages of women in nonjob-related courses, such as home economics, slimnastics, and flower arranging, will decline as the percentages in job-related courses increase.

The National Center's statistics suggest a rather clear pattern and a somewhat unambiguous answer to the question posed in the title of this chapter. As John G. Keane recently stated, "Participation in adult education courses varies directly with educational attainment, employment in professional and technical occu-

pations, and family income'' (1985). Continuing education best and most frequently services the white, non–Hispanic, relatively young, male, professional,
and affluent client (Cross 1984, 33–34; Nordhaug 1983, 29–37; Stacey and
Charner 1982, 331). The conclusion that continuing education is primarily a
Yuppie phenomenon, however, is only the beginning of our task for it simply
answers the least interesting of the questions that can be raised about the data.
The more important and interesting questions are: Should continuing education
be primarily a Yuppie phenomenon? Why is it so? And, how can it be changed?
The remainder of this chapter addresses these questions.

The question of whether continuing education should be a Yuppie phenomenon
raises issues of equity, democratic participation in our social, political, and
economic institutions, and conceptions of human potential. An affirmative answer
would be based on the following assumptions: (1) human potential is fixed
relatively early in life, either by genetic or environmental determination; and (2)
our society is and should be divided into two major groups—a well-educated
minority of experts should be the leaders and pacesetters in all sectors of endeavor, whereas the less able majority should be trained for subordinate roles
and lives. These assumptions are widely held among centerists and right wing
politicians, educators, evangelical religious leaders, and social scientists. They
will lead to a rigidly stratified society, perhaps even efficient social and economic
organization, and will help to keep the cost of education at a minimum. These
assumptions, however, will not allow democratic participation. They condemn
the majority to relative ignorance and social and economic dependency as the
educational gap continues to increase at an accelerating rate (Cross 1985).

An alternative set of assumptions argues that: (1) human potential is limited
only by motivation and the availability of effective educational opportunity; (2)
our society should be genuinely democratic—each participant should have equal
weight in social, political, and economic decisions; and (3) this democratic
participation can best be facilitated by effective education for all segments of
the population. Such assumptions seemed to motivate the U.S. Congress to pass
a series of laws during the late 1970s whose objectives were to extend educational
opportunities to those adults previously underserved by continuing education.
Unfortunately, the Reagan administration caused at least a temporary delay in
the effective implementation of these objectives (Christoffel 1982, 379–389;
Hadley 1982, 8–11). For those of us who subscribe to the latter set of assumptions, the important questions become (1) why does continuing education fail to
serve all segments of the population as effectively as it does the Yuppies; and
(2) what can be done to change this configuration of service? Why does continuing
education serve the young, affluent, well-educated professional and technical
worker more effectively than other groups? The answers are complex and to
some extent specific to various subgroups. It should be emphasized that the
following type of analysis refers to groups rather than specific individuals within
these groups. Whereas group analysis provides vital information for continuing

education planners and administrators, one should recognize that individuals within those groups will differ considerably in motivation, drive, and life experiences.

It is perhaps most expeditious to examine first why Yuppies are so well served. One important reason is the perceived relationship between continuing education and job-effectiveness for this group. Both the individuals and the employers believe that continuing education courses may improve job performance. Thus employers are willing not only to suggest or require participation, but to subsidize it. Moreover, both the Yuppies and their employers have the political and economic power and influence to effect the availability of such courses. In addition, the kinds of courses needed to increase job-effectiveness for Yuppies fit the pattern of traditional higher education. Courses in computer technology or management techniques and quality control circles or laser technology for surgeons or high energy physics for engineers will not offend academic sensibilities or raise the specter of diluted standards in any educational delivery agency. Moreover, the Yuppies need not fear continuing education courses. By definition, they have been successful in educational institutions. Yuppies have been socialized to believe that they will continue to achieve in academic settings and that such academic success will lead directly to economic, social, and political success in life: They are well aware that they are the educational elite. Lastly, Yuppies tend to live in urban and other areas where continuing education is most readily available. This advantage is compounded by a ready access to transportation facilities not enjoyed by many non–Yuppies. To varying degrees, one or more of these factors do not work in favor of non–Yuppie subgroups who are underserved by continuing education.

The most important synthetic analysis of research on why adults do not participate in continuing education has been done by K. Patricia Cross. She has developed an interesting tripartite classification scheme for categorizing the various obstacles to participation in continuing education. Her categories are: (1) "situational barriers"; (2) "institutional barriers"; and (3) "dispositional barriers" (Cross 1981, 97–108). If we apply these categories to groups underserved by continuing education, we can begin to see why the obstacles are indeed considerable. Situational barriers include the obstacles arising from one's life situation, that is, the objective conditions of life, such as home responsibilities, objections of family and friends, lack of time or a place to study, absence of child care facilities, job responsibilities, inadequate finances for tuition, books, or transportation. Cross reports that obstacles in this category are most frequently cited by respondents to survey research (Cross 1981, 100). It is easy to understand that those at the lower end of the socioeconomic structure are most adversely affected by these barriers. One item worthy of detailed analysis as exemplary in this category is the cost of continuing education.

Some studies (Johnstone and Rivera 1965; Penland 1979; Boshier and Baker 1979) suggest that cost is overrated as an obstacle. When applied to low income groups, however, the compelling evidence, as well as common sense, indicates that it is a severe barrier. The substantial use of the G.I. Bill, the dramatic drop in continuing education registration in California following the passage of Proposition 13, and Bishop and Van Dyk's study of Viet Nam veterans (1977) all indicate that cost is highly significant (Geiogue 1982). Cross notes that cost "probably constitutes a significant barrier for precisely those population subgroups who could profit most from adult learning—the young, ethnic minorities, and the educationally and economically disadvantaged" (1981, 103).

It is ironic but not out of character with the structure of educational delivery services in the United States that the more financially advantaged are generally provided the most highly subsidized continuing education. Gregory B. Smith reveals a very large continuing education effort by the private sector. He noted that "the conclusion is inescapable that training through company courses in working hours, the most prevalent mode, was disproportionately concentrated on providing managerial and other white-collar skills" (Smith 1982, 310–311). He emphasizes that "manual workers receive a disproportionately small share of formal training" (313). Moreover, he presents evidence that shows that much of the formal training provided for manual workers is in the area of safety training (308).

Institutional barriers constitute Cross's second category. These barriers include those institutional practices and procedures that make it difficult for adults to become students. They include inconvenient scheduling of courses, complicated red tape involved in enrollment, location of courses, program requirements, and ineffective publicity for courses. Again, it is not difficult to see that these obstacles pertain with special emphasis to those at the lower end of the socioeconomic structure—those least well served by continuing education. The most often cited problems relate to inconvenient location and scheduling.

Whereas relatively few of survey respondents indicate that insufficient information about continuing education opportunities is a problem, Cross indicates that this relative absence of concern itself may indicate lack of information (Cross 1981, 104–105). Gordon G. Darkenwald suggests that between one-fourth to one-third of all adults have little knowledge of continuing education opportunities. He notes, "Low SES [socioeconomic status] adults, and those living in rural areas, are particularly likely to be unaware of adult learning opportunities or sources of information about them" (Darkenwald 1980, 5).

One probable reason for this knowledge gap about continuing education opportunities is that continuing educators too often rely on publicity mediums such as newspapers, posters, radio, and television, which are highly effective with the middle class but relatively ineffective with lower socioeconomic groups (Darkenwald and Larson 1980; Smith 1983).

We focused on the information barrier as an example of institutional barriers because it seems to have a logical priority. Whereas all of the obstacles clustered in this category represent significant barriers especially for the lower socioeconomic groups, solving the others without attending to the information issue would probably affect little change in participation rates.

Cross's third category, "dispositional barriers," relates to attitudes about self that preclude potential learners from participating in continuing education. They include fear of failure, concern for age, lack of self-confidence, and general negative attitudes toward education. Cross indicates these barriers are "probably underestimated in survey data" because individuals hesitate to register what they think may be socially undesirable attitudes (Cross 1981, 106–107). It is all too easy to see dispositional barriers as a "problem" with the learner. Such a conclusion may oversimplify a complex problem in social psychology. It is a mistake that continuing education can ill afford.

Let us analyze the fear of failure and general negative attitude toward education as an example of the dispositional barriers. A frequent but shallow response to learners with these attitudes is the following: they do not like school because of past problems they experienced in school. The problems were caused by a lack of academic ability and/or motivation; probably stemming from a bad home environment and/or low intelligence. These potential students will probably not do well in continuing education just as they did not do well in previous schooling.

An alternate analysis, however, suggests that their past problems in public school were not caused by low intelligence or a lack of innate ability; rather, that the public schools are essentially middle-class institutions that demonstrate a rigid class bias against lower SES students. Class bias is exhibited in the schools' social linguistic and value orientations, which make it extremely difficult for lower SES students to succeed. Lower SES students learn that school is an alien culture in which they are failures. This intensive socialization process results in the attitudes displayed by these students. Our analysis suggests that it is the public schools who have failed to teach (rather than a failure in the students). And even more unfortunately, schools have developed attitudes in lower SES students that make participation in continuing education very unlikely. In point of fact, these students are the very ones who most need the opportunity for continuing education (Bloom 1976, 1981; deLone 1979; Stubbs 1976; Violas 1978). It is the obligation for continuing educators to provide avenues to facilitate these opportunities.

One rarely discussed problematic area that seems to contribute to the dispositional obstacles category is the labor market segmentation or the occupational structure in the United States (Levin and Tobin 1982). Most schooling in the United States, including continuing education, is pragmatically based with economic security and occupational mobility the presumed outcome. In continuing education, this is reflected in the very high proportion of individuals who indicate they are enrolled in continuing education classes for job-related reasons. The rationale that motivates most Americans into educational endeavors asserts that more education will increase the individual's productive capacity, thus making him or her more attractive to present or prospective employers. The result will be promotions up the job ladder, increased wages, security, and higher occupational status. This rationale assumes that most occupations require some manual and/or cognitive skills and that these requirements increase as one ascends the occupational structure. It also presupposes the existence of a hierarchical job ladder in occupations and employing institutions. In social science literature, these ideas are embedded in the theories of human capital and functional stratification. They are most compelling to individuals whose employment experiences demonstrate objective conditions that closely approximate the assumptions of the rationale.

Unfortunately, the occupational structure in the United States does not conform to these assumptions. Since the beginning of this century and with increasing intensity since World War II, the U.S. labor market has been segmented into primary and secondary labor markets. The primary labor market mainly employs white, non–Hispanic, well-educated, affluent males. It is this labor market that most closely approximates the above assumption. This sector, however, has not been increasing in size. The secondary labor market employs the vast majority of females, Hispanics, Blacks, the least well educated and least affluent, and is the only rapidly growing segment of the employment sector. This labor market is characterized with jobs requiring little manual or cognitive skills, repetitive and nonimaginative routine, and does not have job ladders. Many of its jobs are considered "dead-ends" (Braverman 1974; Grubb and Lazerson 1975; Violas 1978, 1981).

It is not surprising that workers from the primary labor market are overrepresented as participants in continuing education. Nor should anyone be entirely puzzled when we discover that those from the secondary labor markets are underrepresented as participants. Neither group of workers are displaying irrational behavior. Their respective responses to continuing education are based in the objective conditions of their work experiences and their realistic expectations.

The rationale that motivates most people to participate in continuing education simply does not conform to the occupational reality experienced by workers from the secondary labor markets. Their jobs are the lowest paid, repetitive, and do not require much, if any, cognitive or manual skill. There are few, if any, promotional rings on the job ladder. The few that exist require little additional skills and hence little additional education. In the secondary labor market, the only way up is out. That is, escape requires an entirely new occupation in a different sector of the labor market. Such a move, however, requires an entirely different set of credentials. It is not accomplished by incremental improvement in existing credentials. Escape generally necessitates full-time study or an extremely long-term commitment to part-time study. Unfortunately, full-time study is usually economically impossible for workers from the secondary labor market and part-time study usually seems like an impossibly difficult road to travel. Sadly, the few who with dogged determination make the arduous journey often find that prospective employers view their part-time degrees as less valuable than the new four-year B.A. graduates.

The above discussion may cause some to speculate that continuing education is an enterprise that can offer little of interest or value for workers from secondary labor markets. This is neither the intended nor the correct conclusion. Continuing education is potentially both interesting to and valuable for all humans. Unfortunately, the current structures and goals of continuing education are not conducive to stimulating interest in all segments of society. Our task is to creatively design structures and goals that render continuing education equally serviceable to non-Yuppie groups.

We have examined the extent and characteristics of participants and nonparticipants and surveyed the barriers to participation in continuing education. What remains is to analyze ways to reduce the barriers with the hope of increasing participation especially among those groups traditionally less well served. This is the most difficult, complex, and important aspect of our task. As Darkenwald and Larson have cautioned, "there are no simple solutions or formulas for success that can be applied to all situations" (Darkenwald and Larson 1980, 89). Furthermore, Shipp and McKenzie have warned that "programs planned on the basis of the personal orientation of the adult educator may meet the needs only of the active learners [those most well served] since the demographic and psychographic profile of the adult educator will in all probability most closely resemble that of the active learner" (Shipp and McKenzie 1981, 196).

Some of us may find our response to the problems of the less well served more constrained because of institutional and/or personal factors. Thus we suggest two different strategies for action. The "modest" strategy will suggest ways of increasing participation of the less well served without major changes in the structure or basic goals of the continuing education delivery systems. The "active" strategy, in addition to incorporating the suggestions of the modest strategy, proposes alternative structures and philosophies for current continuing education delivery systems.

The proposed modest strategy does not assail the current basic assumption underlying participation in continuing education, that is, that the basic objectives are job-related. Nor does it address the extant structure of delivery systems. Rather, it emphasizes the reduction of barriers such as self-image, cost, recruitment, and institutional constraints.

Many of the less well served have been socialized during their early school experiences to believe that they are educational losers. "Lack of self-confidence and low self-esteem, coupled with low verbal facility and the low perceived value of education commonly create high barriers to participation" (Irish 1980, 41). This negative self-image must be corrected if participation of this group is to be increased. There is no magic wand that once waved will turn a negative into a positive self-image. It entails long and difficult work. The beginning of the process will require selection of sensitive and empathic instructors and carefully graded course materials that will allow participants to develop both self-esteem as well as academic and verbal skills. Self-reported success stories may well stimulate interest among peers who might otherwise not have considered participation in continuing education.

It is clear that among the least well served the financial cost of participation represents a serious barrier. Continuing education must make every effort to reduce and when possible eliminate this barrier. Unfortunately, all too often this policy decision is not made directly by continuing educators. Nevertheless, we can attempt to influence decision makers in our state legislatures, the directorships of foundations, the board rooms of industry, business, and higher education. Our task here is to act as educators and as a pressure group.

Recruitment is an area where we can make a direct impact. The important factor to keep in mind is that the least well served often do not respond to the recruitment techniques that are successful with Yuppie types. Mass media publicity has proven a disappointment in recruitment of our target population (Darkenwald and Larson 1980; Irish 1980; Knox 1984; Smith 1983). The traditional media-based publicity campaign must be supplemented with direct recruitment. The most effective is through community agencies, local community personnel as recruiters, and peer recruiters (Irish 1980). M. C. Mulvey has probably not greatly overstated the case when he said, ''Every successful program of recruitment in the United States has relied primarily upon a personal invitation to attend the classes from a member of the student's own peer group'' (Mulvey 1969, 3). The utilization of successful students from the target population to act as recruiters among their nonparticipating peers in the local community may prove effective.

An incisive examination of institutional practices may reveal ways we can reduce institutional barriers. Typical questions we should ask are: Can we schedule classes at a time more convenient for our target population? Have we reduced the red tape for registration and matriculation enough to uncomplicate the process for our target population? Are classes located in places that are familiar to and accessible for the target population? Are the program requirements and course prerequisites realistic for the target population? Too often we erect institutional barriers not by design but from lack of foresight or understanding. We must become intimately acquainted with the life situations of the less well served in order to modify and simplify our institutional practices so they cease being insurmountable barriers to participants.

It should be emphasized that we must move on all the above fronts simultaneously. These barriers act in concert to reduce participation. It will be less than effective to reduce one obstacle while leaving the others in place. Any single barrier may be enough to discourage a potential participant. A multidimensional effort is required.

For those who wish to move rapidly and dramatically to increase participation among the less well served, it may be desirable to supplement the modest strategy outlined above with an active strategy. The proposed active strategy emphasizes nonjob-related goals as basic to the philosophy underlying continuing education programs for the less well served. It also seeks to develop alternative community-based and community-controlled delivery systems. We outline this active strategy with reference to two of the less well served groups: older adults (those over 65 years) and Hispanics.

Older adults represent one of the most rapidly increasing subgroups in our society. By the turn of the century, it is projected that they will constitute over 17 percent of the total U.S. population. Yet they remain one of the most underrepresented groups served by continuing education. Phileon B. Robinson's fine article, "Education for Older Adults" (1983) can be used profitably as a guide for continuing educators concerned with this population. Many of the following ideas are culled from his work.

Program developers should remember that interests and needs of older adults are somewhat different from the general population. They have little interest in amassing credits or developing skills for future employment. The interaction of health and energy levels, concerns for safety and physical access are heightened in this group. They seem most attracted by opportunities to meet people, for recreation, self-improvement, and to examine new and interesting ideas. Typically, they indicate a need for programmatic responses to everyday problems such as how to negotiate governmental bureaucracies, managing retirement incomes, dietary and health concerns.

Few continuing educators have the background, training, and knowledge to develop programs and courses for older adults that will account for their needs and interests without considerable input from them. Moreover, one effective method of publicizing courses is to involve the potential students in the planning stages. For these reasons, it makes a great deal of sense for older adults' continuing education to be community-based and community-controlled. At the very least, there should be an advisory board composed of older adults. Many cities have retirement homes, older adult centers, and even self-contained, older adult communities. These entities often have self-governing boards that could provide an effective entree for the continuing educator to develop a community-based program for older adults.

Hispanic-Americans are the second group we examine with respect to the active strategies for improving participation in continuing education. (The following ideas generally apply to other ethnic minorities such as Blacks, Native Americans, Laotians, or Vietnamese immigrants.) Hispanics number almost 15 million in the United States, have an alarming school dropout rate, high illiteracy, and high unemployment rates. Those who are employed are concentrated in the menial, dead-end jobs in the secondary labor market. They live in areas that receive the poorest and least public services. It is not an overstatement or inflammatory to say that Hispanics have been and continue to be victims of our social, economic, political, and educational structures. Continuing education has been even less successful than the public schools in serving Hispanics.

Nevertheless, Thomas W. Heaney has documented some examples of success—the Universidad Popular and the Instituto del Progreso Latino in Chicago; Liberacion Learning Center in south Florida; and Project Literacy in San Francisco (1983). There are several common characteristics in those programs. They are all community-based and community-controlled. They are action-oriented in the Paulo Freire tradition with the action being collective and aimed against their oppressors, that is, landlords, employers, governmental agencies, and the public schools. Their collective power is also aimed at improving human rights and opening employment opportunities.

Most interestingly, this kind of action not only took place within an educational setting, but it stimulated learning. Universidad Popular's pass record on the G.E.D. examination, for example, was 400 percent higher than that of the City of Chicago. And none of these programs has experienced recruitment difficulties.

Especially for socially and economically oppressed (disadvantaged is perhaps a more polite term) groups, learning becomes meaningful and vital when put in a context of their own daily problems and oppressions. As our participation rates amply demonstrate, these groups do not respond positively to "traditional" programs. What logic and common sense tell us and experience demonstrates is that they need the opportunity and occasion to develop their own goals, programs, and structures for continuing education. The continuing educator who approaches these communities with his or her programs and courses will experience faint response. Those, however, who go into the Hispanic community as resource persons, willing to help Hispanics develop their own educational programs, can expect an enthusiastic response, a great amount of active learning, and community mobilization. Incidentally, they can also expect to be considered mavericks by their superiors and will undoubtedly find the institutional structures poised to cut funding for the programs.

The examples of older adults and Hispanics indicate that for some groups the traditional goals and structures of continuing education are inappropriate. As with any group, educational programs work most effectively if they are aimed at the particular needs, aspirations, and problems of the group. For groups whose demographic characteristics and life situations differ considerably from the continuing education, these goals and structures can best be ascertained by the group itself. Community control not only helps to develop effective programs and courses, but it assures that only sensitive teachers will be retained. As an added bonus, community control publicizes the effort among potential learners. Lastly, it should be remembered that for these groups, the traditional job-related objectives of continuing education are often secondary when they exist at all.

If we are to take seriously the task of increasing significantly the participation of the least well served in continuing education, the effort needed is almost overwhelming. It will require careful planning along multidimensional lines. We must open new sources of funding against a backdrop of general retrenchment in educational spending. It will be necessary to violate some of the cannons of the professoriate and offend long-established sensibilities of our guild. And when most effective, especially with lower socioeconomic groups, we will be considered a nuisance rather than an educator by the establishment. The risk of ignoring the challenge, however, is even greater (London 1981). For if we do, we will be forced to agree with L. Steven Zwerling's conclusions that continuing education is a "breeder of inequality" and "is potentially the most unequal segment of organized educational activity. The key 'entrance requirement' (educational itself) recapitulates all the inequities existing in the social structure'' (Zwerling 1982, 19).

If continuing education continues to be primarily a Yuppie phenomenon, our sense of social justice may suggest that continuing education does not deserve to continue.

13

Teachers, Their World, and Their Work: A Review of the Idea of "Professional Excellence" in School Reform Reports

Richard J. Altenbaugh

Amidst the flurry of recent policy studies in education, three have received considerable notoriety, have been reviewed extensively, and will more than likely significantly influence the current movement for school reform. John Goodlad's (1984) *A Place Called School: Prospects for the Future* has the broadest scope since it encompasses elementary as well as secondary education. This particular study employed a large field staff to record firsthand observations, specifically surveyed 1,350 teachers at all levels, and interviewed 956 of them. Ernest Boyer's (1983) *High School: A Report of Secondary Education in America* and Theodore Sizer's (1984) *Horace's Comprise: The Dilemma of the American High School* represent more specific treatises through their emphasis on secondary education. Boyer's endeavor received substantial backing from the prestigious Carnegie Foundation for the Advancement of Teaching, and included data from 15 high schools. Sizer, meanwhile, personally visited over two score American secondary schools as well as utilized a sizeable field staff. He presents his findings through a series of vignettes and in a readable, almost literary style. The studies treat a broad range of topics, namely educational goals, students, curricula, classroom routines, as well as a host of recommendations for reforming the schools. Of course, each of these policy studies addresses the subject of the teacher—albeit some more comprehensively than others.

This chapter analyzes how these three reform reports collectively treat the topic of teachers and concomitant reforms to improve teaching. First, it summarizes their findings about teachers and their recommendations for the betterment of teaching. Second, through a review of the historical literature, it points to the shortcomings inherent within these reports. Third, it argues that these reform reports fail to grapple with many of the more profound problems plaguing the schools and stresses that history represents a fundamental tool in policy analysis.

THE CONDITIONS OF TEACHING

When addressing the circumstances of teaching, these policy-makers paint a bleak picture. Generally, teachers face poor working conditions. Goodlad observes that the typical work week for the teacher is "a combination of the flexible schedule normally associated with blue-collar jobs and a little of the flexibility associated with a profession . . . " (Goodlad 1984, 169). Teachers work an average week that spans thirty-seven to fifty hours. Goodlad's figure compares favorably with the average forty-seven-hour week found by the National Education Association.

To make matters worse, high school teachers, as Sizer found, largely devote their instructional time to the frustrating chore of motivating uninterested students amidst innumerable, petty interruptions. In addition to actual instructional responsibilities, Boyer notes that teachers must perform a myriad of menial tasks, particularly the dreaded lunchroom, hallway, and chaperone duties. Moreover, teachers must assume clerical burdens, turn in lesson plans to building principals each week (in advance), maintain elaborate student attendance records, and counsel students. Poor job conditions are further evidenced by supply shortages, and sometimes dirty and antiquated facilities. Likewise, the threat of violence plagues many teachers. According to Boyer, "one-third of New York City [high school] teachers and one-fourth of those elsewhere said they had been assaulted. Forty percent reported that violence is a daily concern" (Boyer 1983, 159).

Because they are underpaid, a large portion of teachers are forced to "moonlight" (Goodlad 1984, 170). Sizer reviews salary statistics and reports a "13 percent drop in public school teachers' real salaries from 1970 to 1980, and a 16 percent real reduction in the compensation for independent school teachers" (Sizer 1984, 185–187). Both Goodlad and Boyer cite statistics indicating that 29 percent of teachers in 1982 moonlighted during the school year, whereas 36 percent held extra summer jobs. This, of course, dramatically balloons the number of hours many teachers actually work each week as well as precludes the long "summer vacations" commonly attributed to teachers. "In sum," Boyer argues, "the teachers' world is often frustrating, frequently demeaning, and sometimes dangerous" (Boyer 1983, 159).

Teachers' work is also largely fragmented and isolated. Goodlad and Boyer, like sociologist Dan Lortie (1975), note the rather insular nature of teaching. "There was little in our data to suggest active, ongoing exchanges of ideas and practices across schools, between groups of teachers, or between individuals even in the same school" (Goodlad 1984; Boyer 1983, 158). This often lonely existence appears to contribute to a sense of alienation and powerlessness on the part of teachers. Teachers, to be sure, control classroom pedagogy, but little else. Teachers, Goodlad argues, "felt more potent concerning policies that govern students than policies directed at the teachers themselves" (Goodlad 1984, 190). Teachers conveyed a sense of being objectified to these researchers. Sizer nicely articulates this phenomenon:

Teachers are told the amount of time they are to spend with each class—say, fifty-five minutes five times a week. Even though they are expected to be competent scholars they are rarely trusted with the selection of the texts and teaching materials they are to use, a particularly galling insult. Teachers are rarely consulted, much less given significant authority, over the rules and regulations governing the life of their school; these usually come from "downtown." Rarely do they have any influence over who their immediate colleagues will be; again, "downtown" decides. . . . Teaching often lacks a sense of ownership, a sense among the teachers working together, that the school is theirs, and that its future and their reputation are indistinguishable. Hired hands own nothing, are told what to do, and have little stake in their enterprises. Teachers are often treated like hired hands. Not surprisingly, they act like hired hands. (Sizer 1984, 184)

Thus, a dichotomy exists between the rhetoric and the reality of teaching. Goodlad observes that "the practicing teacher . . . functions in a context when the beliefs and expectations are those of a profession but where the realities tend to constrain, likening actual practice to a trade" (Goodlad, 1984, 193).

How do these policy-makers confront the "proletarianization" of teaching? (Apple 1982). Their recommendations appear to focus on a total restructuring of the teachers' time, based largely on the professional model at the college and university levels. This includes the dissolution of noninstructional duties and the improvement of the intellectual climate of the school by fostering it as a "center of inquiry" (Boyer 1983, 159–160). Other suggestions range from the unrealistic to the pedestrian; specifically, a 25 percent jump in teacher salaries to creating an attractive physical plant and improving student discipline.

Boyer, in particular, dwells on "recognition and rewards" as well as the "professionalization" of teaching as a means of increasing the psychic payoff of teaching. His process to "renew teaching" includes an elaborate plan to honor "outstanding teachers" by school districts, colleges and universities, state governments, and through recognition from newspapers and businesses (Boyer 1983, 164–165). Mercifully, Sizer sees such "Teacher of the Year" awards as "patronizing" and "hollow" (Sizer 1984, 187). The professionalization of teaching, for Boyer, encompasses the recruitment of "gifted students" into teaching; improvement of teacher education; implementation of a "planned program" of continuing education for teachers; creation of a career ladder (again, reminiscent of the college/university professorial model); and, finally, enticement of part-time "lecturers" from business, government, law, and medicine to supplement the regular instructional staff. "If reforms such as those we have outlined were put in place," Boyer concludes, "teachers would, we believe, BE REGARDED as professionals, they would BE TREATED as professionals, and they would

CONSIDER THEMSELVES professionals. Above all, they would be better teachers and the quality of the school would be enhanced'' (Boyer 1983, 185).

WHITHER HISTORY?

Although these analyses of teaching conditions are insightful and necessary, the policy recommendations, given historical precedents, are unrealistic. These policy-makers have overlooked, for the most part, two crucial points. First, they have ignored the historical roots of centralized authority in school administration. Second, they have themselves objectified teachers in their treatment, and this, too, ignores historical tradition.

For all of their criticisms of the deleterious effects of the school bureaucracy, Goodlad, Boyer, and Sizer neither call for its total dissolution nor for its restructuring. They merely want to tinker with it. Ultimately, the teacher will continue to remain at the bottom of the decision-making apparatus. Not only do they offer cosmetic reforms regarding teacher participation in the decision process, but they unquestionably accept the political economy and its concomitant corporate mentality as a given. Yet, many of the problems that beset the schools are inherent in the corporate structure of the schools. Their proposed reforms strongly reflect, to be sure, a consensus outlook (Karier 1984). Boyer even goes so far as to urge closer bonds with corporations.

Ironically, during the early decades of this century, school administrators eagerly embraced the efficiency methods of corporate America as a panacea (Curti 1971; Tyack and Hansot 1982; Berman 1983). Raymond Callahan's (1962) classic historical study *Education and the Cult of Efficiency* illustrates the twofold impact of scientific management on the schools. First, centralized authority was seen as the best means of streamlining the top-down decision-making process. Second, all administrative judgments were based on cost effectiveness rather than on sound educational benefits. The results of these measures, as Callahan notes, were profound: "They saw schools not as centers of learning but as enterprises which were functioning efficiently if the students went through without failing and received their diplomas on schedule and if the operation were handled economically'' (Callahan 1962, 247). The schools were thus viewed as factories, the students as the raw material, and the teachers as workers. In order to increase the cost effectiveness of the teaching force, teachers had to endure efficiency ratings, assume larger classes, instruct for more periods, and participate less in decision making.

This historical process toward the increased segmentation and centralization of labor has not abated as revealed through such works as *Labor and Monopoly Capital: The Degradation of Work in the Twentieth Century* by Harry Braverman (1974) and, more recently, *Segmented Work, Divided Workers: The Historical Transformation of Labor in the United States* by David Gordon, Richard Edwards, and Michael Reich (1982). In this latter study, the authors maintain a historical perspective and argue that three overlapping stages have shaped the development of the labor process and labor markets in the United States since the early nineteenth century. These stages corresponded directly to economic crises that involved continuing and intense social class conflict, resolved only through structural changes that helped to shape the American working class. The first period, "the initial proletarianization of labor," began in the 1820s and continued through the 1890s, and saw the transformation of work to a wage-labor system (Ware 1964). The "homogenization of labor," the second stage, witnessed the profound transition of labor to a largely semiskilled experience. Control of the labor process shifted dramatically from workers to employers and their foremen who used either direct supervision or machines to "drive" the work process. As a result, skills were much less controlled by workers beginning in the 1870s until the onset of World War II (Taylor 1967; Montgomery 1979). The third period, "the segmentation of labor," began in the 1920s and continues to the present. Although the so-called drive-system did not totally disappear, it has been increasingly replaced in many sectors by a series of structured rules and incentives. As Gordon, Edwards, and Reich explicate it: "a crucial part of these arrangements included employer recognition of unions, grievance proce-dures, and seniority rules for layoffs and promotion; in return, employers gained discretion over changes in the organization of work, provided that increases in wages were granted in return for increases in productivity" (Gordon et al. 1983, 16). The work of salaried professionals, among them engineers, nurses, and teachers, has likewise experienced this segmentation process since the 1920s through the imposition of bureaucratic control (Schatz 1984).

Michael Apple (1982) traces the impact of this trend on teachers' work. This experience reflects the political economy, to be sure (Apple 1983). As Beyer states it: "Such processes of segmentation and isolation have, in many cases, become part of our collective consciousness, an unstated assumption in many kinds of activities. Through the tendency toward task analysis and the specialized division of labor, experience becomes increasingly fragmented" (Beyer 1983, 103).

One manifestation of this segmentation process is that curricula have become "commodified." Instructional packages that have standardized objectives, ac-tivities, and exercises, and evaluation instruments have been developed for mass distribution to schools. Teachers are thus divorced from the process of actually constructing materials that could embody specific, personal meanings and values. The routinization and depersonalization of teaching has effectively "deskilled" it, not unlike the segmented work of blue-collar factory workers (Beyer 1983). As Apple asserts, "the development of new forms of control, the process of deskilling, the separation of conception from execution, are not limited to fac-tories and offices. These tendencies intrude more and more into institutions like the school" (Apple 1983, 146).

Apple further outlines three kinds of control that can be employed to help extract more work—simple, technical, and bureaucratic. Simple control refers to blatant authoritarian assertiveness. But this has become less important as the size and complexity of production has increased, thus requiring more sophisticated forms of worker control. Technical control is imbedded in the physical structure of the workplace and relies heavily on advanced technology to direct the pace and skill level of the operation. Bureaucratic control represents the most subtle and least visible mode of control since "its principles are embodied within the hierarchical social relations of the workplace. Impersonal and bureaucratic rules concerning the direction of one's work, the procedures for evaluating performance, and sanctions and rewards are dictated by officially approved policy" (Apple 1983, 146–147). In the schools, this phenomenon is no better illustrated than by a recent statement released by Nancy Noonan (1985), president of the Pennsylvania State Education Association. She calls for the "restructuring of decision-making," which would enable teachers "to assume more responsibility for solving workplace problems." She cites a recent statewide poll that demonstrates how teachers "are excluded from the important educational decisions." With few exceptions, "many administrators ask teachers to rubber-stamp decisions that have already been made. The most autocratic administrators won't involve teachers at any level."

Theodore Sizer appears to be the only policy-maker to confront the issue. In his discussion of the "hierarchical bureaucracy" of the schools, he addresses the concept of scientific management and how it has produced a top-down structure with the trend toward even greater centralization. He elaborates the six defects of "pyramidal governance" as conformity, measurability, norm referencing, specificity, status quo, and stifling initiative. His solution is disappointing, however. He recommends a decentralization of authority, but is vague beyond this point. He does imply that by restructuring the principal's role as a "lead teacher," thus moving away from managerial responsibilities, the decentralization process will somehow evolve.

Still, the most crucial element that Goodlad, Boyer, and Sizer overlook in their solutions is the principal actor, the teacher. The school may have a clearcut grading system, an elaborate organizational chart, a class schedule, a curriculum, and an official motto that suggests the primary goal or purpose of schooling. Yet, people do not always "act" according to what the school is supposed to be, or what administrators say it is, but rather according to how they see it (Bogdan and Biklen 1982). This is especially true with teachers. As Susan Moore Johnson (1984) found in her recent study of the impact of teacher union on the schools, teachers clearly exert their control over the classroom. In this regard, Johnson discusses the concept of "covert insurrection," that is, teachers have always "reserved certain important powers for themselves" (Johnson 1984, 143). Further, teachers have even manipulated their unions to protect their own needs and interests. Johnson states:

The school site is a place where teachers' values rather than union values prevail. Teachers' allegiance to their schools and to their principals often takes precedence over their allegiance to the union. Teachers resist having their schools subsumed as indistinguishable components of the larger district. They fiercely defend their autonomy and use the union and the contract as they see fit, invoking them in some cases, ignoring them in others. (Johnson 1981, 165–166)

Johnson's analysis of teachers' attitudes and actions is substantiated by a historical perspective. Social historians like David Montgomery (1981) and E. P. Thompson (1963) view human agency as an important element in the making of history. And teachers as historical actors have demonstrated an uncanny ability to shape educational policy. During the nineteenth century, for example, female Yankee teachers in the Reconstructed South "resisted" and subverted the large and overbearing male hierarchical, bureaucratic system. Jacqueline Jones' (1980) fine study, *Soldiers of Light and Love: Northern Teachers and Georgia Blacks, 1865–1873*, reveals how female teachers protested against unequal pay scales for male and female teachers, male-dominated supervision, and certain policy decisions. As Jones explicates it:

The teachers accepted the schoolmen's argument that women's special, innate characteristics peculiarly suited them for work in the classroom. But, in the South, they supplemented notions of their own moral superiority with a strong sense of professionalism to produce forthright challenges to their male superiors in the fields of both educational policy and mission-home management. Their successes and failures alike indicate that formal role categories based on sex were not always indicators of actual behavior. (Jones 1980, 107)

Policy-makers must begin to take the active, historical role of teachers into account when they attempt to analyze the process and structure of schooling in America. Students and often administrators are transient, but teachers are more likely to remain in their classrooms and school buildings year after year, sometimes decade after decade. This strategic position guarantees that teachers will ultimately decide the relative success or failure of educational reform. Wayne Urban's (1982) historical examination of teacher groups in Atlanta, Chicago, and New York reveals that teachers were essentially pragmatic (Newman 1985). They "sought policies and procedures which would secure benefits and improve working conditions . . . and they followed their own priorities as they wound their way through the thicket of educational and political affairs" (Urban 1982, 10–11).

In some cases, teachers spearheaded reform when it was deemed beneficial. The experiences of Pittsburgh teachers, as William Issel (1967) discovered, provides a case in point. Pittsburgh teachers advanced progressive educational reform in their schools. "Through their organization, the Pittsburgh Teachers Association, the teachers were active on three broad fronts: they sought to improve their professional status; they worked to make the schools responsible for the well-being of the Pittsburgh community; they attempted to increase the role of the professional educator in the operation of the school system" (Issel 1967, 221). In their efforts, the teachers vigorously lobbied state legislators and, to a great extent, influenced the passage of a major piece of legislation, the Pennsylvania School Law of 1911, that embodied many of their professional objectives. Through publicity and organizational work, Pittsburgh teachers promoted reform in truancy, high school entrance examinations, industrial education, homework, physical education, and public health. "Teachers," Issel concludes, "played an important role in the movement for educational reform in Pittsburgh during the Progressive Era" (Issel 1967, 231).

In other cases, teachers effectively blunted educational reform. As Larry Cuban (1984) found, between 1900 and 1940, teachers emasculated the pedagogical facets of progressive education reforms in many cities. Teachers, during a later period (1965–1975), similarly stultified informal pedagogical innovations such as the open classroom and alternative schools. Thus, in Cuban's study, teachers chose, for any number of personal and professional reasons, to resist educational change! This represents a significant accomplishment given the fact that teachers have little, or no, role in determining class size and composition, length of the workday, number of class periods, textbooks, and grade levels or subjects taught. What teachers do control is how classroom space and furniture are utilized, the role of students, classroom activities, and instructional tools (i.e., audiovisual aids). Goodlad's (1984) findings corroborate Cuban's historical analysis. Whereas teachers apparently perceived themselves as powerless regarding fiscal management and personnel decisions, the "classroom is indeed the teacher's domain, and here . . . teachers saw themselves in control of what they taught and how" (Goodlad 1984, 188, 190). However, Goodlad downplays what implication this may have for educational policy formulation and implementation. For Cuban (1984), teachers have successfully exercised their limited authority to the point that they have extirpated educational reforms that they perceived as imposed upon them or as not serving their interests.

HISTORY AS HUMAN AGENCY

Given historical precedent, how realistic are the recommendations of Goodlad, Boyer, and Sizer?

To generalize, they all conclude, either implicitly or explicitly, that teachers represent one of the main "problems" of the current school "crisis" as well as part of the "solution." The school bureaucracy, as they perceive it, appears to be contributing to the teachers' dilemma, and the means by which to convert teachers to part of the solution—and concurrently transforming the schools—is to simply alter their bureaucratic environment. The fundamental element missing in all of these analyses is the historical perspective that illustrates both the dominance of a corporate mentality in the administration of the schools, which tends to objectify teachers, as well as the inescapable role of teachers as policy setters in spite of their subordinate position. Teachers represent the center of the controversy since they are the central actors. A dialectic is indeed at work (Gitlin 1983).

Commenting on the nagging presentism that often characterizes policy studies, Donald Warren argues that history "can be useful in understanding the extent to which policy and policymaking are influenced by inertia, the weight of established practice, familiar ideas, and traditional approaches to problem solving" (Warren 1978, 16). Warren's point is best illustrated by the following passage:

It seems clear . . . that if we are to attract into the teaching profession a fair percentage of the best boys and girls who are graduating each year from high school, we must insist upon a living minimum salary with a rapid annual increase during the first four or five years of service. *(School and Society, 1921)*

Seemingly echoing current reform reports, this statement about attracting higher quality students into teaching was written in 1921. The solution to solving serious school problems then, as it is now, was simplistic and superficial. Worse yet, the solution proffered in 1921, as history has shown us, was nothing more than empty rhetoric. Educational policy-makers have not learned the lessons of the past.

What is to be done? In order to generate truly effective changes in the schools, policy-makers must avoid the pitfall of ahistorical policy-making. They must begin to come to grips with profound and fundamental problems that have beset the schools for most of this century. They must consider a total restructuring of the school governance process that completely avoids the corporate model. They must also direct their attention to the central actor in the process, the teacher (Clifford 1975). Too long ignored or, worse yet, patronized, the teacher holds the key to the humanistic process of learning. For, as Cuban (1984) warns: "There should be a page in the *Guinness Book of World Records* on failed classroom reforms, for few ever seem to have been incorporated into teachers' repertoires. . . . Most instructional reforms in the last century were generated outside the school and were shoved downward into the classroom" (Cuban 1984, 6). Reform must begin with the teachers; they are the gatekeepers of school reform.

Unless policy-makers confront the historical issues facing the schools in general and address the conditions of teaching in particular, these studies will amount to nothing more than so much "more" empty rhetoric.

Bibliography

BOOKS

Abatso, Y. 1982. *Coping Strategies: Retaining Black Students in College*. Atlanta: Southern Education Foundation.

Adler, M. 1971. *The Common Sense of Politics*. New York: Holt, Rinehart, and Winston.

———. 1982. *The Paideia Proposal: An Educational Manifesto*. New York: Macmillan.

American Council on Education, Business-Higher Education Forum. 1983. *America's Competitive Challenge: The Need for a National Response*. A Report to the President of the United States; from the Business-Higher Education Forum. Washington, D.C.: American Council on Education.

American Enterprise Institute. 1985. *The Private Sector in the Public Schools: Can It Improve Education?* Washington, D.C.: American Enterprise Institute.

American Negro Academy Occasional Papers 1–22. 1969. New York: Arno Press and the New York Times.

American Vocational Association. 1984. *Collaboration: Vocational Education and the Private Sector*. Arlington, Va.: American Vocational Association.

Apple, M. 1982. *Education and Power*. Boston: Routledge and Kegan Paul.

Apple, M., and L. Weiss, eds. 1983. *Ideology and Practice in Schooling*. Philadelphia: Temple University Press.

Appleton, N. 1983. *Cultural Pluralism in Education: Theoretical Foundations*. New York: Longman.

Astin, A. W. 1977. *Four Critical Years: Effects of College on Beliefs, Attitudes and Knowledge*. San Francisco: Jossey-Bass.

Balkan, L. 1970. *Les effets du bilinguisme Francais-Anglais sur les aptitudes intellectuelles*. Bruxelles: Aimav.

Bamgbose, A., ed. 1976. *Mother Tongue Education*. Paris: UNESCO.

Banks, J. A. 1981. *Multiethnic Education: Theory and Practice*. Boston: Allyn and Bacon.

Baumol, W. J., and K. McLennan. 1985. *Productivity Growth and U.S. Competitiveness*. New York: Oxford University Press.

Bell, D. 1973. *The Coming of Post-Industrial Society*. New York: Basic Books.

Bennett, W. 1980. *The Revival of Civic Learning: A Rationale for Citizenship Education in American Schools*. Bloomington, Ind.: Phi Delta Kappan Educational Foundation.

———. 1986. *What Works: Research about Teaching and Learning*. Washington, D.C.: U.S. Department of Education.

Berg, I. 1970. *Education and Jobs*. New York: Praeger.

Berkson, I. B. 1920. *Theories of Americanization: A Critical Study*. New York: Teachers College Press.

Berry, M. F., and J. Blassingame 1982. *Long Memory: The Black Experience in America*. New York: Oxford University Press.

Blackwell, J. E. 1983. *Networking and Mentoring: A Study of Cross-generational Experiences of Blacks in Graduate and Professional Schools*. Atlanta: Southern Educational Foundation.

———. 1984. *Desegregation of State Systems of Higher Education: An Assessment (Conference Report)*. Atlanta: Southern Education Foundation.

Bloom, B. S. 1976. *Human Characteristics and School Learning*. New York: McGraw-Hill.

Bogdan, R. C., and K. Biklen. 1982. *Qualitative Research for Education: An Introduction to Theory and Methods*. Boston: Allyn and Bacon.

Bohannon, M., M. Buckley, and D. Osbourne. 1983. *The New Right in the States: The Groups, the Issues, and the Strategies*. Washington, D.C.: Conference on Alternative State and Local Policies.

Borman, K. M., and J. H. Spring. 1984. *Schools in Central Cities: Structure and Process*. New York: Longman.

Bowers, C. 1974. *Cultural Literacy For Freedom*. Eugene, Ore.: Elan Press.

Bowles, S., and H. Gintis. 1976. *Schooling in Capitalist America*. New York: McGraw-Hill.

Boyer, E. L. 1983. *High School: A Report on Secondary Education in America*. New York: Harper and Row.

Bradford, D. L., and A. R. Cohen. 1984. *Managing for Excellence: The Guide to High Performance in Contemporary Organizations*. New York: John Wiley and Sons.

Braverman, H. 1974. *Labor and Monopoly Capital: The Degradation of Work in the Twentieth Century*. New York: Monthly Review Press.

Business-Higher Education Forum, American Council on Education. 1983. *America's Competitive Challenge: The Need for National Response*. Washington, D.C.: American Council on Education.

Butler, S. M., M. Sanera, and W. B. Weinrod, eds. 1984. *Mandate for Leadership II: Continuing the Conservative Revolution*. Washington, D.C.: Heritage Foundation.

Callahan, R. E. 1962. *Education and The Cult of Efficiency: A Study of the Social Forces that Have Shaped the Administration of the Public Schools*. Chicago: University of Chicago Press.

Carnegie Corporation of New York. 1983. *Education and Economic Progress: Toward a National Economic Policy*. New York: Carnegie Corporation.

Carnegie Council on Policy Studies in Higher Education. 1980. *Giving Youth a Better Chance: Options for Education, Work, and Service.* San Francisco: Jossey-Bass.

Carnegie Forum on Education and the Economy. 1986. *A Nation Prepared: Teachers for the 21st Century.* The Report of the Task Force on Teaching as a Profession of the Carnegie Forum on Education and the Economy. New York: Carnegie Corporation.

Carnevale, A. 1982. *Human Capital: A High Yield Corporate Investment.* Baltimore: American Society for Training and Development.

Carnoy, M., and H. M. Levin. 1985. *Schooling and Work in the Democratic State.* Stanford, Calif.: Stanford University Press.

Castells, M. 1980. *The Economic Crisis and American Society.* Princeton, N.J.: Princeton University Press.

Cetron, M. 1985. *School of the Future.* New York: McGraw-Hill.

Chamber of Commerce of the United States. 1984. *Business and Education: Partners for the Future.* Washington, D.C.: Chamber of Commerce.

Children's Defense Fund. 1985. *Black and White Children in America: Key Facts.* Washington, D.C.: Children's Defense Fund.

Chomsky, N., and E. S. Herman. 1979. *The Washington Connection and Third World Fascism.* Boston: South End Press.

Church, R. 1976. *Education in the United States.* New York: Free Press.

Clark, R. M. 1983. *Family Life and School Achievement: Why Poor Black Children Succeed or Fail.* Chicago: University of Chicago Press.

College Entrance Examination Board. 1984. *Academic Preparation for the World of Work.* New York: College Entrance Examination Board.

————. 1983. *Academic Preparation of College.* An Educational Equality Project. New York: College Entrance Examination Board.

Committee for Economic Development. 1983. *Productivity Policy: Key to the Nation's Economic Future.* New York: Committee for Economic Development.

————. 1984. *Strategy for U.S. Industrial Competitiveness.* New York: Committee for Economic Development.

————. 1985. *Investing in Our Children: Business and the Public Schools.* New York: Committee for Economic Development.

Committee for Survival of a Free Congress and Education Foundation. 1984. *A Blueprint for Education Reform.* Washington, D.C.: Committee for Survival of a Free Congress and Education Foundation.

Conant, J. B. 1959. *The American High School Today.* New York: McGraw-Hill.

Cooper, R. N., K. Kaiser, and M. Kosaka. 1977. *Towards a Renovated International System.* New York: New York University Press.

Counts, G. 1927. *Social Composition of Boards of Education: A Study in the Social Control of Education.* Chicago: University of Chicago Press.

Croni, D. 1968. *Black Moses—The Story of Marcus Garvey and the Universal Negro Improvement Association.* Madison: University of Wisconsin Press.

Cronin, J. 1973. *The Control of Urban Schools.* New York: Free Press.

Cross, K. P. 1981. *Adults as Learners.* San Francisco: Jossey-Bass.

Crozier, M. J., S. P. Huntington, and J. Watanuki. 1975. *The Crisis of Democracy.* New York: New York University Press.

Cuban, L. 1984. *How Teachers Taught: Constancy and Change in American Classrooms, 1890–1980.* New York: Longman.

Curti, M. [1935] 1971. *The Social Ideas of American Educators*. Totowa, N.J.: Littlefield, Adams & Co.

Dabney, W. [1926] 1970. *Cincinnati Colored Citizen*. Reprint. New York: Negro University Press, division of Greenwood Press.

Darling-Hammond, L. 1984. *Beyond the Commission Reports: The Coming Crisis in Teaching*. Santa Monica, Calif.: The Rand Corporation.

————. 1985. *Equality and Excellence: The Educational Status of Black Americans*. New York: College Entrance Examination Board.

deLone, R. 1979. *Small Futures: Children, Inequality, and the Limits of Liberal Reform*. New York: Harcourt Brace Jovanovich.

Doyle, D. P., and T. W. Hartle. 1985. *Excellence in Education: The States Take Charge*. Washington, D.C.: American Enterprise Institute.

DuBois, W. E. B., and A. G. Dill, eds. 1911. *The Common School and the Negro American*. The Atlanta University Publications, no. 16. Atlanta: Atlanta University Press.

Educational Commission of the States, Task Force on Education for Economic Growth. 1983. *Action for Excellence: A Comprehensive Plan to Improve our Nation's Schools*. Denver: Educational Commission of the States.

————. 1985. *Reconnecting Youth*. Denver: Education Commission of the States.

Educational Equality Project, College Entrance Examination Board. 1983. *Academic Preparation for the World of Work*. New York: College Entrance Examination Board.

Edwards, J. R. 1979. *Language and Disadvantage*. London: Edward Arnold.

Etizioni, Amitai. 1984. *Self-Discipline, Schools, and the Business Community*. Washington, D.C.: National Chamber Foundation.

Everhart, R. 1983. *Reading, Writing, and Resistance: Adolescence and Labor in a Junior High School*. Boston: Routledge and Kegan Paul.

Fagen, R. R., ed. 1979. *Capitalism and the State in US-Latin American Relations*. Stanford, Calif.: Stanford University Press.

Feinberg, W., and J. Soltis. 1985. *School and Society*. New York: Teachers College Record Press.

Feistritser, C. E. 1985. *Cheating Our Children: Why We Need School Reform*. Washington, D.C.: National Center for Educational Information.

Finn, C. E., D. Ravitch, and R. H. Roberts, eds. 1985. *Challenges to the Humanities*. New York: Holmes and Meier.

Fleming, J. E., G. R. Gill, and D. Swinton. 1978. *The Case for Affirmative Action for Blacks in Higher Education*. Washington, D.C.: Howard University Press.

Ford Foundation. 1984. *City High School: A Recognition of Progress*. New York: The Ford Foundation.

Foster, P. 1965. *Education and Social Change in Ghana*. London: Routledge and Kegan Paul.

Francis, A. 1986. *New Technology at Work*. Oxford: Clarendon Press.

Franklin, V. P. 1979. *The Education of Black Philadelphia—The Social and Educational History of a Minority Community, 1900–1950*. Philadelphia: University of Pennsylvania Press.

Franklin, V. P., and J. Anderson, eds. 1978. *New Perspectives on Black Educational History*. Boston: G. K. Hall & Co.

Gardner, E. 1985. *A New Agenda for Education*. Washington, D.C.: Heritage Foundation.

Garvey, M., and A. Jacques, eds. 1925. *Philosophy and Opinions of Marcus Garvey*. New York: Atheneum.

Gilder, G. 1981. *Wealth and Poverty*. New York: Basic Books.

Ginsburg, A., and S. Hanson. 1985. *Values and Educational Success among Disadvantaged Students*. Final Report to the U.S. Department of Education. Washington, D.C.: Department of Education.

Ginzberg, E., D. P. Mills, J. D. Owen, H. L. Sheppard, and M. L. Wachter. 1982. *Work Decisions in the 1980's*. Boston: Auburn House.

————. 1985. *Technology and Employment*. Boulder, Colo.: Westview Press.

Glasgow, D. G. 1980. *The Black Underclass*. San Francisco: Jossey-Bass.

Goble, F. G., and B. D. Brooks. 1983. *The Case for Character Education*. Ottawa, Ill.: Green Hill Publishers.

Gold, M., and D. Mann. 1984. *Expelled to a Friendlier Place*. Ann Arbor: University of Michigan Press.

Gollnick, D. M. 1979. *Comparative Study of Multicultural Teacher Education in Teacher Corps and Other Institutions*. Washington, D.C.: American Association of Colleges for Teacher Education.

Gollnick, D. M., and P. C. Chinn. 1983. *Multicultural Education in a Pluralistic Society*. St. Louis: C. V. Mosby.

Goodlad, J. I. 1984. *A Place Called School: Prospects for the Future*. New York: McGraw-Hill.

Gordon, D. M., R. Edwards, and M. Reich. 1982. *Segmented Work, Divided Workers: The Historical Transformation of Labor in the United States*. New York: Cambridge University Press.

Gramsci, A. 1971. *Selections from Prison Notebooks*. Trans. and ed. by Moore and Smith. New York: International Publications.

Gruneberg, M. M., and D. J. Osborne, eds. 1981. *Psychology and Industrial Productivity: A Reader*. London: Macmillan Press.

Hall, R. M., and B. R. Sandler. 1984. *Out of the Classroom: A Chilly Campus Climate for Women?* Project on the Status and Education of Women. Washington, D.C.: Association of American Colleges.

Hanson, S., and A. Ginsberg. 1985. *Gaining Ground: Values and High School Success*. Final Report to the U.S. Department of Education. Washington, D.C.: Department of Education.

Hargreaves, D. 1967. *Social Relations in a Secondary School*. New York: Humanities Press.

Hart, G. 1983. *A New Democracy*. New York: Quill Press.

Hart, P. S. 1984. *Institutional Effectiveness in the Production of Black Baccalaureates*. Atlanta: Southern Education Foundation.

Heatherly, C. L., ed. 1981. *Mandate for Leadership: Policy Management in a Conservative Administration*. Washington, D.C.: Heritage Foundation.

Heilbronner, R. L. 1965. *The Limits of American Capitalism*. New York: Harper and Row.

Held, C. 1980. *Introduction to Critical Theory—Horkheimer to Habermas*. Berkeley: University of California Press.

Hispanic Policy Development Project. 1984. *Make Something Happen*, Vols. I and II. Washington, D.C.: Hispanic Policy Development Project.

Holmes Group. 1986. *Tomorrow's Teachers*. East Lansing: Michigan State University.

Honig, B. 1985. *Last Chance for Our Children: How You Can Help Save Our Schools*. Boston: Addison-Wesley.

House, E. 1974. *The Politics of Educational Innovation*. Berkeley, Calif.: McCutchan.

Howard, R. 1985. *Brave New Workplace*. New York: Viking Press.

Janowitz, M. 1983. *The Reconstruction of Patriotism: Education for Civic Consciousness*. Chicago: University of Chicago Press.

Jay, M. 1973. *The Dialectical Imagination—A History of the Frankfort School and the Institute of Social Research, 1923–1950*. Boston: Little, Brown.

Johnson, S. M. 1984. *Teacher Unions in Schools*. Philadelphia: Temple University Press.

Johnstone, J. W., and R. J. Rivera. 1965. *Volunteers for Learning*. Chicago: Adelaine.

Jones, J. 1980. *Soldiers of Light and Love: Northern Teachers and Georgia Blacks, 1865–1873*. Chapel Hill: University of North Carolina Press.

Kanter, R. 1983. *The Change Masters: Innovation for Productivity in the American Corporation*. New York: Simon and Schuster.

Karier, C. 1975. *Shaping the American Educational State*. New York: Free Press.

Karier, C., P. Violas, and J. Spring. 1973. *Roots of Crisis*. Chicago: Rand McNally.

Keddie, N., ed. 1973. *The Myth of Cultural Deprivation*. Baltimore: Penguin Books.

Kliebard, H. 1986. *The Struggle for the American Curriculum*. Boston: Routledge and Kegan Paul.

Kloss, H. 1977. *The American Bilingual Tradition*. Rowley, Mass.: Newbury House.

Koerner, J. 1968. *Who Controls American Education?* Boston: Beacon Press.

Kolko, G. 1969. *The Triumph of Conservatism*. Chicago: Quadrangle Books.

Kornweibel, T., Jr. 1975. *No Crystal Stair: Black Life and the Messenger, 1917–1928*. Westport, Conn.: Greenwood Press.

Lappe, F. M. 1975. *Diet for a Small Planet* (rev. ed.). New York: Ballantine Books.

Leuchte, P. F. 1985. *A Report on the Perceptions Held by Three Levels of Management at a High Technology Facility*. Internal unpublished document.

Levin, H. M. 1984. *Improving Productivity Through Education and Technology*. Stanford, Calif.: Stanford University, Institute for Research on Educational Finance and Governance.

Levin, H. M., and R. W. Rumberger. 1983. *The Educational Implications of High Technology*. Stanford, Calif: Stanford University, Institute for Research on Educational Finance and Governance.

———. 1984. *Forecasting the Impact of the New Technologies on the Future Job Market*. Stanford, Calif.: Stanford University, Institute for Research on Educational Finance and Governance.

Levin, M. 1985. *The Private Sector in the Public School: Can It Improve Education?* Washington, D.C.: American Enterprise Institute.

Lightfoot, S. 1983. *The Good School*. New York: Basic Books.

London, J., R. Wenkert, and W. Hagstrom. 1963. *Adult Education and Social Class*. Cooperative Research Project No. 1017. Berkeley: University of California Survey Research Center.

Long, R. 1980. *American Education*. New York: H. M. Wilson Co.

Lortie, D. C. 1975. *Schoolteacher: A Sociological Study*. Chicago: University of Chicago Press.

Lund, R., and J. A. Hansen. 1986. *Keeping America at Work: Strategies for Employing the New Technologies*. New York: John Wiley and Sons.

Mabee, C. 1979. *Black Education in New York State—From Colonial to Modern Times*. Syracuse: Syracuse University Press.

McGraw, O. 1980. *The Family, Feminism, and the Therapeutic State*. Washington, D.C.: Heritage Foundation.

McKenzie, R. B. 1985. *Competing Visions: The Political Conflict over America's Economic Future*. Washington, D.C.: The Cato Institute.

McNeil, L. 1986. *Contradictions of Control*. Boston: Routledge and Kegan Paul.

McNett, I. 1983. *Demographic Imperatives: Implications for Educational Policy*. Washington, D.C.: American Council on Education.

McNett, I. 1982. *Let's Not Reinvent the Wheel: Profiles of School/Business Collaboration*. Washington, D.C.: American Enterprise Institute.

Magaziner, I., and R. Reich. 1982. *Minding America's Business*. New York: Harcourt, Brace, Jovanovich.

Magrath, C. P., et al. 1985. *A Call for Change in Teacher Education*. Washington, D.C.: National Commission for Excellence in Teacher Education.

Martin, R. L. 1984. *Business and Education: Partners for the Future*. Washington, D.C.: National Chamber Foundation.

Melman, S. 1970. *Pentagon Capitalism: The Political Economy of War*. New York: McGraw-Hill.

Minsky, M., ed. 1985. *Robotics*. Garden City, N.Y.: Anchor Press.

Montgomery, D. 1979. *Worker's Control in America: Studies in the History of Work, Technology, and Labor Struggles*. New York: Cambridge University Press.

Moss, A. A., Jr., 1981. *The American Negro Academy—Voice of the Talented Tenth*. Baton Rouge: Louisiana State Press.

Moynihan, D. P. 1986. *Family and Nation*. New York: Harcourt, Brace, Jovanovich.

Mulvey, M C. 1969. *Recruitment in Adult Basic Education Handbook*. Lexington, Mass.: New England Regional Conference.

Murray, C. 1984. *Losing Ground: American Social Policy, 1950–1985*. New York: Basic Books.

Naisbett, J. 1982. *Megatrends: Ten Directions Transforming Our Lives*. New York: Warner Books.

NARMIC/American Friends Service Committee. 1982. *Automating Apartheid: U.S. Computer Exports to South Africa and the Arms Embargo*. Philadelphia: NARMIC/American Friends Service Committee.

Nasaw, D. 1979. *Schooled to Order: A Social History of Public Schooling in the United States*. New York: Oxford University Press.

National Academy of Sciences. 1983. *Education for Tomorrow's Jobs*. Washington, D.C.: National Academy Press.

———. 1984. *High Schools and the Changing Workplace: Employers' View*. Washington, D.C.: National Academy Press.

National Advisory Council on Economic Opportunity. 1981. *The American Promises: Equal Justice and Economic Opportunity—Final Report*. Washington, D.C.: U.S. Government Printing Office.

National Alliance of Business. 1984. *A Nation at Work: Education and the Private Sector*. Washington, D.C.: National Advisory Council on Vocational Education and National Alliance on Business.

———. 1986. *Employment Policies: Looking to the Year 2000*. Washington, D.C.: National Alliance of Business.

National Center for Educational Statistics. 1982. *Participation in Adult Education, 1981.* Washington, D.C.: National Center for Educational Statistics.

National Center for Research in Vocational Education, The Ohio State University. 1981. *Productivity Primer: General Introduction.* Columbus: National Center for Research in Vocational Education.

————. 1985. *Toward Excellence in Vocational Education: Improving Teaching.* Columbus: National Center for Research in Vocational Education.

National Coalition of Advocates for Students. 1985. *Barriers to Excellence: Our Children at Risk.* Boston: National Coalition of Advocates for Students.

National Commission on Excellence in Education. 1983. *A Nation at Risk: The Imperative for Educational Reform.* Washington, D.C.: U.S. Government Printing Office.

————. 1985. *A Call for Change in Teacher Education.* Washington, D.C.: American Association of Colleges for Teacher Education.

National Commission on the Reform of Secondary Education. 1973. *The Reform of Secondary Education.* New York: McGraw-Hill.

National Education Association. 1893. *Report of the Committee on Secondary School Studies.* Washington, D.C.: U.S. Government Printing Office.

————. 1918. *Cardinal Principles of Secondary Education: A Report of the Commission on the Reorganization of Secondary Education.* Washington, D.C.: U.S. Government Printing Office.

————. 1985. *Report of the Committee of Fifteen on Elementary Education.* (With the reports of the subcommittees; On the reports of the subcommittees; On training of teachers; On the correlation of studies in elementary education; On the organization of city schools systems). Washington, D.C.: U.S. Government Printing Office.

National Science Board Commission of Precollegiate Education in Mathematics, Science, and Technology. 1983. *Educating Americans for the 21st Century.* Washington, D.C.: National Science Foundation.

National Society for the Study of Education. 1982. *Education and Work*; 81st Yearbook. Chicago: National Society for the Study of Education.

Navarro, P. 1984. *The Policy Game.* New York: John Wiley and Sons.

Newitt, J., ed. 1979. *Future Trends in Education Policy.* Lexington, Mass.: Lexington Books.

Oakes, J. 1985. *Keeping Track: How Schools Structure Inequality.* New Haven, Conn.: Yale University Press.

O'Connor, J. 1973. *The Fiscal Crisis of the State.* New York: St. Martin's Press.

Office Automation Reporting Service, May 1985.

Ogbu, J. 1978. *Minority Education and Caste: The American System in Cross-Cultural Perspective.* New York: Academic Press.

Ohme, K. 1985. *Triad Power: The Coming Shape of Global Competition.* New York: Free Press.

O'Toole, J. 1981. *Making America Work: Productivity and Responsibility.* New York: Continuum.

Peters, T. J., and N. Austin. 1985. *A Passion for Excellence: The Leadership Difference.* New York: Random House.

Peters, T. J., and R. H. Waterman. 1982. *In Search of Excellence: Lessons from America's Best-Run Companies.* New York: Harper and Row.

Phillips, K. P. 1984. *Staying on Top: The Business Case for a National Industrial Strategy*. New York: Random House.

Pivan, F. F., and R. A. Cloward. 1982. *The New Class War: Reagan's Attack on the Welfare State*. New York: Pantheon Books.

Pratte, R. 1977. *Ideology and Education*. New York: David McKay.

———. 1979. *Pluralism in Education: Conflict, Clarity and Commitment*. Springfield, Ill.: Charles C. Thomas.

Reagan, M. D., and J. G. Sanzone. 1981. *The New Federalism*. New York: Oxford University Press.

Reich, R. B. 1983. *The Next American Frontier*. New York: Times Books.

Robinson, T. 1910. *A Primer of Libertarian Education*. New York: Free Life Editions.

Rumberger, R. W. 1981. *Overeducation in the U.S. Labor Market*. New York: Praeger.

Sandbrook, R. 1982. *The Politics of Basic Needs: Urban Aspects of Assaulting Poverty in America*. Toronto: University of Toronto Press.

Schiller, H. I., and J. D. Phillips. 1970. *Super State: Readings in the Military-Industrial Complex*. Urbana: University of Illinois Press.

Schroyer, T. 1973. *The Critique of Domination—The Origins and Development of Critical Theory*. Boston: Beacon Press.

Seeley, D. 1985. *Education Through Partnership*. Washington, D.C.: American Enterprise Institute.

Servan-Schreiber, J. J., and B. Crecine. 1985. *The Knowledge Revolution*. Pittsburgh: Carnegie Mellon Press.

Shaiken, H. 1984. *Work Transformed: Automation and Labor in the Computer Age*. New York: Holt, Rinehart and Winston.

Silberman, C. E. 1970. *Crisis in the Classroom*. New York: Random House.

Simmons, J., and W. Mares. 1983. *Working Together*. New York: Alfred A. Knopf.

Simon, P. 1980. *The Tongue-Tied American: Confronting the Foreign Language Crisis*. New York: Continuum.

Sizer, T. R. 1984. *Horace's Compromise: The Dilemma of the American High School*. Boston: Houghton-Mifflin.

Sklar, H. 1980. *Trilateralism: The Trilateral Commission and Elite Planning for World Management*. Boston: South End Press.

Slater, P. 1977. *Origin and Significance of the Frankfurt School—A Marxist Perspective*. London and Boston: Routledge and Kegan Paul.

Smith, J. P., and F. R. Welch. 1986. *Education Is Key to Economic Equity*. Santa Monica, Calif.: The Rand Corporation.

Sola, P. 1972. *Plutocrats, Pedagogues and Plebes: Business Influences on Vocational Education and Extra-Curricular Activities in the Chicago High Schools 1899–1925*. Unpublished Ph.D. dissertation, University of Illinois, Urbana-Champaign.

Sola, P., and J. DeVitis, eds. *New Horizons in Teacher Education* (forthcoming).

Spring, J. 1976. *The Sorting Machine*. New York: David McKay.

———. 1985. *American Education*. New York: Longman.

———. 1986. *The American School, 1642–1985*. New York: Longman.

Stubbs, M. 1976. *Language, Schools and Classrooms*. London: Methuen.

Swing, E. S. 1980. *Bilingualism and Linguisitic Segregation in the School of Brussels*. Quebec: Centre International de Recherche sur le Bilinguisme.

Taskforce on Education for Economic Growth, Educational Commission of the States.

1983. *Action for Excellence: A Comprehensive Plan to Improve Our Nation's Schools*. Denver: Educational Commission of the States.

Taskforce on Federal Elementary and Secondary Education Policy, Twentieth Century Fund. 1983. *Making the Grade*. New York: Twentieth Century Fund.

Taylor, F. W. [1911] 1967. *The Principles of Scientific Management*. New York: Norton.

Thee, M. 1986. *Military Technology, Military Strategy, and the Arms Race*. New York: St. Martin's Press.

Thomas, G. E. 1984. *Black College Students and Factors Influencing Their Major Field Choice*. Atlanta: Southern Education Foundation.

Thompson, E. P. 1963. *The Making of the English Working Class*. Middlesex: Penguin Books.

Thurow, L. 1982. *The Zero Sum Society: Distribution and the Possibilities for Economic Change*. New York: Basic Books.

Tiedt, P. L., and I. M. Tiedt. 1986. *Multicultural Teaching*, 2d ed. Boston: Allyn and Bacon.

Timpane, M. 1981. *Corporations and Public Education*. New York: Teachers College.

Toffler, A. 1983. *Previews and Premises*. New York: William Morrow.

Troike, R. C. 1978. *Research Evidence for the Effectiveness of Bilingual Education*. Rosslyn, Va.: National Clearinghouse for Bilingual Education.

Twentieth Century Fund Taskforce. 1983. *Making the Grade*. Report of the Twentieth Century Fund Task Force on Federal Elementary and Secondary Educational Policy. New York: Twentieth Century Fund.

Tyack, D., and E. Hansot. 1982. *Managers of Virtue: Public School Leadership in America, 1820–1980*. New York: Basic Books.

UNESCO. 1953. *The Use of Vernacular Language in Education*. Paris: UNESCO.

Union of Concerned Scientists. 1984. *Empty Promise: The Growing Case against Star Wars*. Boston: Beacon Press.

United States Department of Education. 1984(a). *The Nation Responds: Recent Efforts to Improve Education*. Washington, D.C.: U.S. Government Printing Office.

————. 1984(b). *Progress of Education in the United States of America 1980–1981 through 1982–1983*. Washington, D.C.: U.S. Government Printing Office.

Urban, W. J. 1982. *Why Teachers Organized*. Detroit: Wayne State University Press.

Velikhov, E. P., ed. 1986. *Weaponry in Space: The Dilemma of Security*. New York: Pergamon Press.

Violas, P. C. 1978. *The Training of the Urban Working Class: A History of Twentieth Century American Education*. Chicago: Rand McNally.

Ware, N. [1924] 1964. *The Industrial Worker, 1840–1860: The Reaction of American Industrial Society to the Advance of the Industrial Revolution*. Chicago: Quadrangle Books.

Warren, D. R. 1978. *History, Education and Public Policy*. Berkeley, Calif.: McCutchan.

Weis, L. 1985. *Between Two Worlds: Black Students in an Urban Community College*. Boston: Routledge and Kegan Paul.

Weiss, B. J., ed. 1982. *American Education and the European Immigrant: 1840–1940*. Urbana: University of Illinois Press.

Whitehead, A. N. 1929. *The Aims of Education*. New York: Macmillan.

Willis, P. 1977. *Learning to Labor: How Working Class Kids Get Working Class Jobs*. Westmond, England: Saxon House Press.

Wynne, E., and H. Walberg. 1984. *Developing Character: Transmitting Character.* Posen, Ill.: ARL Services, Inc.

Yarmolinsky, A. 1971. *The Military Establishment: Its Impacts on American Society.* New York: Harper and Row.

Zeigler, L., and M. Jennings. 1974. *Governing American Schools: Political Interaction in Local School Districts.* North Scituate, Mass.: Duxbury.

ARTICLES

Adams, G. 1986. "Star Wars—A Dangerous Chimera." *Dissent* 1, 261–264.

Adelson, J., and C. E. Finn. 1985. "Terrorizing Children." *Commentary* (April), 29–36.

Alter, A. E. 1986. "Creating the Future: Business Innovators Say What It Will Take." *Mass High Tech* (February).

Althusser, L. 1978. "Ideology and Ideological State Apparatuses: Notes Toward and Investigation." In *Lenin and Philosophy and Other Essays.* London: New Left Books.

Ampene, L. 1981. "Reaching Unreached Adults." In *Comparing Adult Education Worldwide*, eds. A. N. Charters et al. San Francisco: Jossey-Bass, pp. 175–196.

Anderson, J. 1978. "Northern Philanthropy and the Training of the Black Leadership." In *New Perspectives on Black Educational History*, eds. V. P. Franklin and J. Anderson. Boston: G. K. Hall & Co.

Ansara, M., and S. M. Miller. 1986. "Opening Up Progressive Thought." *Social Policy*, 3 (Summer), 3–10.

Apple, M. W. 1978. "Ideology Reproduction and Educational Reform." *Comparative Educational Review* (October).

———. 1982. "Work, Gender, and Teaching." *Teachers College Record*, 84.

———. 1983. "Curriculum in the Year 2000: Tensions and Possibilities." *Phi Delta Kappan* (January).

Bain, B. C. 1974. "Bilingualism and Cognition: Towards a General Theory." In *Biculturalism and Education: Proceedings from the Conference at College Universitaire Saint-Jean*, ed. S. Carey. University of Alberta.

Baker, G. A. 1983. "Serving Undereducated Adults: Community As Learning Center." *New Directions in Continuing Education*, 20 (December).

Bauer, G. 1986. "The Moral of the Story: How to Teach Values in the Nation's Classrooms." *Policy Review* (Fall), 24–27.

Bennett, W. 1985. "Educators in America: The Three R's." *Vital Speeches of the Day*, 51 (May).

Berman, C. 1983. "Business Efficiency, American Schooling and the Public School Superintendency: A Reconsideration of the Callahan Thesis." *History of Education Quarterly*, 23.

Berman, E. H. 1985. "The Improbability of Meaningful Educational Reform." *Issues in Education*, III.

Berman, E. H. 1984. "State Hegemony and the Schooling Process." *Journal of Education*, 166 (3) (Fall).

Beyer, L. 1985. "Educational Reform: The Political Roots of National Risk." *Curriculum Inquiry*, 15 (1).

Beyer, L. E. 1983. "Aesthetic Curriculum and Cultural Reproduction." In *Ideology and*

Practice in Schooling, eds. M. W. Apple and L. Weiss. Philadelphia: Temple University Press.

Boshier, R., and G. Baker. 1979. "Effects of Fees on Clientele Characteristics and Participation in Adult Education." *Adult Education*, XXIX (3).

Boykin, A. W. 1979. "Psychological/Behavioral Verve: Some Theoretical Explorations and Empirical Manifestations." In *Research Directions of Black Psychologists*, eds. A. W. Boykin, A. J. Franklin and J. F. Yates. New York: Russell Sage Foundation.

Brandeis, L. D. 1954. "True Americanism." In *American Thought: Civil War to World War I*, ed. P. Miller. New York: Holt, Rinehart, and Winston.

Bridgman, A. 1985. "Children's Fund Will Work to Reduce Teen-age Pregnancy, Infant Mortality." *Education Week* (March 3), 6.

British Radical Science Collective. 1985. "Compulsive Technology." In *Compulsive Technology: Computers as Culture*, eds. T. Solomonides and L. Levidow. London: Free Association Books.

Brophy, J. 1982. "How Teachers Influence What Is Taught and Learned in Classrooms." *Elementary School Journal*, 83.

Burns, A. F. 1986. "The Condition of the World Economy." *AEI Memorandum* (Summer) 5.

Butts, R. F. 1973. "Assaults on a Great Idea." *The Nation*, 216 (April 30).

———. 1976. "Once Again the Question for Liberal Public Educators: Whose Twilight?" *Phi Delta Kappan*, 58 (11) (September).

———. 1977(a). "The Public School as Moral Authority." In *The School's Role as Moral Authority*, eds. R. F. Butts et al. Washington, D.C.: Association for Supervision and Curriculum Development.

———. 1977(b). "Public Education in a Pluralistic Society." *Educational Theory*, 17 (Winter).

———. 1982. "The Revival of Civic Learning Requires a Prescribed Curriculum." *Liberal Education*, 68.

Charp, S. 1985. "Editorial." *T. H. E. Journal*. 13 (September).

Chavez, L. 1984. "Citizenship Education: Recovering a Lost Dimension." In *A Blueprint for Education Reform*, ed. C. Marshner. Chicago: Regnery.

Clifford, G. J. 1975. "Saints, Sinners and People: A Position Paper on the Historiography of American Education." *History of Education Quarterly*, 15.

Christoffel, P. H. 1982. "An Opportunity Deferred." *Education and Urban Society*, 14 (3).

Collins, R. 1977. "Functional and Conflict Theories of Educational Stratification." In *Power and Ideology in Education*, eds. J. Karabel and A. Halsey. New York: Oxford University Press.

Cook, E. 1984. "Sex Equity and National Reports in Education." Unpublished paper, College of Education, University of Cincinnati.

Cookson, P. S. 1978. "Adult Education Participation and Occupational Achievement: A Regression Analysis." *Adult Education*, XXIX (1).

Cooley, M. 1980. "Computerization—Taylor's Latest Disguise." *Economic and Industrial Democracy*, 1, 523–539.

Cooper, D. E. 1978. "Linguistics and 'Cultural Deprivation.' " *Journal of Philosophy of Education*, 12.

Cope, R. G. 1985. "Six Management Propositions for Economic Vitality in the Pacific

Basin: A World Ocean Perspective.'' *Asia Pacific Journal of Management*, 2 (2), 81–95.

Couch, K. A. 1986. "How Economic Change Shapes New Dreams." *Public Opinion* (Sept/Oct).

Cross, K. P. 1984. "The Rising Tide of School Reform Reports." *Phi Delta Kappan* (November).

———. 1985. "The Changing Role of Higher Education in the Learning Society." *Continuum*, 49 (2).

———, and A. McCartan. 1984. "Adult Learning: State Policies and Institutional Practices." ASHE-ERIC, Higher Education Report No. 1. Washington, D.C.: Association for the Study of Higher Education.

Cuban, L. 1984. "Transforming the Frog into a Prince: Effective Schools Research, Policy and Practice at the District Level." *Harvard Educational Review*, 54 (2).

Cummins, J. 1976. "The Influence of Bilingualism on Cognitive Growth: A Synthesis of Research Findings and Explanatory Hypotheses." *Working Papers in Bilingualism*, 9, 1–43.

Darkenwald, G. 1980. "Continuing Education and Hard-to-Reach Adults." *New Directions for Continuing Education* (8).

Douglas, E., and D. Bryant. 1985. "Implementing Computer-Assisted Instruction: The Garland Way." *T. H. E. Journal*, 13 (September).

Doyle, D. P., and C. E. Finn. 1984. "American Schools and the Future of Local Control." *The Public Interest* (Fall).

Draper, R. 1985. "The Golden Ram." *New York Review* 32 (October 28), 46–49.

Editorial. 1984. "High-Tech and Health." *Dollars and Sense*, 99 (September).

Editorial. 1985(a). "Computing the Future." *Science for the People*, 17 (March/April).

Editorial. 1985(b). *The Christian Science Monitor* (October 25).

Education Week Staff. 1985. "1983: Dip in Birth Rate, Rise in Unwed Mothers." *Education Week* (October 16), 1.

———. 1986. "Here They Come, Ready or Not" (Special Report). *Education Week* (May 14), 13–40.

Evans, D. 1983. "We Must Begin Educational Reform Every Place at Once." *Phi Delta Kappan*, 65 (November).

———. 1984. "Business Has Rediscovered the Schools." *Phi Delta Kappan*, 65 (6) (February).

Feinberg, W. 1985. "Fixing the Schools: The Ideological Turn." *Issues in Education*, III (2).

Fernández, D. 1985. "Bennett's Statement on Bilingual Policy Called 'Erroneous' " (Letter). *Educational Week* (October 30), 20.

Filene, P. 1970. "An Obituary for the Progressive Movement." *American Quarterly* (Spring).

Finkelstein, J., and D. Newman. 1984. "The Third Industrial Revolution: A Special Challenge to Managers." *Organizational Dynamics* (Summer).

Finn, C. E. 1983. "The Drive for Educational Excellence: Moving Towards a Public Consensus." *Change* (April), 14–22.

———. 1984. "Gee, Officer Krupke." *Policy Review* 72–76.

———. 1986. "Decentralize, Deregulate, Empower." *Policy Review* (Summer), 58–61.

Futrell, M. H. 1986. "A New Threat to Proud Schools." *Education Week* (April 2).

Gardner, E. 1985. "The Growth of the Federal Role in Education." In *A New Agenda for Education*, ed. E. Gardner. Washington, D.C.: Heritage Foundation.

Geiogue, H. E. 1982. "Tax Limitation Measures: Their Impact on Recurrent Education in California." *Education and Urban Society*, 14 (3) (May).

Geiser, K., and B. Harrison. 1985. "The High-Tech Industry Comes Down to Earth." *Boston Globe*, Focus Section (June 23).

Gill, J. 1980. "Affirmative Action: The Bakke and Weber Cases." In *Meanness Mania: The Changed Mood*. Washington, D.C.: Institute for the Study of Educational Policy, Howard University.

Giroux, H. 1984. "Public Philosophy and the Crisis in Education." *Harvard Educational Review*, 54 (May).

————. 1985. "Thunder on the Right: Education and the Ideology of the Quick Fix." *Curriculum Inquiry*, 15.

Gitlin, A. 1983. "School Structure and Teachers' Work." In *Ideology and Practice in Schooling*, eds. M. W. Apple and L. Weiss. Philadelphia: Temple University Press.

Goldman, L. 1983. "The Hidden Agenda of the Report on Excellence." *Educational Leadership*, 41 (2).

Gordon, B. 1985. "Toward Emancipation in Citizenship Education: The Case of African-American Cultural Knowledge." *Theory and Research in Social Education*, 12 (4).

————. 1986. "Institution Building and Knowledge Production: Implications for Curriculum Theorizing and Education Praxis." Paper presented at symposium: Curriculum, Critical Science, and the Race-Class Issue: Implications for Educational Theory and Praxis. Annual meeting of the American Educational Research Association, San Francisco, April 1986.

Gordon, D. 1986. "Do We Need to Be Number 1?" *Atlantic Monthly* (April).

Greenbaum, G. 1976. "Division of Labor in the Computer Field." *Monthly Review* (July/ Aug.), 40–55.

Grissom, T. 1973. "Education and the Cold War: The Role of James B. Conant." In *Roots of Crisis: American Education in the Twentieth Century*, eds. C. J. Karier, P. C. Violas, and J. Spring. Chicago: Rand McNally.

Grubb, W. N., and M. Lazersen. 1975. "Rally 'Round the Workplace." *Harvard Educational Review*, 45 (4).

Gutkind, P. C. W. 1983. "Workers are Workers and Marxist Intellectuals are Mere Intellectuals (said Alice)." *Contemporary Marxism*, 7.

Hadley, P. E. 1982. "The Changing Philosophy of Our Federal Government and Its Impact on Adult Education." *Life Long Education: The Adult Years* (May).

Hartle, T. W. 1986. "Dream Jobs?" *Public Opinion* (Sept/Oct), 11–12.

Harvey, W., and D. Scott-Jones. 1985. "We Can't Find Any: The Elusiveness of Black Faculty Members in American Higher Education." *Issues in Education*, 3 (1).

Hawley, W. 1985. "False Premises, False Promises: The Mythical Character of Public Discourse About Education." *Phi Delta Kappan*, 67.

Hayashi, A. 1985. "Government Makes a Super Effort." *Electronic Business* (June 15).

Hays, S. 1964. "The Politics of Reform in Municipal Government in the Progressive Era." *Pacific Northwest Quarterly* (October).

Heaney, T. W. 1983. "Hanging on or Gaining Ground: Educating Marginal Adults."
    New Directions for Continuing Education, 20 (December).
Heisner, J. D. 1980. "The Brouhaha over Bilingual Education." *Instructor*, 39 (Decem-
    ber).
Hentoff, N. 1985. "Census Reports Sharp Increase in Single-Parent Households." *Ed-
    ucation Week* (May 19).
————. 1985. "Federal Study Finds Dramatic Rise in Number of Poor Children."
    Education Week, 5 (May 29).
Hertling, J. 1985. "Monihan, Citing Poverty Rate Calls for New Family Policies."
    Education Week (April 17).
Honig, B. 1985. "Jobs and Education." *Education Week* (May 29), 23.
Howe, F. 1979. "The First Decade of Women's Studies." *Harvard Educational Review*,
    49.
Howe, H., et al. 1984. "Symposium on the Year of the Reports: Responses from the
    Educational Community." *Harvard Educational Review*, 54 (1).
Ianco-Worrall, A. D. 1972. "Bilingualism and Cognitive Development." *Child Devel-
    opment* (43), 1390–1400.
Irish, G. H. 1980. "Reaching the Least Educated Adult." *New Directions for Continuing
    Education*, 8.
Issel, W. H. 1967. "Teachers and Educational Reform During the Progressive Era: A
    Case Study of the Pittsburgh Teachers Association." *History of Education Quart-
    erly*, 7.
Jacobson, R. L. 1986. "Carnegie School-Reform Goals Hailed: Achieving Them Called
    'Tall Order.' " *Chronicle of Higher Education*, 32 (13).
Jain, A. K. 1985. "Education for Factory Automation." *Manufacturing Systems* (Sep-
    tember).
Johnson, F. E. 1985. "Installing a Solution Center: Think Big, Start Small." *Infosystems*.
    32 (June).
Karabel, J. 1974. "Community Colleges and Social Stratification." In *The Education
    Establishment*, eds. E. L. Useem and M. Useem. Englewood Cliffs, N.J.: Pren-
    tice-Hall.
Karier, C. J. 1984. "The Image and the Reality: A Review of Ernest L. Boyer's *High
    School.*" *Curriculum Inquiry*.
Kaus, M. 1986. "The Work Ethic State." *The New Republic* (July 7), 22–23.
Keane, J. G. 1985. "Higher Education, Some Trends Stressing the Need for Strategic
    Focus." *Continuum* 49 (2) (Spring).
Keesbury, F. E. 1984. "Who Wrecked the Schools? Thirty Years of Criticism in Per-
    spective." *Educational Theory*, 34.
King, M. L. 1968. "Preface." In *Dusk by Dawn*, W. E. B. DuBois. New York: Schocken
    Books.
Kirkpatrick, J. 1986. "The United States and the World: Setting Limits." *AEI Memo-
    randum*, 9 (Spring) (Abstracted).
Kirst, M. 1986. "Sustaining the Momentum of State Educational Reform: The Link
    Between Assessment and Financial Support." *Phi Delta Kappan*, 67.
Kjolseth, R. 1973. "Bilingual Education Programs in the United States: For Assimilation
    or Pluralism?" In *Bilingualism in the Southwest*, ed. P. R. Turner. Tucson: Uni-
    versity of Arizona Press.

Knox, A. 1984. "Serving the Noncollege Bound." *New Directions for Continuing Education*. 20 (March).

Kraemer, K. L., and R. Kling. 1985. "The Political Character of Computerization in Service Organizations: Citizen Interests or Bureaucratic Control." *Computer and the Social Sciences*, 1 (April–June).

Kuttner, B. 1983. "The Declining Middle." *Atlantic*, 252 (July).

Landry, R. G. 1974. "A Comparison of Second Language Learners and Monolinguals on Divergent Thinking Tasks at the Elementary School Level." *Modern Language Journal*, 58: 10–15.

Lather, P. 1981. "Reeducating Educators: Sex Equity in Teacher Education." *Educational Horizons*, 60 (1).

Leinhardt, G., and A. Palley. 1982. "Restrictive Educational Settings: Exile or Haven?" *Review of Educational Research*, 52.

Levin, H. M. 1984. "Jobs: A Changing Workforce, A Changing Education?" *Change*, 16 (7).

Levin, H. M., and K. Tobin. 1982. "Introduction, Recurrent Education in the United States." *Education and Urban Society*, 14 (3).

Little, J. 1982. "Norms of Collegiality and Experimentation: Workplace Conditions of School Success." *American Educational Research Journal*, 19.

Lockhead, M., and Klein, S. 1985. "Sex Equity in Classroom and Climate." In *Handbook for Achieving Sex Equity Through Education*, ed. S. J. Klein. Baltimore, Md.: Johns Hopkins University Press.

London, H. 1981. "The Future of Continuing Education." *Life Long Learning: The Adult Years* (December).

Loury, G. C. 1985. "Beyond Civil Rights." *The New Republic* (October 7), 22–25.

McCracken, P. W. 1986. "Reluctant to Prosper." *AEI Memorandum*, 2 (Fall).

Marable, M. 1981. "Common Program: Transitional Strategies for Black and Progressive Politics in America." *New Political Science*, 5, 6.

Melman, S. 1983. "Manager's Debacle." *New York Times* (May 4).

Miller, L. S. 1986. "Nation-Building and Education." *Education Week* (May 14), 52.

Mohr, C. 1985. "Weapons in Space—the Controversy over Star Wars, What Moscow Might Be Doing in Replying to Star Wars." *New York Times*, March 6.

Newman, F. 1981. "Reducing Student Alienation in High Schools: Implication of Theory." *Harvard Educational Review*, 51.

Newman, J. W. 1985. "Teachers as Workers: Listening to the Rank and File." *Journal of Thought*, 20.

Noonan, N. M. 1985. "The Teacher's Side: Democracy in Our Schools." *Pittsburgh Press*, Section A, 10 (September 15).

Nordhaug, O. 1983. "Distribution of Adult Education: The Norwegian Case." *Adult Education Quarterly*, 4 (1) (Fall).

Olson, L. 1984. "Shocking Waste of Youths Cited in Study of Hispanics' Schooling." *Education Week* (December 12).

Oreffice, P. F. 1985. "Playing Football with the World." *AEI Memorandum* (Spring).

Packard, D. 1986. "Improving Weapons Acquisition." *Policy Review* (Summer), 11–15.

———. 1987. "Management of America's National Defense." *AEI Memorandum* (Winter), 4.

Passow, A. 1984. "Tackling the Reform Reports of the 1980's." *Phi Delta Kappan* (April).

Peal, E., and Lambert, W. 1962. "The Relation of Bilingualism to Intelligence." *Psychological Monographs*, 76.

Pearson, R. 1985. "Avoiding Skill Shortages in the New Technologies." *Long Range Planning*, 18 (4).

Penland, P. 1979. "Self-Initiated Learning." *Adult Education*, 24 (3).

Pink, W. 1984. "Schools, Youth and Justice." *Crime and Delinquency*, 30.

———. 1986. "Facilitating Reform at the School Level: A Missing Factor in School Reform." *Urban Review*, 18.

Pink, W., and R. Leibert. 1986. "Reading Instruction in the Elementary School: A Proposal for Reform." *Elementary School Journal*, 87.

Pink, W., and M. Sweeney. 1978. "Teaching Nomination, Deviant Career Lines and the Management of Stigma in the Junior High School." *Urban Education*, XLVIII.

Pratte, R. 1983. "Multicultural Education: Four Normative Arguments." *Educational Theory*, 33, 21–32.

Prentice, S. 1985. "OSU Near Bottom in Enrolling Blacks." *Columbus Citizen Journal* (November 11, 1985).

Ratner, G. 1985. "A New Legal Duty for Urban Schools: Effective Education in Basic Skills." *Education Week* (October 30), 24. Times Books.

Reagan, G. M. 1985. "Criticism of Public Schools in the Eighties: Reports, Retorts, Recommendations and Rationalizations." Symposium paper presented at the University of Pittsburgh of Johnstown.

Reagan, T. 1980. "Bilingual Education: A Reevaluation of Objectives." *Journal of the Midwest History of Education Society*, 8.

———. 1984. "Bilingual Education in the United States: Arguments and Evidence." *Education and Society*, 2.

Rhodes, B. 1985. "Micro Security That Makes Sense." *Computer Decisions* (May 7).

Rist, R. 1970. "Social Class and Teacher Expectation." *Harvard Educational Review*, 49.

Robins, K., and F. Webster. 1985. "Higher Education, High Tech, High Rhetoric." In *Compulsive Technology: Computers as Culture*, eds. T. Solomonides and L. Levidow. London: Free Association Books.

Robinson, C. A. 1986. "Is Strategic Defense Criticism Obsolete?" *Policy Review* (Summer), 16–23.

Robinson, P. B. 1983. "Education for Older Adults." *New Direction for Continuing Education*, 20 (December).

Rose, E. 1985. "Child-Care Options Limited for Black Families." *Education Week* (October 30).

Rule, J. E. 1986. "How We Got Government Off Our Backs." *Dissent*, 1, 258–259.

Rumberger, R. 1984. "The Growing Imbalance Between Education and Work." *Phi Delta Kappan*, 65 (5) (January).

Sadker, D., and M. Sadker. 1985. "The Treatment of Sex Equity in Teacher Education." In *Handbook for Achieving Sex Equity Through Education*, ed. S. J. Klein. Baltimore, Md.: Johns Hopkins University Press.

Samater, I. M. 1984. "From 'Growth' to 'Basic Needs': The Evolution of Development Theory." *Monthly Review*, 36 (5), 1–13.

Schatz, R. W. 1921. "Teachers' Salaries." *School and Society* (August 21).

————. 1984. "Labor Historians, Labor Economics, and the Question of Synthesis." *Journal of American History*, 71.

Scheffler, I. 1984. "On the Education of Policymakers." *Harvard Education Review*, 54 (2).

Schwartz, H. 1984. "Affirmative Action." In *Minority Report: What Has Happened to Blacks, Hispanics, American Indians and Other Minorities in the Eighties*, ed. L. W. Dunbar. New York: Pantheon Books.

Select Committee, Amherst College. 1980. *Report of the Select Committee on the Quality of Undergraduate Life, Amherst College*. Amherst, Mass.: Amherst College.

Shapiro, S. 1983. "Schools, Work and Consumption: Education, and the Cultural Contradictions of Capitalism." *The Journal of Educational Thought*, 17 (3) (December).

Shapiro, S. 1985. "Capitalism at Risk: The Political Economy of the Educational Reports of 1983." *Educational Theory*, 35 (Winter).

Shipp, T., and L. R. McKenzie. 1981. "Adult Learners and Non-Learners: Demographic Characteristics as an Indicator of Psychographic Characteristics." *Adult Education*, 31 (4).

Shor, I. 1978. "No More Teacher's Dirty Looks: Conceptual Teaching from the Bottom Up." In *Studies in Socialist Pedagogy*, eds. T. M. Norton and B. Ollman. New York: Monthly Review Press.

Smith D. 1983. "Strategies for Serving Select Populations: Issues and Perspectives." *New Directions for Continuing Education*, 20 (December).

Smith, G. B. 1982. "Employer-sponsored Programs of Recurrent Education." *Education and Urban Society*, 14 (3) (May).

Sola, P. 1976. "Vocational Guidance: Integrating School and Society in Chicago 1912–16." *The Vocational Aspect of Education*, 28 (71), 117–123.

Sola, P. 1978. "The Chicago Association of Commerce and the Organization of Extra-Curricular Activities in the Chicago High Schools, 1914–1925." *The Vocational Aspect of Education*, 30 (77), 119–127.

Sparks, R. M. 1986. "High Technology and the 99th Congress." *AREA Development*, pp. 10–14.

Staples, R. 1984. "Racial Ideology and Intellectual Racism: Blacks in Academia." *The Black Scholar*, 15 (2).

Stacey, N., and I. Charner. 1982. "Unions and Postsecondary Education." *Education and Urban Society*, 14 (3) (May).

Tanner, D. 1984. "The American High School at the Crossroads." *Educational Leadership* (March).

Thompson, C. 1986. "Military Direction of Academic CS Research." *Communications of the ACM*, 29 (July).

Timpane, M. 1984. "Business Has Rediscovered the Schools." *Phi Delta Kappan*, 65 (6) (February).

Toure, S. 1969. "A Dialectical Approach to Culture." *The Black Scholar*, 1 (1).

Troike, R. C. 1981. "Synthesis of Research on Bilingual Education." *Education Leadership* (March), 498–504.

Troike, R. C., and Savalle-Troike, M. 1982. "Teacher Training for Bilingual Education: An International Perspective." In *Issues in International Bilingual Education: The Role of the Vernacular*, eds. B. Hartford, A. Valdman, and C. R. Foster. London: Plenum.

Tugend, A. 1986. "Half of Chicago Students Drop Out, Study Finds." *Education Week* (March 6).

———. 1986. "Over 12 Percent of Adults Illiterate, Census Says." *Education Week* (April 30).

Uhlenberg, P., and D. Eggebeen. 1986. "The Declining Well-Being of American Adolescents." *The Public Interest* (Winter).

Valentine, C. A. 1971. "Deficit, Difference and Bicultural Models of Afro-American Behavior." *Harvard Educational Review*, 41.

Valli, L. 1985. "Office Students and the Meaning of Work." *Issues in Education*, 3 (1).

Violas, P. C. 1981. "Reflecting on Human Capital Theories, Skill Training and Vocational Education." *Education Theory* 31 (2) (Spring).

Wagner, A. P. 1982. "Postcompulsory Education and Training: In Inventory of Programs and Sources of Support." *Education and Urban Society* 14 (3) (May).

Walberg, H. 1984. "Improving the Productivity of America's Schools." *Educational Leadership* 41 (8), 19–27.

Walsh, J. 1986. "Family Ties, Feminism's Next Frontier." *The Progressive* (September), 21–23.

Wehlege, G. 1983. "The Marginal High School Student: Defining the Problem and Searching for a Policy." *Children and Youth Service Review*, 5.

Weis, L. 1985. "Excellence and Student Class, Race and Gender Cultures." In *Excellence in Education*, eds. P. Altback, G. Kelly, and L. Weiss. Buffalo, N.Y.: Prometheas Books.

Whitman, D., et al. 1986. "Broken Lives—America's Underclass." *U.S. New and World Report* (March).

Williams, R. 1976. "Base and Superstructure in Marxist Cultural Theory." In *Schooling and Capitalism: A Sociological Reader*, eds. I. R. Dale, G. M. Esland, and M. MacDonald. Boston: Routledge and Kegan Paul.

Wilson, J. Q. 1985. "The Rediscovery of Character: Private Vice and Public Policy." *The Public Interest*.

Wilson, R. 1987. "Bennett Calls Character Training, Not New Federal Programs, Key to Competitiveness." *Education Week* (February 25).

Wolfe, A. 1981. "Radical Intellectuals in a Conservative Time." *New Political Science* 5 (6).

Wright, T., F. Rodriguez, and H. Waitzkin. 1985. "Corporate Interests, Philanthropies, and the Peace Movement." *Monthly Review* (February), 19–34.

Wu, S., W. Pink, R. Crain, and O. Moles. 1982. "Student Suspension: A Critical Reappraisal." *Urban Review*, 18.

Wynne, F. 1985. "On Pedagogy and Time-Honored Virtues." *Education Week* (May 8), 36.

Zimmerman, J. S. 1985. "PC Security: So What's New." *Datamation* (November 8).

Zuboff, S. 1982. "New Worlds of Computer-Mediated Work." *Harvard Business Review* (September–October).

Zwerling, L. S. 1982. "Adult Education: Breeder of Inequality?" *New York Times*, Summer Survey of Education (August 22).

Index

About the Editors and Contributors

RICHARD J. ALTENBAUGH is assistant professor and coordinator of Secondary Social Sciences/History Program, Department of History, College of Arts and Sciences at Northern Illinois University. His research includes twentieth-century social/educational history.

EDWARD H. BERMAN is professor of Education in the Department of Foundations of Education, School of Education at the University of Louisville, Louisville, Kentucky. His research areas include comparative education and the history of education.

KATHRYN M. BORMAN is professor and associate dean of Graduate Studies and Research, College of Education, University of Cincinnati. Her research includes sociology of education with emphasis on childhood and youth, focused on gender and urban education.

JOSEPH L. DEVITIS is associate professor of Education and Human Development and coordinator of Master of Arts in Social Sciences, Department of Career and Interdisciplinary Studies, School of Education and Human Development, State University of New York at Binghamton. His research interests are teacher education, social and psychological theory, and social change and moral development.

BEVERLY M. GORDON is assistant professor in the Department of Educational Policy and Leadership, College of Education at Ohio State University, Columbus.

Her areas of interest include curriculum theory and development, specifically the historical and ideological aspects of knowledge production and dissemination; teacher education; and African-American epistemology.

ERNEST KAHANE received his Ph.D. in the Philosophy of Education from the University of Illinois, Urbana-Champaign. He is presently a training consultant for a number of leading computer and high tech firms along the Boston beltway. He conducts workshops in management consulting and training innovation. Dr. Kahane is also an adjunct professor at Boston University.

DON T. MARTIN is associate professor, Department of Administration and Policy Studies, School of Education, University of Pittsburgh, Pennsylvania. His research interests include the history of education, critical theory, social theory, and the politics of education.

STUART A. McANINCH is assistant professor of History, Central Michigan University, Mount Pleasant. His areas of interest include the history of American education and the history of teaching methods.

ANDREW D. ORAM is senior technical writer at Concurrent Computer Corporation, Westford, Massachusetts. His research interests are in the principles of computer engineering and their impact on training needs.

PATRICIA O'REILLY is associate professor of Child Development and Psychology as well as head of the Department of Educational Foundations, College of Education, University of Cincinnatti, Ohio. Her research interests include the impact of sexual stereotyping on human development and the psychology of women.

WILLIAM T. PINK is associate dean of the Graduate School of Education, National College of Education, Evanston, Illinois. His research areas include the sociology of schools, at-risk students, and school change.

TIMOTHY G. REAGAN is associate professor of educational foundations in the Department of Teacher Education, School of Education, Central Connecticut State University, New Britain. Research areas include the education of cultural and linguistic minority groups.

JOHN MARTIN RICH is professor of Cultural Foundations of Education, University of Texas at Austin. His research includes moral education and educational policy issues.

CHRISTINE M. SHEA is currently a center fellow at the North Carolina Center for the Advancement of Teaching. She is on leave from her position as assistant professor of the History of Education at West Virginia University. Her research area is the history of twentieth-century school and social reform movements. She is currently completing work on a social history of the Progressive-era mental hygiene movement.

PETER SOLA is associate professor of Foundations of Education at Howard University, Washington, D.C. He has published a book on ethics and educational decision-making and another dealing with innovative teacher certification programs. He is currently working on a multicultural education textbook.

PAUL C. VIOLAS is professor of Educational Policy Studies, College of Education, University of Illinois at Urbana-Champaign. His research includes the nineteenth-century common school and Horace Mann as well as British public schooling.